Biographical Texts from Ramessid Egypt

Society of Biblical Literature

Writings from the Ancient World

Theodore J. Lewis, General Editor

Associate Editors

Edward Bleiberg
Billie Jean Collins
F. W. Dobbs-Allsopp
Edward L. Greenstein
Niek Veldhuis
Raymond Westbrook
Terry Wilfong

Number 26
Biographical Texts from Ramessid Egypt
by Elizabeth Frood
Edited by John Baines

BIOGRAPHICAL TEXTS FROM RAMESSID EGYPT

by

Elizabeth Frood

edited by

John Baines

Society of Biblical Literature
Atlanta

BIOGRAPHICAL TEXTS FROM RAMESSID EGYPT

Library of Congress Cataloging-in-Publication Data

Frood, Elizabeth.
  Biographical texts from Ramessid Egypt / by Elizabeth Frood ; edited by John Baines.
    p. cm. -- (Society of Biblical Literature writings from the ancient world ; no. 26)
  Includes bibliographical references and index.
  ISBN 978-1-58983-210-7 (paper binding : alk. paper)
  1. Egypt--History--New Kingdom, ca. 1550-ca. 1070 B.C.--Biography. 2. Egypt--Civilization--To 332 B.C. I. Baines, John, 1946- II. Title.

DT87.F76 2007
932'.014--dc22

                                              2007016651

Printed in the United States of America on acid-free, recycled paper
conforming to ANSI/NISO Z39.48-1992 (R1997) and ISO 9706:1994
standards for paper permanence.

For my parents

Fig. 1. Standing Pillar Statue of Wenennefer (no. 14a).

CONTENTS

III. Civil Officials

IV. The Military

CHRONOLOGICAL TABLE

This table is based on Baines and Malek 2000. All dates are approximate and are B.C.E. unless otherwise indicated.

Old Kingdom Dynasties 4–8	2575–2150
First Intermediate Period Dynasties 9–11	2125–1975
Middle Kingdom Dynasties 11–14	1975–1640
Second Intermediate Period Dynasties 15–17	1630–1520
New Kingdom	1539–1075
Dynasty 18	1539–1292
Ahmose	1539–1514
Amenhotep I	1514–1493
Thutmose I	1493–?
Thutmose II	?–1479
Thutmose III	1479–1425
Hatshepsut	1473–1458
Amenhotep II	1426–1400
Thutmose IV	1400–1390
Amenhotep III	1390–1353
Amenhotep IV/Akhenaten	1353–1336
Smenkhkare	1335–1332
Tutankhamun	1332–1322
Ay	1322–1319
Horemheb	1319–1292

Dynasty 19	1292–1190
Ramesses I	1292–1290
Sety I	1290–1279
Ramesses II	1279–1213
Merenptah	1213–1204
Sety II	1204–1198
Amenmesse (usurper in reign of Sety II)	
Siptah	1198–1193
Tawosret	1198–1190
Dynasty 20	1190–1075
Sethnakht	1190–1187
Ramesses III	1187–1156
Ramesses IV	1156–1150
Ramesses V	1150–1145
Ramesses VI	1145–1137
Ramesses VII	1137–1129
Ramesses VIII	1129–1126
Ramesses IX	1126–1108
Ramesses X	1108–1104
Ramesses XI	1104–1075

Third Intermediate Period   1075–715
Dynasties 21–25

Late Period   715–332
Dynasties 25–30

Greco-Roman Period   332 B.C.E.–395 C.E.

ABBREVIATIONS

ÄAT   Ägypten und Altes Testament. Studien zu Geschichte, Kultur und Religion Ägyptens und des Alten Testaments
AF   *Altorientalische Forschungen*
ADAIK   Abhandlungen des Deutschen Archäologischen Instituts Abteilung Kairo
AHAW   Abhandlungen der Heidelberger Akademie der Wissenschaften
AOAT   Alter Orient und Altes Testament
ASAE   *Annales du Service des Antiquités de l'Egypte*
AVDAIK   Archäologische Veröffentlichungen des Deutschen Archäologischen Instituts Abteilung Kairo
BIFAO   *Bulletin de l'Institut Français d'Archéologie Orientale*
BiOr   *Bibliotheca Orientalis*
BSEG   *Bulletin de la Société d'Egyptologie de Genève*
BSFE   *Bulletin de la Société Française d'Egyptologie*
CdE   *Chronique d'Egypte*
FIFAO   Fouilles de l'Institut Français d'Archéologie Orientale
GM   *Göttinger Miszellen: Beiträge zur Ägyptologischen Diskussion*
IFAO   Institut Français d'Archéologie Orientale
JANER   *Journal of Ancient Near Eastern Religions*
JARCE   *Journal of the American Research Center in Egypt*
JEA   *Journal of Egyptian Archaeology*
JNES   *Journal of Near Eastern Studies*
KRI   Kitchen, Kenneth A. 1975–1991. *Ramesside Inscriptions, Historical and Biographical.* 8 vols. Oxford: Blackwell.
l.p.h.   "life, prosperity, health" (see glossary)
MÄS   Münchner Ägyptologische Studien
MDAIK   *Mitteilungen des Deutschen Archäologischen Instituts Abteilung Kairo*
OBO   Orbis Biblicus et Orientalis
OLA   Orientalia Lovaniensia Analecta
OLP   *Orientalia Lovaniensia Periodica*
OLZ   *Orientalistische Literaturzeitung*
PdÄ   Probleme der Ägyptologie

PM   Porter, Bertha, and Rosalind L. B. Moss, with Ethel W. Burney and
          Jaromír Málek (from 1973). 1927–1952. *Topographical Bibliography of
          Ancient Egyptian Hieroglyphic Texts, Reliefs, and Paintings.* 7 vols. 2nd
          edition 1960–. Oxford: Griffith Institute.
RdE   *Revue d'Égyptologie*
SAGA   Studien zur Archäologie und Geschichte Altägyptens
SAOC   Studies in Ancient Oriental Civilization
SAK   *Studien zur Altägyptischen Kultur*
Urk. IV   Sethe, Kurt and Wolfgang Helck. 1906–1958. *Urkunden der 18. Dynas-
          tie.* Leipzig: Hinrichs; Berlin: Akademie-Verlag.
WZKM   *Wiener Zeitschrift für die Kunde des Morgenlandes*
ZÄS   *Zeitschrift für Ägyptische Sprache und Altertumskunde*

EXPLANATION OF SIGNS

[ ]   lost or very damaged text that is partly or fully restored
ᴦ ᴉ   damaged text where the restoration is confident
...   extensive lacunae, or words and phrases that cannot be translated. An
           ellipsis that is enclosed in square brackets models the extent of the
           lacunae or untranslatable section. Thus the loss of two hieroglyphic
           groups is indicated [... ...].
[italic]   comments give details of extensive lacunae
( )   explanatory additions to translations
(?)   uncertain renderings of words or phrases
< >   omissions or, occasionally, errors in the original

ACKNOWLEDGMENTS

I have been privileged to have John Baines as both advisor for the doctoral thesis from which this book was developed, and as editor. I am grateful for his guidance, insight, and encouragement which have encompassed every stage of its development.

Work on the volume has been supported by my colleagues and students at two institutions: the School of Archaeology, Classics and Egyptology, University of Liverpool, from 2003–2006, especially Mark Collier, Roland Enmarch, and Christopher Mee; and the Oriental Institute, University of Oxford, especially Mark Smith who initially suggested the project.

The following people and institutions have provided invaluable assistance and resources: James Allen (Brown University, formerly Metropolitan Museum of Art, New York), Elisabeth Delange (Louvre, Paris), Mamdouh Eldamaty (formerly director of the Egyptian Museum, Cairo), Elizabeth Fleming (Griffith Institute, Oxford), Ken Kitchen (University of Liverpool), John Larson (Oriental Institute, University of Chicago), Geoffrey Thorndike Martin, Adel Mahmoud† (Egyptian Museum, Cairo), Jaromir Malek (Griffith Institute, Oxford), Ingeborg Müller (Ägyptisches Museum, Berlin), Boyo Ockinga (Macquarie University, Sydney), Maarten Raven (Rijksmuseum van Oudheden, Leiden), Elsa Rickal (Paris), Christina Riggs (formerly Manchester Museum, University of Manchester), JJ Shirley (Swansea University), Jacobus van Dijk (Rijksuniversiteit, Groningen), Tania Watkins (Department of Ancient Egypt and Sudan, British Museum), Helen Whitehouse (Ashmolean Museum, Oxford), and Dietrich Wildung (Ägyptisches Museum, Berlin). Richard Jasnow (Johns Hopkins University) offered invaluable advice at the book's early stages. My thanks also go to Billie Jean Collins (Society of Biblical Literature) and Theodore Lewis (Johns Hopkins University) for their patient and thorough editing of the manuscript.

I benefited from discussion with a number of colleagues and friends, including Tom Hardwick, Anthony Leahy, Antonio Loprieno, Lynn Meskell, Cynthia Sheikholeslami, and Martin Stadler. Anthony Spalinger developed my early interest in Egyptology in New Zealand and continues to provide important advice and resources.

I am grateful to Richard Parkinson, Yvonne Harpur, and Paolo Scremin for discussion, reassurance, and friendship. Joanne Roberts has been a source of understanding and perspective for more years than we care to remember. Special thanks go to Christoph Bachhuber for his support, care, and the endless hours he spent editing and formatting. I would also like to thank Jenny Cashman and Angela McDonald who listened to, read, and commented on chapters, and have been guides and inspirations. I could not have achieved this without the constant support of my parents, Hilary Wynyard and James Frood, who have encouraged me throughout every transformation of my life and work.

List of Figures

INTRODUCTION

The self-presentation of members of the nonroyal elite through biographical inscriptions is a central element in ancient Egyptian high culture and was a component of its monumental discourse from the Old Kingdom, in the mid-third millennium B.C.E., until Roman times. The inscriptions that I present in this book were produced during the Ramessid period (ca. 1290–1075 B.C.E.), a time of significant development in domains of representation. Among monuments of individuals from this period, scholars have focussed on tombs, in which there were major changes, including a reduction in the number of biographies inscribed in them. Thus, these texts, which are inscribed on statues, stelae, and temple walls, as well as in tombs, have not been gathered together as a corpus. Yet, they form a distinctive and wide-ranging body of material that is significant both for historical and social reconstructions of the period and for exploring the highly individual ways in which a self could be fashioned and presented in these diverse contexts.

Most of the texts selected for this collection are narrative inscriptions that present one or several events from an individual's life, that were formative, transformative, or culminating. I include a smaller number of inscriptions, often based on sequences of epithets, that characterize an individual's moral character and adherence to norms of behavior. Since the inscriptions were set up to commemorate and celebrate the lives of members of the elite for whom their official role and position in society was the central and defining element, I organize the translations according to the office of their protagonists. This arrangement makes it easy to compare and contrast texts belonging to individuals whose spheres of action were related and who may have had similar concerns.

The texts presented here are relatively few in number. Although a central genre, biography was never a common strategy of self-presentation, and in the Ramessid period it was used by relatively few people. This restriction relates to broader changes in representation, which I discuss in more detail below (4.2). Those who did select biography reanimated and reinterpreted the conventions of the genre, often using unprecedented forms or media of self-presentation including, for example, placing the inscriptions on temple walls. They also developed new motifs, such as communication with the gods in dreams and oracles, as well as admissions of wrongdoing. These and other innovations stand alongside traditional formulations that draw more directly upon earlier New Kingdom and Middle Kingdom models. In this book, I present a range of these different approaches to biography and self-presentation.

1. Approaching Egyptian Biography

Egyptian biography is far removed from modern Western biographical and autobiographical traditions.[1] Although the Egyptian texts do relate aspects of character and/or events in the career of a single person, the chronologically ordered development of a life and personality, which is an expectation of various genres of more recent life-writing, is not a feature of these inscriptions. The texts were inscribed in hieroglyphs, the monumental form of the Egyptian script, in tombs or on statues and stelae in temples. They are thus context-bound, functional, and not intended for general dissemination. They present an idealized image of the individual that is oriented to maintaining self and memory after death through mortuary cult in tomb and temple. Differences between modern life-writing and Egyptian biography can generate issues of definition and interpretation, some of which I treat here.

In the following introductory survey and discussion, I divide Egyptian biographies into two basic types, namely, texts that present narratives of aspects of career or of particular events and texts that center on the individual's moral character and behavior.[2] This thematic division has structural implications. While career and event biographies are usually composed with narrative forms that move the protagonist forward in time, ethical biographies consist of nominal, timeless statements of qualities and attributes: "I was effective, the possessor of a perfect name, without fault in the palace" (no. 18). These statements often have the form of strings of epithets, which make condensed declarations of adherence to codes of moral and ideal behavior that are often incorporated within lists of titles. Epithets have "biographical potential" (Baines 1999c, 30; Baud 2005, 93–95) and some may allude to culminating events or historical contexts. For example, an epithet of the chancellor Bay seems to allude to his role as kingmaker in the late Nineteenth Dynasty: "one who placed the king on the throne of his father" (KRI IV, 364,5; 371,8–9; Schneider 2003, 142–43; see no. 32).

Although the division of biography into "types" is a valuable descriptive and analytical tool, it is also reductive. Many texts display features of both career-based and ethical biography and do not fit easily into a single category. The complexity and variety of Egyptian biographical material is demonstrated by the texts presented in this volume.

1.1. Biography and Autobiography

In the definition and categorization of Egyptian texts, the terms biography and autobiography can designate a range of formulations of the self, most, but not all, of which are composed in the first person. The use of both terms encapsulates a problem of definition for both the ancient material and our own modern context. This problem relates most specifically to issues of authorship. The term "autobiography" in particular implies an identification between the subject of the text and its author. For the Egyptian texts, the use of the first-person is a fiction, mobilizing the immediacy of the individual's presence in the tomb or temple where the text was set up (Baines 1999b, 37). It seems likely that the texts were commissioned by the owner or his family rather than composed by him. In a memorial context, the first-person voice is that of the deceased, rather than that of the text's author. I therefore use "biography" and not "autobiography" to designate the texts presented here. Biography is a more flexible term because it leaves the relationship between the subject and the implied author open. This flexibility is particularly valuable for the Ramessid texts, some of which make explicit play with the potentials of the voice in biography, especially in the use of the third-person (e.g., nos. 11a, 17).

1.2. Content

Egyptian biographies are highly crafted compositions. In the case of career-based narratives, the events selected often crystallized key aspects of the individual's performance of office, in particular in relation to his peers, the king, or the gods. Experiences and events that we might consider crucial for telling a life are not included. For example, although biographies often evoke relationships between parents and children (e.g., no. 3c), detailed aspects of the family setting and the domestic sphere fall outside the decorum of the narrated life. In part for this reason biographies are not generally attested for women. Women were largely excluded from the administrative, official sphere and therefore could not have texts that were focussed in that domain, such as biographies. Biographies of women do not appear until the first millennium, when the genre underwent significant transformation.[3]

Egyptian biographies are almost always idealizing, presenting an individual's adherence to social codes and his fulfillment of duties, and thus providing the model of a proper life. Some texts seem to mobilize this didactic potential explicitly, addressing the living not only in order to solicit them to maintain the protagonist's offering cult but perhaps also to serve as an example. In the biography of Userhat, this point is made explicitly, unlike in most others: "O nobles, great and small, all the elite, all people, all sun-folk, I will tell you (about) what has happened to me—(for) I was distinguished above others—so that you may report it from generation to generation, elders teaching the young" (no. 19b).

Within this idealizing frame, Egyptian biographies can present problematic situations such as famine or social isolation. However, these motifs are usually included in order to demonstrate the protagonist's ability to overcome them. Such motifs are a particular feature of biographies of the First Intermediate period. Untoward actions or experiences of the individual are, in contrast, very rarely expressed. A few texts that center on personally problematic situations such as illness (Strudwick 2005, 317, no. 234; 318–20, no. 235; 322–23, no. 240) or incidents involving the king (Strudwick 2005, 305–6, no. 227) are known from the Fourth and Fifth Dynasties when biography was still emerging as a textual genre and its central elements had not yet been formalized (see also Baines 1999c, 23–24). Significantly, narration of the untoward was not again a feature of biography until the Ramessid period when themes relating to personal misconduct and suffering may have developed as part of an exploration of new motifs to express individual relationships to the gods (4.4).

In biography, the self is primarily constituted through interactions with the gods, the king, and the human sphere, as well as the dead, to whom the individual may be partly assimilated. Most actions are presented in relation to these groups, for example, service to the king in official duties, military engagement, and expeditions to foreign lands; service to the gods in pious actions and priestly duties in maintaining the cult; and care for dependant people and a role as a mediator in disputes (to name but a few motifs). Biographical texts articulate, participate in, and enact these social relationships, detailing aspects of interaction that could not be presented visually, therefore complementing pictorial motifs in tombs in particular. Among the domains mentioned, the divine sphere is central in the Ramessid period.

1.3. Fictionality

Many Egyptian biographies appear to be closely and concretely grounded in specific historical and social contexts. A few from the early Eighteenth Dynasty are key sources for the wars of reunification that began that epoch (e.g., Lichtheim 1976, 12–15). From the corpus in this book, the detailed list of years in office by the high priest Bakenkhons (no. 2a) has been used in the reconstruction of genealogies and chronologies, as well as for mapping the development of priestly careers (Jansen-Winkeln 1993, with references).

Although the elite context of biography and the specificity of some texts means that they can speak to social and historical issues, caution should be exercized in using them as sources, especially in view of their functional and aesthetic aims, which are not simply to relate facts.

All narrative is fictively shaped; it is not possible simply to "tell the truth." As Hayden White (1987, 178) observes in his analysis of Paul Ricœur's conception of history, "narrative discourse does not simply reflect or passively register a world already made; it works up the material given in perception and reflection, fashions it, and creates something new, in precisely the same way that human agents by their actions fashion distinctive forms of historical life out of the world they inherit as their past." This process of selection, omission, and fashioning applies to the Egyptian material as well. Crucial questions when reading and interpreting Egyptian biographies are: Why are certain selections made? What are the priorities in shaping a life for display in monumental contexts? For the statue text of Bakenkhons, the list of years may have been in part a way of emphasizing service to the god Amun by enumerating a lifespan dedicated to, and bounded by, the temple (see also Frood 2003, 75–78).

Some biographies incorporate more clearly fictional, as opposed to fictively shaped, motifs. The clearest example is the presentation of the individual as someone of lowly background. This motif is present in biographies from the Old Kingdom onward, but is seen as a particular feature of those from the Amarna period. In many cases, the protagonists in question were from elite backgrounds, as sometimes demonstrated by other texts on their monuments, which give the names and titles of their fathers. An early example is the Sixth Dynasty official Weni who bears lower-ranking titles in his biography but whose father is now known to have been a vizier and thus a man of high standing (Richards 2002, 79, 90, 95). The allusion to, or expression of, humble origin emphasizes advancement through personal abilities as in Weni's case, or, in texts included in this volume, through the intervention of the king (no. 19b) or a god (no. 11a).

While most texts "mask" their fictionality (Iser 1993, 12), some make explicit play with their fictionalizing potential, especially the blurred boundaries between biography and literary tales. The Middle Kingdom Tale of Sinuhe begins as a biographical text before departing from this frame to narrate its protagonist's self-imposed exile from Egypt (Parkinson 1997, 21–53; 2002, 150–53). The biography of Samut (no. 11a), in contrast, begins in the third person as a "Tale of Samut," using an introductory formula known from two Middle Kingdom tales, thus assimilating his text with these high cultural forms (see Morenz 1998).

The concept of "aesthetic referentiality," developed by Paul John Eakin for studies of modern autobiography (1992, esp. 50–53, 193–99), is useful when approaching these issues in Egyptian biographical texts. This concept characterizes how autobiographical texts maintain the potential to refer to the real world but, as aesthetically created objects, are deeply immersed in fictionalizing representation. In the Egyptian context, both the referential and the aesthetic are further bound to, and shaped by, the monumental form.

1.4. IMPLICATIONS OF CONTEXT

Central to the interpretation of Egyptian biographies is their physical setting within tombs and temples. Their meanings are shaped by their funerary and commemorative contexts, as well as more broadly by architectural setting and landscape. Set up for display within these contexts, biographies were integrated with other modes of self-presentation and were oriented to particular functions and spheres of action.

Characteristic of ancient Egyptian high culture is significant elite investment in monumental perpetuation of self and memory beyond death. Armando Petrucci (1998, xviii), who has studied written traditions in Western cultures, foregrounds the social implications of a "written death" as "a substantially and profoundly 'political' practice aimed at celebrating and recording the power and social presence of the group, corporate or familial, to which the deceased belonged and … directed at consolidating its wealth, prestige, endurance over time, vitality, and capacity for reproduction and expansion." The "political" and functional dimensions of Egyptian mortuary monuments are similarly interconnected.

Tombs were the resting place of the deceased's body, creating a domain for the maintenance of cult while celebrating and commemorating his life. The New Kingdom Theban tomb had a tripartite structure that provides a model for interpreting the different zones of tomb space (Kampp-Seyfried 2003). The upper, exterior sections were oriented to the solar cult and often incorporated a pyramid or pyramidion. The middle level, generally termed the chapel, consisted of a hall at the front leading to a shrine in the rear. The hall is usually decorated with scenes and texts relating to lived experience and official duties, and can include biographical texts or "daily life" scenes such as harvesting and fishing and fowling. Scenes linking this world with the next and mobilizing the transition between them, for example banqueting scenes and funerary processions, could also be shown in this area. The shrine was the focal point of actions relating to the deceased's cult. Its decoration was often more overtly religious in focus, including offering scenes and the continuation and culmination of funerary scenes.[4] Rock-cut statues of the tomb owner, or in the Ramessid period of gods (see 3.3), were often present in the shrine. The final zone is the sealed burial chamber, which sometimes incorporated long sloping passages, especially in the late Eighteenth Dynasty and Ramessid period. This zone was rarely decorated.

Statues and stelae extended some of the meanings and functions of the tomb into temple domains where they were instrumental in ensuring the owner's afterlife through the maintenance of his cult and his continuing interaction with the divine cult. Stelae, and especially statues, were also a way for elite individuals to assert their presence in sacred spaces, particularly the restricted areas of temples.

Biographies are not isolated within tomb or temple. In the tomb, they interconnect with other scenes and texts and in the temple with the iconography of statues and stelae. In the Nineteenth Dynasty tomb of Samut (no. 11), the biographical texts and offering scenes that fill the upper registers of the west side of the hall center on his relationship with deities, especially the goddess Mut. In contrast, the scenes on the east side show his transition to and transformation in the next world, including the funerary journey and procession, rituals performed before the tomb, and his judgment and introduction before Osiris (Negm 1997, esp. 14). Thus, different spheres of visual and textual presentation present complementary and interdependent aspects of the self and of transformation in relation to the gods.

Text and context are more tightly integrated on temple statues. The biography on the rear surface of the pillar statue of Wenennefer, the high priest of Osiris (no. 14a), places him at the center of rituals relating to Osiris. He narrates how he enlivened and transfigured the god's statue through his access to ritual objects, and this in turn enables his own transformation: "I was equipped, bound in red linen, the *ames*-club in my hand to smite the disaffected, the *iaat*-weapon to smite the rebel." This leading role in cult performance is also presented through the statue's unusual architectural form. With the pillar almost subsuming the priest's body (see fig. 1: frontispiece), the statue seems to become part of a structure, metaphorically supporting a temple and, by implication, the god.

Monumental contexts weave image, text, and architecture into complex visual, verbal, and sensory experiences. An inscription in the Theban tomb of Ibi, constructed some four hundred years after the Ramessid period, mobilizes this potential explicitly, inviting its reader to "immerse (*dfy*)" himself in the tomb space and to "enter/comprehend (*ꜥq*)" its written dimensions through "seeing" and "hearing" (Kuhlmann and Schenkel 1983, I, 71–72; II, pl. 21). A number of the biographies in this volume similarly express concepts relating to aesthetic pleasure and experience. The biography in the tomb of

Nefersekheru invites people to "joyfully receive what I have said [concerning my life on] earth" (no. 24). The inscription on the stela of Bakaa, perhaps set up in his tomb or memorial chapel, suggests that visitors might "delight" in his biography and "take pleasure, for this is no burden that would be heavy on your hearts" (no. 39). Such appeals also speak to the biographies' potential for factual or symbolic audiences who could read the texts or have them read out.

Although written and spoken forms of Egyptian were far apart, the texts probably relate to oral performance. Within the tomb, biographies may have been declaimed during funerary ceremonies in a practice comparable to the biographical eulogies that are a component of funerals in many cultures, and discussed by Ralph Houlbrooke (1998, 295–330) for Medieval and Early Modern England. Tombs ideally remained a domain of cult activity long after the death of the owner and could be accessible to curious, pious visitors. Maya begins his biography by addressing such visitors as "the people who will come and who wish to take recreation in the West (the necropolis), to walk about in the district of ⌜eternity⌝" (no. 23).

Appeals to the living are also common on statues and stelae, while biographies are often framed as appeals or instructions. The modeling of audience in temples, however, remains problematic. Access to state temple complexes was generally restricted to high officials and the priesthood. Therefore statues set up in Karnak, for example, would have been seen by relatively few people (nos. 2, 3a–c, 21). Some statues were set up in perhaps more open temple contexts, such as the Deir el-Bahri complex, which was a focus of personal religion. Such pieces had the potential for a wider audience, something that both the form and the texts of the statue of Amenemone (no. 36) from the site specifically mobilize. It is, however, uncertain how far the texts on statues could have been read; one inscribed on a back pillar may not have been visible if the statue was set up against a wall. In such contexts, as well as in tombs, performances during creation and dedication may have been central to the monument's meaning. Many of these texts were also overtly directed beyond the human sphere to the gods and the next world.

2. Biography before the Ramessid period[5]

In order to set Ramessid biographies in relation to the development of biography, I outline the main features of the genre before the Nineteenth Dynasty, drawing in particular on Andrea Gnirs's global survey (1996, 219–41; English summary 2001).

Biographical texts were first inscribed on tomb walls in Memphite cemeteries during the early Old Kingdom and were restricted to the tomb throughout that period.[6] Both career and ethical biographies developed out of extended title strings, which were the earliest form of written self-presentation (Baud 2005, 93–96). The oldest extended texts relating to an individual life are those in the early-Fourth Dynasty tomb of Metjen, which include lengthy property decrees (Baud 2005, 98–105; Strudwick 2005, 192–94, no. 108). Biographies centered on single, significant events also emerged in the Fourth Dynasty including, for example, a fragmentary slab from Giza, which records the owner's illness and the king's response: "Now with regard to the period when he was ill, his majesty had brought for him a carrying-chair from the Residence so that he might supervize from it the work for which he was responsible" (Baud 2005, 115–16; Strudwick 2005, 322, no. 240). These early texts are presented in the third person; the first person became the standard voice for biography only in the Fifth Dynasty.

The Fifth Dynasty also witnessed the emergence of ethical biography and the elaboration of this type and career biography in length, theme, and structure. These developments are particularly well-illustrated by the long texts in provincial tombs of the Sixth Dynasty, such as the inscriptions of Harkhuf at Aswan, which narrate his expeditions in Nubia and incorporate a letter from the king (Lichtheim 1973, 23–27; Strudwick 2005, 328–33, no. 241). Old Kingdom biographies are characterized by experimentation in both form and content including, for example, the narration of untoward events such as illness. A defining feature is the role of the king as the primary initiator of and focus for individual action.

This king-centered world contrasts with texts from the First Intermediate period, the years of political decentralization that followed the Old Kingdom (for examples, see Lichtheim 1988, 21–37). The concerns of these biographies are local, often focusing on the actions of individuals in caring for their towns and communities. The texts also highlight their role in intervening in problems such as social unrest (e.g., Baines 1999a) or hunger. The ideals are those formulated in the Fifth and Sixth Dynasties, but the texts stress the autonomy of the individual as a self-made man who acts independently for the benefit of his community: "I made a water-way for this town; (the rest of) Upper Egypt was in an evil state, no water to be seen" (Khety, Asyut: Griffith 1889, pl. 15; Lichtheim 1988, 28). Claims to the veracity of biographical statements also emerge in this period (Coulon 1997), indicating some scepticism in relation to proclaimed ideal actions. Truth claims are found in biographies from this time on (see no. 24).

Expansion in theme is paralleled by an expansion and elaboration in media and location. In the late Old Kingdom, expedition inscriptions carved in the rock at quarrying and mining sites begin to incorporate biographical elements (Strudwick 2005, 149, no. 75) and this becomes a particularly productive domain for new themes and phraseology (e.g., Anthes 1928; Gardiner and Peet 1952–1955). Biography can also be detached from its tomb context through its incorporation on stelae, which were often quite small, potentially portable, and could be set up in temple areas in addition to tombs.

With the reestablishment of centralized royal authority in the late Eleventh Dynasty and its powerful consolidation in the Twelfth, biographies shift focus again to assert the individual's relationship with the king, while retaining the emphasis on personal initiative and self-sufficiency: "I undertook journeys at the command of the king, joining the ranks of the favored. The king placed me as an up-and-coming person; I was born as one who understands and acts. It was my heart that advanced my position and I surpassed the deeds of my ancestors" (Wepwawetaa, Leiden V4: Sethe 1928, 72, ll. 13–16; Lichtheim 1988, 76).[7] Ethical biography was highly developed during the Twelfth Dynasty with the composition of artful "catalogues of virtues" that emphasized an individual's adherence to official codes of behavior through elaborate metaphor and phraseology (e.g., Parkinson 1991, 61–63).

A significant transformation in the Middle Kingdom is the opening up of the world of the temple as theme and dedicatory context. The dedication of biographical monuments within temple complexes is rare, but attested (e.g., Fischer-Elfert and Grimm 2003). This development is especially salient at Abydos where stelae and statues set up in chapels dedicated to individual cults are oriented to practices in the main temple complexes. Individuals express a desire to participate in festivals and relate aspects of priestly duties and activities. Some biographies link acts of piety with ethical concerns (Espinel 2005) and strongly express the protagonist's involvement with the divine sphere: "I brought ⌐Osiris Khentimentu, lord of⌐ Abydos, to his palace, I followed the god to his domain. His cleansing was performed and his seat was widened. I loosened the knot within [...]; [he came to rest among (?)] his [followers], his attendants" (Ikhernofret, Berlin 1204: Sethe 1928, 79, ll. 20–23; Lichtheim 1988, 99).

Temple-based biographies expand in the Eighteenth Dynasty with the widespread use of statues, especially block statues, as a medium for display.[8] A striking example is the statue set up in Karnak by Hapuseneb, the vizier and high priest of Amun under the female king Hatshepsut, the full body surface of which bears biographical texts narrating works and activities in Karnak and other temples and sacred sites (Delvaux 1988). This statue can be compared with the Nineteenth Dynasty tradition of biographical block statues of high priests in Karnak (nos. 2, 3a–c). Hapuseneb also dedicated at least two other statues in that temple complex. The increased focus on temples that characterizes the New Kingdom is connected with the expression of religious concerns in biography. In the decades before the Amarna period, biography was incorporated within hymns and prayers, explicitly linking the self and lived experience with the gods (e.g., Lichtheim 1976, 86–89; discussion: Gnirs 1996, 215–17). This practice continued in the Ramessid period.

Biography generally gains prominence in the Eighteenth Dynasty both through its expansion into temple domains and through the increased space accorded it in tombs, particularly on stelae in Theban tombs (see Hermann 1940). In the earlier Eighteenth Dynasty, career biographies developed in new directions, a phenomenon that Gnirs (1996, 230) relates to increased competition among elites. Accounts of travel and military exploits, which can be compared with royal narratives and annals, include complex presentations of dramatic setting and action: "And then the great elephant which was among them became belligerent near His Person. I was the one who cut off its trunk while it was alive before His Person, while I was standing in the water between two rocks" (Amenemhab, Thebes: Freier in Blumenthal et. al. 1984, 312; Baines in preparation). The king is the central mediator of events, particularly promotion and the transformation of personal status. The action is generally oriented to the king and numerous texts emphasize their protagonist's close relationship with him.

The expression of loyalism to the king intensifies in the Amarna period.[9] The main actor in biographies is the king, while the individual passively receives his favor and acts according to his instructions: "I am a servant of his (the king's) creating ... my lord advanced me so that I might execute his teachings as I listened to his voice without cease" (May, Amarna: Murnane 1995, 144). For Gnirs (1996, 232–33), this extreme loyalism opens the way to a new form of biography, which she terms "confessional," where the king's intervention transforms the individual from a lowly and humble status into a member of the elite. She argues that this motif is a precursor for Ramessid biographies in which a god enacts a similar transformation (nos. 11a, 45–48). Temples ceased to be a domain for nonroyal self-presentation during the Amarna period when biography was restricted to tombs.

I include some biographies from the immediate post-Amarna period in this volume (nos. 20, 23, and possibly no. 19), but the corpus as a whole deserves separate study. They mark a return to traditional themes, exemplified by the ethical biography on the massive stela of Minnakht (*Urk. IV*, 1530–33; Barbotin 2005, 167–69), which contrasts with the general absence of moral characterization in Amarna biography. Other texts with innovative approaches include the complex fusion of prayer and biography on one of Horemheb's scribe statues dedicated under Tutankhamun (Winlock 1924; Lichtheim 1976, 100–103), which points toward Ramessid developments.

3. The Nineteenth and Twentieth Dynasties

3.1. Historical Outline

The Nineteenth Dynasty is usually understood to begin with the accession of Ramesses I in ca. 1292 B.C.E.[10] However, kinglists such as that set up by Sety I in his temple at Abydos suggest that Horemheb, whom Egyptologists count as the last king of the Eighteenth Dynasty, was associated with the establishment of the new dynasty, and many of his actions shaped its early character. Horemheb was military commander during the immediate post-Amarna period. He took the throne after the deaths of Tutankhamun and Ay, both of whom, unlike Horemheb, were considered too closely linked with Akhenaten to be included in later kinglists. During Horemheb's reign, estimates of the length of which range from twelve to more than twenty-five years, the return to traditional religion was consolidated and administrative and legal structures reformed. The king's army background and his selection of his vizier and former general Pramesses (later Ramesses I) as heir set in place the military character of the Nineteenth Dynasty. Although few biographies from this period narrate military action (exceptions are nos. 41b, 42), a military orientation can be found in the texts of priests who relate their early careers in the army (nos. 2a, 18).

Ramesses I ruled for less than two years but, with a son and grandson, had an assured and established succession by the time of his accession. Although his son, Sety I, aligned himself in display with his father and Horemheb, he also proclaimed a significant break with the past. His reign was termed a "repeating of manifestations (*wḥm mswt*)," a phrase that encapsulates the themes of tradition and innovation that characterize his kingship. He secured Egypt's empire in Syria-Palestine through campaigns to reclaim vassal states held in the mid Eighteenth Dynasty, and undertook an extensive program of temple restoration and new construction. Innovations in royal action and display in his reign are exemplified by the temple complex he built at Abydos. Although modeled on Middle Kingdom and Eighteenth Dynasty structures at the site, features of the temple, such as multiple axes to nine distinct sanctuaries and the cenotaph complex at the rear, created new structures for royal relationships with the gods.

It is Sety's son, Ramesses II, who dominates the historical landscape of the Nineteenth Dynasty. His sixty-seven-year reign was a period of consolidation externally, with military campaigns and developing diplomacy, and of internal expansion, involving large-scale building programs. His early years are characterized by extensive campaigns in Syria-Palestine, strengthening and attempting to extend, Egypt's power base in the region. This strategy brought him into conflict with the interests of the Hittite Empire, based in central Anatolia, against which he was unable to prevail. His temple reliefs and texts claimed victory against Hittite forces at the city of Qadesh in western Syria when the reality was stalemate and Egyptian withdrawal from their advance position. In the second decade of his reign, unsettled political affairs in Anatolia exerted pressure toward a treaty between the two empires, a significant elaboration of Egyptian foreign policy (Morris 2005, 372–76). This alliance was reinforced by two diplomatic marriages between Ramesses and Hittite princesses.

Within Egypt, Ramesses undertook building programs on an unprecedented scale. He established a new capital city, Piramesse, near Avaris, which had been the capital of the foreign rulers of Egypt during the Second Intermediate period. He also undertook works of expansion in most major temple complexes. A salient feature of this building work is the focus on Nubia: Ramesses II built eight rock-cut temples in Nubia, some of which, such as the pair at Abu Simbel, are innovative in their form, scale, and decorative programs. This comprehensive monumental display of power and prestige across Egypt and its territories can be compared with other forms of political expression such as the emphasis on the roles and positions of his sons in administrative and religious offices, which may have been a way to ensure royal presence at every level of the bureaucratic system (Fisher 2001, I, 135).

Many of Ramesses' children predeceased him, and it was his thirteenth son Merenptah who succeeded to the throne after his death. During his nine year reign, Merenptah maintained the stability and prosperity of the Egyptian empire, and was engaged in military campaigns, especially in the Levant, and ongoing building works. In his fifth year, he defended Egypt against an invasion by Libyan chiefs allied with mobile populations from other parts of the Mediterranean referred to in Egyptian sources as "Sea Peoples." These groups were to play a significant role in changing political and cultural dynamics in the Near East and Egypt in the transition to the early Iron Age (ca. 1200 B.C.E.).

The end of the Nineteenth Dynasty is characterized by dynastic crisis, seemingly related to two conflicting lines of succession from Merenptah. The details and chronology are unclear and much debated. Merenptah was succeeded by Sety II, probably his son. The throne was also claimed by a rival, Amenmesse, who held power for a couple of years, perhaps largely in the south. Most of Amenmesse's inscriptions were later usurped or erased by Sety II. The dynastic struggles continued after Sety's death. He was succeeded by Siptah, but other powerful individuals dominate the record at this time: Tawosret, Sety II's widow, who may have acted as regent or rival to the young king (see no. 33), and the chancellor Bay (no. 32). Although Bay is depicted as an intimate of the king early in his reign, he seems to have fallen from favor: an ostracon records the execution of "the great enemy Bay" in year 5, shortly before Siptah's own death (Grandet 2000). Tawosret then ruled as king for a short period. The length of time between the accession of Sety II and the death of Tawosret was probably less than fifteen years.[11]

Later sources describe the end of the Nineteenth Dynasty retrospectively as a time of chaos, foreign rule, and lawlessness, and there may have been some conflict at the accession of the founder of the Twentieth Dynasty Seth-nakht following the death of Tawosret. He had no known connections with the preceding dynasty. Sethnakht was succeeded by his son Ramesses III, who ruled for thirty-one years, a period of relative stability in spite of political and cultural transformations impacting the wider Mediterranean.[12] This changing world is demonstrated in the early part of his reign with attempted invasions by Libyans (years 5 and 11) and "Sea Peoples" (year 8), the latter being credited in his texts with the collapse of the Hittite Empire: "No land could stand before them, from Hatti, Kode, Carchemish, Arzawa, and Alasiya" (Peden 1994, 29). Ramesses III's victories are narrated and depicted on walls of his mortuary temple at Medinet Habu on the Theban West Bank, the latest preserved major royal building work of the New Kingdom. Labor strikes at the workmen's village of Deir el-Medina due to non-payment of rations may indicate economic problems toward the end of Ramesses III's reign, but these may have been confined to the Theban area, and the situation in other parts of Egypt is not known. The records of a harem conspiracy which probably resulted in the king's death speak to ever-present rivalries and intrigues in royal courts rather than reflecting deep-seated problems specific to his reign.

The seven-year reign of Ramesses III's son, Ramesses IV, seems to have been relatively untroubled. He was able to gather resources to mount major quarrying expeditions and begin building projects, although these were not completed. Little firm evidence from the reign points to military campaigns or active involvement in the maintenance of empire.

The history of the latter part of the Twentieth Dynasty (ca. 1150–1075 B.C.E.) is one of decline, exacerbated by a quick succession of kings, all probably related to Ramesses III. Egypt progressively lost its vassal states in Syria-Palestine and more gradually its control of Nubia. Libyan incursions into Middle and Upper Egypt contributed to political, economic, and social insecurity. Although the tomb and temple thefts recorded in papyri from the reigns of Ramesses IX onwards may not have been exceptional events, the associated trials attest to corruption in Thebes and the failure of local authorities to maintain order.

Diminishing royal authority was balanced to some extent by continuity in some major elite families. The vizier Neferrenpet was active from the reign of Ramesses IV to Ramesses VI and the high priest of Amun, Ramessesnakht, held office for over thirty years, from Ramesses IV to Ramesses IX (Polz 1998). The longer reigns of Ramesses IX (ca. 18 years) and Ramesses XI (ca. 30 years) also offered a degree of continuity toward the end of the dynasty. Ramesses IX engaged in small-scale building works and military actions, and Ramesses XI was able to muster an army when civil war engulfed Upper Egypt (no. 8). However, this civil war speaks to profound fragmentation of governmental systems, leading ultimately to the devolution of power to local officials, such as Herihor, the general and high priest of Amun, who governed Upper Egypt in the final years of Ramesses XI's reign. These developments in royal and elite power structures look toward, and usher in, the culturally vital and politically decentralized world of early-first millennium Egypt.

3.2. Cultural Transformations

The Ramessid period, in particular the early Nineteenth Dynasty, is often seen as a largely reactionary phase when traditional beliefs and practices were reinstated after the "heresy" of the Amarna period. The nature of this reaction and the levels at which it was negotiated and enacted are widely debated. Innovation in nonroyal monumental discourse and representation, including biography, is part of broader interplays of tradition and change that characterize the late New Kingdom and for which Amarna is viewed as a major catalyst. Most relevant to biographies are linguistic change, the Ramessid conception of the past, and developments in religion.

Discussion of cultural change in the Ramessid period has centered on the impact of what Antonio Loprieno (1996, 522) terms "cultural diglossia" (Baines 1996; Fischer-Elfert 2003, with references). This refers to the transmission of Middle Egyptian literary texts, including for example the Tale of Sinuhe, as a canon in educational contexts, such as scribal training at the workmen's village of Deir el-Medina. At the same time, new literary genres emerged, composed in and enabled by a new form of the written language, Late Egyptian. Something like Late Egyptian was first broadly used in monumental contexts in the Amarna period, although many related features can be found in earlier texts. In the Ramessid period, Late Egyptian was the language of non-literary documents such as legal and economic texts, as well as letters. Literary and monumental texts vary in the level to which they incorporate later forms. Monumental texts, in particular, tend to be composed in a more elevated and traditional register termed "Neo-Middle Egyptian" or

"Traditional Egyptian (égyptien de tradition)."[13] Biographical texts participate in this linguistic proliferation in complex ways, from the formal texts of Bakenkhons (no. 2), composed in "Traditional Egyptian," to the mix of registers, from Middle Egyptian to Late Egyptian, in the biography of Samut (no. 11a; see 4.3).

The separation of formal high literary forms from contemporary compositions has been interpreted as showing Ramessid veneration of an ideal age in the past, particularly the Middle Kingdom, together with a sense of separation from and inferiority to it (Assmann 2002 [1996], 276–77; Fischer-Elfert 2003, 125). This interpretation is reinforced by sources such as a tomb relief, "Fragment Daressy," which depicts revered "authors" and sages from the past, and the so-called "students' miscellany" of Papyrus Chester Beatty IV, which laments their passing: "None of our time is like Neferti, or Khety, the foremost among them" (Lichtheim 1976, 177). But to view this treatment simply as veneration and "inferiority" glosses over complex interactions and tensions between tradition and innovation. A magical papyrus in Athens, probably from Deir el-Medina, incorporates sages of the past into a protective spell because of their magical efficacy (Fischer-Elfert 2002, 177–79; 2003, 128–30, fig. 7:1). This text reinforces the significance of verses of P Chester Beatty IV that refer to the magical power of these individuals, exemplifying how various pasts were redefined and transformed by new contexts. The Fragment Daressy is unprovenanced; its lost tomb may have mobilized similar plays (Baines 1989, 143). Such reformulations of traditional structures, themes, and settings are also a feature of Ramessid biography.

In religion and religious display, response to the Amarna period can be encapsulated in two broad spheres, the development of what Jan Assmann (1995 [1983]) terms "Theban Amun-Re theology," an extension of the solar religion of the pre-Amarna New Kingdom (Baines 1998b, 277–88), and "personal piety." Definitions of, and approaches to, this latter phenomenon are crucial for Ramessid biography. Assmann (e.g., 1995 [1983], 190–210; 2002 [1996], 229–46) defines "personal piety" narrowly as a textual or literary phenomenon that negotiates broader changes in the understanding of the world and the gods and is thus distinct from "popular," local practices such as domestic shrines and votive offerings. "Personal piety" would express a new religiosity, concerned with the direct experience of god and crystallized in the phrase "to place god in one's heart."[14] Assmann locates the beginnings of this religious movement in the Theban festivals of the early New Kingdom, but sees its most developed form in such texts as the Ramessid biographies of Samut and Djehutyemheb (nos. 11–12) and in contemporary hymns and prayers that express a direct experience of the divine within a view of the world as dependent on the will of god (including nos. 45–48). He links what he sees as the radical nature of this development to Amarna reforms, which positioned the king as sole intermediary between the human sphere and his god, the Aten.

Such a view of Ramessid discourse as incorporating a new reality "in which time, destiny, and history become intelligible in a religious sense" (Assmann 2002 [1996], 243) depends on addressing a restricted selection of sources and on dismissing as irrelevant different, earlier forms of evidence for direct interaction with the divine sphere (e.g., Baines 1991, 172–78). A Middle Kingdom stela, probably from Wadi el-Hudi, links the moral phraseology of provision for others with the performance of temple ritual (Espinel 2005; compare Fischer-Elfert and Grimm 2003, 71, 73–74), a motif emphasized in Ramessid texts. A study by Susanne Bickel (2003) of evidence from Amarna shows how direct communication with and experience of the Aten could be displayed by elite individuals in various contexts. She draws on representations and formulations of prayers in tombs, as well as introductory formulae in letters which evoke the Aten specifically and may attest to religious practices across a broader social scale.

Bickel's study strengthens and extends John Baines's argument (1991, 194–98; Baines 2001) that the Ramessid developments form part of changes in and expansion of decorum in representation, in addition to displaying an intensified interest in religious matters, rather than expressing fundamental shifts in world-view and religious belief. This expansion can be understood both as a reaction against Akhenaten's centralizing reforms and as being enabled by them. Some of the ways in which Ramessid individuals exploited and extended these domains and boundaries can be explored through the texts translated in this book.

3.3. CHANGE IN REPRESENTATION: THE NONROYAL TOMB

Developments in the architecture and decorative programs of elite tombs had an important effect on the use of biography in these spaces; they are also central to discussions of religious thought in the Ramessid period (e.g., Assmann 2001, 259–68; 2003b, 51–52). In architecture and decoration, the Ramessid tomb can be envisaged on the model of a temple, presenting images of the tomb owner, rather than the king who is shown in temples, adoring the gods, as well as depicting the transition to the next world. This is an extension of the traditional function of the nonroyal tomb, whose decoration focused on celebrating and commemorating the owner's life and the world of the living. Many of these developments can be traced back to the pre-Amarna Eighteenth Dynasty (Seyfried 1987; Strudwick 1994). Thus, the Ramessid tomb does not mark a radical change so much as the culmination of a longer process of development and transformation.[15]

The architectural model of the temple is most clearly visible in tombs built in post-Amarna and Ramessid cemeteries at Saqqara. These structures, many of which are free-standing rather than rock-cut, display the organization and structure of cult temples, from large pylons and columned courtyards at the front to tripartite sanctuary areas at the rear where the cult was focused (Raue 1995; general introduction: Martin 1991). Theban tombs, in contrast, were rock-cut. Although the external, upper levels of these tombs tend to be poorly preserved, there is evidence for temple-style architecture in the remains of pylons and courts. Large pillared courts that bear a close affinity to temple architecture are also a feature of some high elite Theban tombs from the reign of Amenhotep III in the Eighteenth Dynasty (e.g., Kheruef, Theban Tomb 192: PM I[2], 1, 296; Ramose, Theban Tomb 55: PM I[2], 1, 106; also Eigner 1983, esp. fig. 5).

The temple-like character of Theban Ramessid tombs is emphasized through the decorative program of their chapels. The scenes in this zone are more explicitly religious in character than earlier tomb scenes, foregrounding the tomb owner's adoration of a range of deities together with depictions relating to preparation for, and transition to, the next world (for which see Barthelmess 1992). Both types are known in pre-Amarna tombs, but such adoration scenes are generally then limited to particular walls and deities directly related to access to the afterlife, such as Osiris and Hathor. The predominance of these scenes in Ramessid tombs can be contrasted with the reduction in those that relate to the office and career of the owner and still more in "daily life" scenes. Although rare, such scenes do occur in Ramessid tombs, where they may be connected to the owner's occupation. Nigel Strudwick (1994, 324) argues this connection, for example, for the gold-working scenes in the shrine of the tomb of the overseer of the treasury in the domain of Amun, Neferrenpet (Hofmann 1995, pls. 39, 40). Scenes of counting cattle and offering calves to Amun in the tomb of the assessor of cattle of the domain of Amun, Samut (no. 11: Negm 1997, pls. 8, 10–11, 18–19), may have a similar function, setting his official role in service of the gods (also Hofmann 2004, 125–29).

Religious themes are integrated into the tomb through a new organization of wall decoration (Assmann 1987, 34–36). Earlier arrangements were governed by architectural features of the tomb so that, for example, a group of scenes would be developed within, and confined to, one section of wall. Register lines were used to distribute the elements within compositions. In Ramessid tomb decoration the register line is the primary organizing principle for the decoration. Strips or bands wrap around tomb walls and are not governed by architectural boundaries. In the tomb of Samut, scenes of the

funerary journey on the east end wall continue onto the north wall with depictions of the carrying of the coffin toward the tomb and ritual acts performed
in front of it (Negm 1997, pls. 23, 25). While Assmann (1987, 36) compares
this changed scene presentation with the organization of scenes on Eighteenth
Dynasty stelae, the new arrangement may also emphasize processes of transition and movement that lead to, and culminate in, the shrine area of tombs.

   Another new feature of Ramessid tombs that reinforces their temple-like
character is the inclusion of rock-cut or free-standing statues of deities in
the shrine. At Thebes and Saqqara, these usually consist of single statues of
Osiris, Hathor as a cow, or sacred bulls (the latter at Saqqara). The only statue
groups from the two cemeteries so far attested are triads of Osiris, Isis, and
Horus (see Kampp-Seyfried 1996, I, 51 for Thebes; van Dijk 1988, 43–44 for
Saqqara). More elaborate groups occurring in provincial tombs often include
local gods. The tomb of Anhurmose at el-Mashayikh (no. 18) has two triads
of deities on either side of a Hathor cow emerging from the rock. The triads
are Horus, Osiris, and Isis on the left, with Thoth flanked by damaged figures
of Onuris/Shu and Mehit/Tefnut on the right (Ockinga and al-Masri 1990,
26–28, pl. 1; compare no. 24).

   Biographical texts that focus on an individual's achievements in this world
have been seen as sitting rather uncomfortably within this densely religious
setting. This would then explain why biography rarely occurs in Ramessid Theban tombs, which form by far the largest surviving group. However,
expansions in boundaries of decorum that made possible the transformation
of tomb function in the Ramessid period also meant that, when biography
was selected as a focus for the tomb, its character could shift to make play
with these religious concerns. I explore these possibilities below (4.2).

4. Biography in the Ramessid Period

4.1. Selection of Material

   The selection of monuments presented in this book is not comprehensive, but intended to illustrate the diversity and complexity of biography and
elite self-presentation in the Ramessid period. Most texts are longer narrative inscriptions, but I include some shorter statements or epithet-based
formulations in order to highlight the range of what was created.

   The material clusters around the reign of Ramesses II in the Nineteenth
Dynasty. The post-Amarna Eighteenth Dynasty sources point to the importance of Memphite contexts (discussed below), as well as giving a sense
of how traditional motifs were reestablished after Amarna. Distinctions

between the post-Amarna period and the Nineteenth Dynasty are also not sharply drawn (3.1). A smaller number of examples comes from the Twentieth Dynasty; the latest datable texts included are the inscriptions of the high priest of Amun, Amenhotep, from its closing years (nos. 4–9).

The majority of the monuments I treat were set up in southern (Upper) Egypt, especially Thebes. However, throughout the Ramessid period, the court was based in the north at Memphis and Piramesse, the city founded by Ramesses II in the Delta. Thus, many of the inner elite no doubt built their tombs in cemeteries at Saqqara or elsewhere in the north and dedicated monuments in temples in the same regions. Few objects from these temples survive (nos. 27 and 29 for the Memphite area), and only a small number of tombs there have been excavated and fully published. I include biographical texts from two post-Amarna tombs at Saqqara (nos. 20, 23) to give a sense of the potential significance of the tombs. There are also strong indications that biography remained a component of Memphite tombs into the Nineteenth Dynasty. Excavators in the tomb of Tia and Tia, a sister of Ramesses II and her husband, found the shattered fragments of a large stela bearing biographical material, which had been the focal point of the central cult chapel (van Dijk 1997, 51–52; see no. 27). Some published Memphite tombs contain shorter biographical statements, and further unpublished examples have been reported.[16]

I include a small number of texts whose content does not fall within a narrow definition of biography, such as an oracle relating to a land dispute (no. 15) and the endowment deed set up in the tomb of Penniut at Aniba in Nubia (no. 44a). These provide selected examples of alternative strategies for the presentation of biographical events. Other monuments of individuals not included in this book contain long legal texts (Gaballa 1977), fragmentary pictures of works of art the owner supervized (S. Schott 1957, 2–5, pl. 1; compare Gaballa and Kitchen 1981, 172–75, figs. 8–11), or scenes of a sed-festival with which the owner was probably involved (Gardiner 1910). These different modes of self-presentation give a sense of the wider context within which biography was produced. A further example is the statue of Panehsy (no. 28) whose inscriptions include speeches directed to the statue itself, vividly setting out its role within the temple. His texts mobilize alternative ways of thematizing the self and offer insights into the meaning of temple statues, a central medium for biography in the Ramessid period.

4.2. CHANGING CONTEXTS

When interpreting Ramessid nonroyal monuments, it is vital to take into account space and setting because demarcations of decorum were relaxed and contexts of self-presentation were changing. Many of the monuments included in this book are distinctive in their media or setting. I highlight a few examples here, in part synthesizing scattered remarks in the introductions to individual texts.

Biographies were only seldom incorporated into tombs, which focused increasingly on the deceased's relationship to the divine sphere (3.3). Where biographies were included, the texts often extended the boundaries of traditional forms of self-presentation, reformulating and elaborating biographical motifs in distinctive settings, as in the tombs of the Theban temple staff, Samut and Djehutyemheb (nos. 11–12). Samut's biography (no. 11a) fills one side of the tomb's hall and centers on his relationship to the goddess Mut, who is depicted receiving the texts. He dedicates his life and his property exclusively to her in return for protection and provision of a funeral: "Burial, it is in your hands, unique one." The fragmentary legal text inscribed below the biography (no. 11b) seems to record Samut's receipt of a "pension" from her domain in return for this dedication. The biography and legal text therefore incorporate the tomb into Mut's domain. A similar dedication of space occurs in Djehutyemheb's tomb. Its temple-like setting culminates with the biographical text in the shrine, which narrates Hathor's designation of land for Djehutyemheb's tomb in a dream (no. 12a). For a biography to be included in the shrine of a tomb is striking; traditionally such texts had been inscribed in the hall. Thus Djehutyemheb narrated direct, lived experience of the divine in the inner, most sacred part of the tomb. The text marks, governs, and protects the space for Djehutyemheb's mummy in the burial chamber below by mobilizing his intimate connection with the goddess. In both these tombs, the biography says little about other events in the protagonist's life but heightens the meaning of the monument as a whole.

Both in these cases and in tombs where more traditional biographies are inscribed in the hall, close to the entrance (e.g., nos. 18, 24, 25c), the texts participate in the transition between this world and the next. Most tombs with biographies also include appeals to the living, so that living social groups are drawn into the context. The standard, otherworldly decoration of Ramessid tombs does not usually exhibit this feature. Important exceptions include the entrances to the tombs of Djehutyemheb (no. 12: Seyfried 1995, 23–24, 29–30, pl. 25) and Anhurmose (no. 18: Ockinga and al-Masri 1988, 19, pl. 10 [b]), which are framed with appeals (not translated in this book). Thus, tombs with biographical inscriptions balance the connections of the individual and his tomb to the lived world with expressions of a direct relationship with the gods.

In the Ramessid period, the temple was the central domain of elite self-presentation. The temple statue became increasingly popular from the early Eighteenth Dynasty onward (Gnirs 1996, 198–99), and, in the Third Intermediate period, statues were the primary medium for biographical inscriptions (Jansen-Winkeln 1985). Already during the Ramessid period, the majority of elite biographies are on statues and relatively few use the older stela format. A number of these statues make play with the implications of their medium through distinctive forms (e.g., nos. 14a, 16, 21). Other owners dedicated multiple statues, bearing complementary texts, in different parts of the same temple complex, perhaps refiguring earlier practices with stelae (compare nos. 41b, 42). This strategy is a characteristic of the high priesthood at Karnak in the Nineteenth Dynasty (nos. 2, 3a–c; see Barbotin 1994 for the Twentieth Dynasty).

Ramessid interest in developing the form of statues is also significant for self-presentation. Examples of such developments include the use of statue surfaces for images and the creation of new types, such as "begging statues," which show the figure's hand cupped to the mouth (Clère 1995). These latter statues display their role as mediators for the gods explicitly (see also Clère 1968a) and foreground desired physical interactions with audiences. The voice of the inscriptions can be drawn into this play: statues can be addressed as an aspect of the self (no. 28) or speak themselves. The "begging" statue of Amenemone (no. 36) has a traditional biography on its right side, while the left bears an address made by the statue to a potential audience in which it stresses its exclusive role as an intermediary for Hathor, evoking its own physical form: "Give me beer upon my hand, *sermet*-beer for my mouth, sweet ointment for my bald head … (for) I am a bald one (priest) of Gold (Hathor)."

The most striking Ramessid innovation is the inscription of biography on temple walls, especially in the preeminent state complex of Karnak. Such walls, especially in inner areas, had been restricted to depicting the interaction of king and gods. For a nonroyal to be foregrounded in this domain is quite exceptional. In the late Nineteenth Dynasty, the high priest of Amun, Roma, inscribed a long text on the east massif of the eighth pylon in Karnak (no. 3d). This reworking of a particular area of the temple as a zone for individual display can be compared with the inscriptions set up on the walls of less central and less restricted cult structures at Elkab, by the viceroy Setau (no. 41a), and on the Theban West Bank, by the chancellor Bay (no. 32). These expansions in decorum for nonroyal self-presentation culminated with the high priest Amenhotep at the end of the Twentieth Dynasty, who made extensive use of the walls of the southern processional route in Karnak for his biographical scenes and texts (nos. 5–9) in order to display his own power and position in the temple and in relation to the gods. The priest's role in these texts and scenes approaches royal prerogatives, although images of the king are retained. There is, therefore, no complete break between religious and political authority. These inscriptions signify instead a redefinition of the meanings of some spheres of sacred space as well as a reformulation of the potentials for priestly representation in these areas.

4.3. FORM AND LINGUISTIC FEATURES

The structure and language of many Ramessid biographies is highly innovative. Some texts maintain traditional forms, with a narrative, often composed in "Traditional Egyptian," or sequences of nonverbal statements following an offering formula or title string. Others depart from these structures through framing devices, play with voice, and the range of linguistic registers made possible by the diglossia of the period (3.2).

Hymns and prayers, characterized by such titles as "giving praise to" a deity, were occasionally used as frames for biography in the mid Eighteenth Dynasty and become increasingly frequent in the Ramessid period (e.g., nos. 12a, 45–50). Incorporation within a hymn enhances a text's potential to display personal concerns in relation to the gods, which is a central feature of Ramessid nonroyal discourse. This expansion of meaning through setting extends to other contexts. The stela of Setau, the viceroy of Kush, alludes to the frame of royal inscriptions by starting with a date and full royal titulary, followed by a eulogy of the king: "Viceroy of Kush ... says in extolling this Perfect God, Horus beloved of Maat ... [I was a servant] ..." (no. 41b). In a striking mix of settings, the damaged front surface of the stela from Bilgai (no. 33) relates to royal display through its inclusion of such motifs as the goddess Seshat recording years of rule. In contrast, part of the text on the reverse is addressed to a named nonroyal individual, thus focusing on a personal context comparable to that mobilized in letters; the use of Late Egyptian and the detailed but hyperbolic enumeration of quantities of goods strengthens the analogy.

Numerous linguistic registers are deployed in the biographies. Part of this development is temporal: the Nineteenth Dynasty texts of Bakenkhons (no. 2) and Nefersekheru (no. 24) are in formal Traditional Egyptian, while those of the late Twentieth Dynasty such as Hori (no. 34: Ramesses VIII) and Amenhotep (especially no. 7: Ramesses IX–XI) are almost entirely in Late Egyptian. Alternatively, oscillation between Middle and Late Egyptian in earlier Nineteenth Dynasty texts, such as the stela of Wenennefer (no. 17), may indicate that there was no good model for their particular themes, while the texts in Late Egyptian on the statue of Panehsy (no. 28: Ramesses II) point to the development of new genres of monumental texts.

The literary Late Egyptian influence visible in the stelae from Deir el-Medina (chapter VI) may reflect the level of education in the village, which involved training in high literary forms, as well as aspiration toward elite models. The distinctive motifs and phraseology developed in the texts also speak to a highly productive compositional milieu interested in new forms of expression within traditional settings.[17] A further example is the Twentieth Dynasty scribe Amennakht who composed a number of literary texts, including an instruction, as well as hymns and prayers (Bickel and Mathieu 1993).

One of the most complex interweavings of frame, register, and voice is the biographical inscription of Samut (no. 11a). In his treatment of the text, Pascal Vernus (1978, 137–41) emphasizes the conscious and artful selection and fusion of different linguistic registers to characterize the different sections. He contrasts the classic Middle Egyptian of the opening five stanzas of the literary narrative, which tell the "Tale of Samut," with the Late Egyptian of the legal statements and the hymn with which the text closes. He considers that the different linguistic levels generate distinctions between generalizing statements expressed through traditional (Middle Egyptian) forms, on the one hand, and aspects of the individual and personal marked by later structures, on the other. In a complementary study, Ludwig Morenz (2000, 315–16) emphasizes the numerous shifts in voice that are signalled by specific narrative forms. The intimacy of the appeals to Mut, which are made in the second person, are framed by, and contrast with, the third-person narrative and the final hymn to Mut, in which the voice of Samut ceases to be present. Vernus (1978, 119) suggests that this hymn enacts a final dissolution of the self that had been so powerfully present at the beginning of the text: Samut is finally surrendered to Mut. These few examples demonstrate the artful and careful composition of the texts in order to maximize both their meaning and their aesthetic qualities.

4.4. Being Near to God

The central relationship that Ramessid individuals develop in their self-presentations is with the gods. This relationship and other aspects of religious self are articulated in multiple, highly personal ways, the diversity of which exemplifies the increasing flexibility of pictorial and textual decorum. This focus is not simply a novel form of "piety," but rather a new display of personal concerns that had existed for many centuries.

The priestly biographies from Karnak and Abydos (chapter I) develop themes relating to their protagonist's role and life in temples, such as ritual performance in key festivals at Abydos (e.g., nos. 14a, 16) and ceremonial roles shouldering the portable barque shrine of the cult statue when it was taken out in processions (e.g., nos. 3c, 16, 17). Distinctive features of these texts include emphasis on vital moments of divine presence, such as initiation into the priesthood and oracular action. Processes of initiation may be alluded to in some Old Kingdom biographies (see Strudwick 2005, 369, no. 270) and are a component of biographies from the Middle Kingdom (Fischer-Elfert and Grimm 2003, 71) and the early New Kingdom (Kruchten 1989, 178, 188–89). In Ramessid texts, its significance is emphasized as the culminating moment in an individual's life and his relationship to king and god (e.g., nos. 2, 3b, 17), as well as enabling him to be present at the center of divine action. The biography of the high priest of Isis, Wenennefer, extends the implications of this motif: his initiation, together with the lively celebration surrounding it, opens the way for his assimilation to the divine child Horus-Ihy (no. 17).

Oracles, as singular moments of divine intervention, are first attested as the focus of royal monumental narratives in the early Eighteenth Dynasty (Kruchten 2001). They become a component of nonroyal, priestly biographical narrative in the Nineteenth Dynasty. The phrase "I was high priest as the gift of Amun" in the biography of Roma (no. 3c) alludes to oracular appointment (see also nos. 1, 3b, 18). One of the most elaborate developments of this motif comes from outside the priestly domain. In a striking departure from traditional biographical structures, the stela of the military officer Penre uses the frame of the oracle to present a speech of the goddess directed to the protagonist (no. 37); this inclusion of a divine speech in a biographical context is exceptional.

Outside the temple domain, other models were used to relate the self to the divine sphere. New motifs such as dreams in which goddesses appear (nos. 12, 50), or the complex interaction of fictionalizing tale and juridical text of Samut (no. 11), narrate singular moments when the self became the focus of divine presence. The dream motif also assimilates and extends earlier royal models (for which see Szpakowska 2003, 47–54, 140). Both the dreams of Djehutyemheb and Ipuy and Samut's "search within himself" for divine protection show a new interest in exploring the internal experiences of the protagonist rather than presenting his external social actions.

Motifs like these are developed in a different direction in the group of stelae from Deir el-Medina, which narrate their protagonist's acceptance of personal responsibility for wrongdoing and the consequential divine punishment that they experienced (nos. 45–48). These texts are framed as hymns, transforming a negative experience into an intervention that they offer back to a deity, evoking divine power at a specific, personal level. This motif is attested only on monuments from Nineteenth Dynasty Deir el-Medina, but echoes of the same ideas can be found in elite biographies that foreground notions of divine rescue and protection without admitting wrongdoing (e.g., no. 11a). In a further extension, the king can also be called upon for aid at a moment of crisis: "I am your servant who stood suffering for you (Amun or the king) … Amun-Re, king of the gods, heard my plea immediately, for he did not permit delay … and I appealed to Pharaoh, my lord …" (no. 8; compare nos. 10 and 34). Thus, religious motifs and settings offer alternative ways of contouring and shaping a life which, through their singular focus on the internal experience of the individual, seem more personal.

4.5. ROYAL PRESENCE

Although many of the biographical texts have a strong religious focus, the king remained central to events and transitions in people's lives such as appointment, promotion, and reward, as in earlier texts. While, in theory, most elite individuals would be able to present a close relationship between themselves and gods, the king was directly accessible to far fewer. His presence in people's lives is more salient in monuments of very high status individuals and may have been crucial for display in some contexts. For example, the use of a figure of the king may have been necessary for the extensive inscription and decoration on the walls of Karnak temple by the high priest of Amun, Amenhotep (nos. 5–9).

The texts translated in this volume present clearly delineated aspects of the king's role, in some cases specifically in cult and ritual. These developments may have parallels in core depictions of the king where he is depicted as supplicant, priestly actor, and the semi-divine recipient of a cult (Baines 1998a, 39). For example, in sanctuaries in Sety I's temple at Abydos the king is shown performing priestly duties, such as cleansing altars and clothing the gods, as part of a detailed evocation of the daily temple ritual that is not attested in other temples. This is a more active and intimate presentation of care for the gods than traditional formal temple scenes of the king offering to them and receiving life and dominion in return. Outside temples, numerous colossal statues of Ramesses II were created as focal points of cult practice at major temple sites in Egypt and Nubia (Habachi 1969; Wildung 1973), following earlier practices particularly of the Eighteenth Dynasty king Amenhotep III.

In nonroyal contexts, a comparable royal role can be displayed in images of cult statues through which Nineteenth and Twentieth Dynasty reward scenes are mediated (e.g., no. 44b). In the reward scene in the Theban tomb of Paser, Sety I is displayed in undifferentiated, effigy-like form with the souls of Pe and Nekhen, evoking his mediatory role in Paser's transition to the next world (no. 25c, fig. 8). Texts that center fully on the lived experience of the king also make play with this cultic potential. In the biography of Nefersekheru (no. 24), language of initiation and purification, which presents the protagonist's advancement through different zones of the royal palace, resonates with priestly narratives of temple space. The culminating scene of Nefersekheru's reward ends the biographical component of the text. As in Paser's scene, royal reward in this life is linked with reward in the next and the king facilitates both. The mobilization of the king's divinized image may correlate with increased representation of individual relationships with the divine sphere. However, this aspect was already developed in Eighteenth Dynasty self-presentation, as in the effigy-form depiction of Thutmose III in the tomb of his vizier Rekhmire (N. de G. Davies 1943, II, pl. 13) or the king's cult presence in the Opet festival narrated in the biography of the soldier Amenemhab under Thutmose III and Amenhotep II (Freier in Blumenthal et. al. 1984, 313). The Ramessid texts seem then to draw on and elaborate such earlier strategies.

The most fully developed narration of actions performed for the king in the Ramessid corpus is in the biography of Setau, the viceroy of Nubia (no. 41b), one of the few to report military exploits. In this text however, Setau becomes the embodiment of royal power in Nubia, acting as "the powerful forearm of Pharaoh," and plundering the land of Irem, in place of the king. Setau presents himself in a quasi-pharaonic role, a strategy that is characteristic of viceregal display in Nubia (see also no. 43; Raedler 2003) and one that may be partly enabled by Setau's emphasis on the king's deified, cultic presence within the temple of Wadi el-Sebua. Here, the deified image of Ramesses II may distance him to some extent from the human sphere, so that a non-royal individual can step into parts of his role.

A central feature of many biographies is the shift in emphasis from actions performed for the king, such as the military exploits in some Eighteenth Dynasty biographies and the biography of Setau, to situations enabled by him. In many texts, the king's central role is as a mediator. In the priestly biographies he ratifies divine interventions such as initiation and oracles relating to promotions (nos. 1, 3b, 17). In the biography of the chief sculptor Userhat (no. 19b), it is the king's recognition and promotion that enables Userhat to create the cult images he lists. Royal action gives him access to the divine sphere, leading to his transformation into a priestly actor with which the text culminates. A different pattern is visible in the late Twentieth Dynasty biography of Hori (no. 34), where the protagonist places himself as the mediator between the king and the gods, forcefully requesting divine protection for himself and the king.

Ramessid developments in self-presentation favor strategies through which people could approach gods directly. The image of the king in some biographies can be understood to reflect this different focus. However, these developments do not all point in the same direction; the king's role in both core and elite representation was a domain of contention and experimentation. The biographies in this book therefore speak to the various ways individuals could allude to and mobilize royal presence in relation to personal status and transformation.

4.6. Social Self

In shaping and displaying a self and life, Ramessid biographies remain grounded in ancient motifs of service to the gods and the king, exemplified by narratives of temple construction, which are central to the biographies of the high priests of Amun in Karnak (chapter I, part 1) and the viceroy Setau (no. 41b). In contrast, themes of social responsibility are less central than in earlier periods. Interactions with the human sphere may have been represented in other domains, such as the mapping of kinship and collegial relationships on late-New Kingdom elite stelae and statues (e.g., Pirelli 1998). This motif is developed in biography, for example, through Roma's listing of offices held by his sons and grandsons in the domain of Amun (no. 3c). The role of the individual as mediator between human and divine spheres, which is mobilized in several texts, notably that of Amenemone (no. 36), may also evoke another aspect of social role.

The most detailed elaboration of the ideal social self is the inscription of the high priest of Onuris, Anhurmose (no. 18). The central theme of his biography is social responsibility through providing for and protecting dependants and as an impartial judge, themes that had been central to self-presentation since the Old Kingdom and reached their most developed form in the Twelfth Dynasty. Anhurmose's text is, however, much longer than most earlier examples. In the priestly biography of Bakenkhons (no. 2b), social responsibility is associated with, and located within, temples. This focus is visible also in Anhurmose's text, where the long sections dealing with his social role are preceded by verses relating to his duties in the temple.

Some of the most ancient and formulaic motifs relating to social action are extended to, and linked with, transition to and judgment in the next world. The thickness of the entrance to the tomb of Paser (see no. 25) depicts his father, who is probably deceased, offering a hymn to the setting sun that closes with the phrases: "(I) gave bread to the [hungry], water to the thirsty, and clothes to the naked" (KRI I, 285,14). Similar phrases are spoken by Paser in a prayer to Osiris on a stela from the tomb (KRI I, 289,6–7) and can be compared with the moral characterization that closes Bakaa's hymn to Osiris (no. 39 and compare no. 10). The most extended presentation of the connection between ethical behavior and life after death is on the four-sided stela of Tia, where the patterning of texts across the surfaces links virtuous action with funerary preparation and transformation (no. 27). The relationship between moral and ethical statements and judgment in the next world had been largely implicit in earlier biography and literary texts. In the Ramessid examples, they are fully integrated with the display of religious concerns and the connection between them is made explicit.

5. Approaching Translation

In my translations, I stay close to the Egyptian while trying to maintain readability and accessability in English. The Egyptian of most of the texts is well-understood, but some passages remain problematic. These are discussed in accompanying notes. In many cases, multiple translations of a passage are possible. Ambiguities and alternative translations are treated in notes when they are crucial to the understanding of a text. A number of Egyptian words are left untranslated; these are vocalized and written in italic (in roman in the italic text introductions). In some cases, the exact meaning of an untranslated word is unknown, but in many the relevant concept has no easy equivalent in English. For these, definitions or explanations are given in the Glossary. Some names of objects or locations, for example in temples or in the next world, are also included there.

The translations are arranged in metrical form following the system developed by Gerhard Fecht (especially 1965: 28–38 for a list of rules; 1993). Fecht's system is based on stressed "units of meaning," that are also prosodic units in the Egyptian language. Small sense groups, usually composing a statement (a clause or pair of epithets, for example), are organized into metrically structured lines of two or three stresses (Fecht's "cola"), called "verses." Verses are grouped by content and theme into larger stanzas. Although this system has been disputed (Lichtheim 1971–1972; Burkard 1996), later research, by Richard Parkinson (in preparation) in particular, on physical features of texts that correlate with metrical units, confirms the reality of the system for the Egyptians. Moreover, the metrical presentation of the translations brings out their poetic character, while also fostering a clearer understanding of the texts' meaning.

6. CONTEXT

Biographical monuments are works of architectural, visual, and verbal art. My treatment of the texts in this book attempts to present all of these dimensions. An introduction to each monument provides a description, together with information on its context and the career of the owner where available, as well as an outline of key themes. For stelae and statues, I translate all the texts inscribed on the object. Shorter texts, such as scene captions, are included in the introductory discussion. Biographies and other longer texts are set out in stanzas.

Although the context of architectural monuments, such as tombs and chapels, is salient for interpretation, it is not possible to present this material in detail. My descriptions are intended to provide an overview of the layout and decorative program, highlighting key areas of interest. Both the texts on the architectural elements of the chapel of Userhat (no. 19a) and the inscriptions of Amenhotep on temple walls at Karnak (esp. no. 6) are translated in full, giving some sense of how surrounding texts relate to biographical material. The selected line drawings and photographs are also intended to bring the visual and monumental setting of the biographies to life. I hope that these more fully presented examples give a sense of how context contributes to the meaning of self-presentations.

In this collection I seek to present an insight into the flexibility and creativity of Egyptian elite self-presentation, of the multiple ways in which Ramessid individuals chose to display themselves and to transform monumental contexts. Biographies of the Ramessid period exemplify the personal character of such strategies of self-presentation, showing how specific members of the elite artfully fashioned enduring commemorations of their lives through a convergence of text, image, and space, in monuments that had power and presence both in this life and for the next.

Fig. 2. Map of Egypt showing the locations of the sites from which the texts translated in this book come.

TRANSLATIONS

I

THE PRIESTHOOD AND RELATED OFFICES

PART 1. THE HIGH PRIESTS OF AMUN

1. THE THEBAN TOMB OF NEBWENENEF

The importance of the office of high priest in the early Ramessid period is apparent both in Nebwenenef's ownership of a mortuary temple southwest of the temple of Sety I on the Theban West Bank at Qurna (now largely destroyed) and the location of his tomb in the high-status sector of Dra Abu el-Naga in the northern part of the Theban necropolis. His later successors Bakenkhons (no. 2) and Roma (no. 3) were buried in the same area. The text recording Nebwenenef's appointment to his position in year 1 of Ramesses II is carved on the south wall of his tomb's transverse hall. The remaining walls of the hall include adoration and ritual scenes typical of Ramessid tombs. The decoration also includes distinctive motifs such as the tomb owner spearing a turtle and hippopotamus (Säve-Söderbergh 1956; and see Hofmann 2004, 39–40).

The scene accompanying the biography shows the king standing at a window of appearances, his right arm outstretched toward the figure of Nebwenenef below; behind the king are traces of the figure of his queen, Nefertari. Their cartouches are carved above them: Dual King, Usermaatre Setepenre, son of Re, Ramesses Meryamun; great royal wife, Nefertari Merytmut. Nebwenenef stands in a court of slender columns with his right arm held out toward the king. This setting may depict a public space in the royal palace. An entourage of five damaged figures stands behind Nebwenenef, the first of them wearing long, plain robes, possibly those of viziers, and bearing the standards of that office. The first seven columns of text are inscribed between the pillars of the hall in a distinctive fusion of text with royal architecture.

Scenes and texts recording an individual's appointment or reward by the king began to be included in nonroyal tombs in the early Eighteenth Dynasty. Unlike the rulers in these earlier narratives, the king in Nebwenenef's text does not initiate the appointment; his role has become that of a mediator for the oracle of Amun.

Year 1, third month of *akhet* [ ],[1]
after His Person traveled north from Thebes,
having performed what his father favors,
(that is for) Amun-Re, lord of the thrones of the Two Lands,
great bull, chief of the Ennead,

and for Mut the great, lady of Asheru,
Khonsu in Thebes, perfect of peace,
and the Ennead who are in Thebes,
in his perfect festival of Opet.

Returning from there in favor,
when favors had been received on behalf of the life, prosperity, and
          health
of the Dual King, Usermaatre Setepenre (Ramesses II), may he live
          forever.

Landing was made at Tawer,
and the high priest of Amun
Nebwenenef, true of voice, was ushered into the presence of His
          Person.

Now he was (then) high priest of Onuris,
high priest of Hathor, lady of Dendara,
and ⌜overseer⌝ of priests of all the gods
to his south as far as Heriheramun,[2]
and to his north as far as Thinis.

Then His Person said to him:
"You are (now) high priest of Amun;
his treasuries and his granary are under your seal.
You are chief spokesman for his temple;
all his endowments are under your authority.
The domain of Hathor, lady of Dendara, will be under the authority
          of [your son],
the proper [heir (?)] of the offices of your fathers, the seat which you
          used to occupy.

As Re lives for me and loves me,
and as my father Amun favors me,
I presented to him the ⌜whole⌝ entourage,

(including) the chief spokesman of the ⌜troops⌝.
The priests of the gods
and the officials of his domain ⌜who were before him⌝ were
	proclaimed for him,
(but) he was not content ⌜with⌝ a single one among them
except when I spoke ⌜your⌝ name to him.[3]

⌜Perform beneficent acts for him⌝ inasmuch as he desired you.
I know your excellence;
do more and his ⌜*ka* will favor you⌝,
and my *ka* will do so too.

He will cause you to endure at the head of his estate,
he will give to you old age ⌜within it⌝,
and he will bring you to mooring upon the soil of his city.[4]
He will give (you) the bow-line and the stern-line,[5]
for he ⌜himself⌝ desired you and ⌜no other⌝ who was suggested to
	him.

He will give the West to you,
because, as for my father Amun,
(he is) a great god, ⌜without equal⌝,
⌜who investigates⌝ bodies, who reveals hearts.
(He is) Perception, who knows what is in bodies.

⌜No god will have power over what he has done,
for his plans cannot be thwarted;
one relies⌝ on his speech.
He, the lord of the Ennead,
is the one who chose [you on account of your character (?)],
he [advanced (?)] you on account of your excellence."

Then the courtiers and the council of thirty ⌜together
praised the perfection of His Person,
kissing the ground profusely⌝ in the presence of this Perfect God,
performing adorations and propitiating [... ... ...]
paying honor before him,
magnifying his qualities to the height of the sky.

⌜They said: "O ruler for Amun,
who will be forever, whom he brought up from extreme⌝ youth,

may you perform *sed*-festivals [... ... ...]
your [...] like sand.
May you be reborn every dawn
and rejuvenate for us ⌐like⌐ the sun.
May you be youthful like the moon,
as the child of [... ... ...]

[May] you [rule (?)] as king of the Two Banks,
the nine bows at your command.
Your boundary is set to the limits of this sky,
its every circuit under your command.

That which the sun encircles is under your charge
and what [the ocean] washes [is under your control]
while you are upon earth, on the Horus throne,
having appeared as ruler of the living.

You marshal the troops of Egypt,
yet you kill as a lord,
one enduring of kingship upon earth.
[... ... ...]

May (?) you rule as he (Amun?) did
while you are upon earth,
(as) the sun in the sky,
your lifetime being as his lifetime.

May he give you eternity and perpetuity united,
joined in life and power.
O perfect ruler, beloved of Amun,
he [will ... ...]."

[Then] His Person [gave to him (Nebwenenef)] his two seals of
          gold,
and his staff of electrum,[6]
being appointed as high priest of Amun,
⌐overseer⌐ of the treasuries,
overseer of the granary, overseer of works,
and overseer of all craftsmen throughout Thebes.

A royal message was sent out [to inform the entire land (?)]

that the domain of Amun, all his property, [was assigned (?)] to
  him,
all his staff, … [*ca. 11 groups lost*]
[by the favor of (?)] the ruler of Amun who will be for eternity.

2A–B. Two Block Statues of Bakenkhons from Karnak

Bakenkhons was probably appointed high priest of Amun in the third decade of the reign of Ramesses II. He held the office for about twenty years, predeceasing his king. Bakenkhons dedicated two block statues in the temple of Amun at Karnak during his time in office, both of which bear biographical inscriptions; one is now in the Cairo Museum and the other in the Staatliche Sammlung Ägyptischer Kunst in Munich. The statues are very similar in appearance; both are made of limestone, about 1.4 meters high (4' 6"), and bear zones of inscription on the front of the knees, the back pillar, and around the base. The style of the statues suggests that they were made in the late Eighteenth Dynasty, drawing on earlier models, and were reused by Bakenkhons (Schoske 1987). Cartouches of Ramesses II are inscribed on the right and left shoulders of both statues. The Cairo statue was found by Georges Legrain (1909, 21) in 1904 on the east side of the door of the seventh pylon. Notes of the excavator of the Munich statue, J. J. Rifaud, who recorded its discovery in 1818, suggest that it was found in the temple of Amun-Re-Horakhty, located between the eastern gate to Karnak and the temple of Amun (Yoyotte 1957, 85). This temple, built by Bakenkhons for his king on the foundations of an Eighteenth Dynasty temple, is often called a "temple of the hearing ear" and is believed to have been at least symbolically accessible to ordinary people. Unusually, the texts on the base and plinth of the Munich statue read from left to right, rather than right to left, probably to suit the specific location in which it was set up.

The spatial contexts of both statues no doubt influenced the expression of their owner's identity and relationship to the royal and divine spheres. The central theme developed in the Cairo statue is Bakenkhons's responsibility toward temple staff. The Munich statue presents a distinctive list of offices held with the number of years in each, and a detailed description of building works in the Eastern temple. The differences in emphasis of the two textual programs are the more striking when their thematic interconnectedness and parallel phraseology are taken into account. Their concerns intersect at key points, especially moments of promotion, as well as seeming to summarize their different central themes, so that their contents speak to each other across the temple space.

2A. Munich Statue

Front of knees:
An offering which the king gives to Amun-Re-Atum-Horakhty,[7]
ram of heaven,
who lives on Maat,
(divine) image who resides in his barque,
to Mut the great, principal of the Two Lands,
and to Khonsu, perfect of peace,
that they may place my name enduringly in Thebes,
firmly established for eternity,

for the *ka* of the member of the *pat*, count,
overseer of the priests of all the gods,
high priest of Amun in Karnak,
Bakenkhons, ⌈true of voice⌉;

he says: O priests, god's fathers,
⌈*wab*-priests⌉ of the domain of Amun:
give bouquets to my statue,
libations to my form,

(for) I was a servant, effective for his lord,
one silent, truly assiduous,
who was pleased with Maat and hated evil,
one who magnified the renown of his god;
high priest of Amun,
Bakenkhons, ⌈true of voice⌉.

Back pillar:
Member of the *pat*, count,
high priest of Amun,
Bakenkhons, true of voice,
he says: I was truly assiduous, effective for his lord,
who respected the renown of his god, who went forth upon his path,
who performed acts of beneficence within his temple
while I was chief overseer of works in the domain of Amun,
as an excellent confidant for his lord.

O all people who are discerning in their hearts,
who exist, who are upon earth,

and who will come after me,
for millions and millions (of years), after hoary old age,
whose hearts are skilled in recognizing worth,
I will cause you to know my character when (I) was upon earth,
in every office which I performed since my birth.

I spent 4 years as an excellent youngster.
I spent 11 years as a youth,
as a trainee stable-master
for king Men⌜maat⌝re (Sety I).

I was a *wab*-priest of Amun for 4 years.
I was a god's father of Amun
for 12 years.
I was third priest of Amun
for 15 years.
I was second priest of Amun for 12.

He favored me; he perceived me because of my character.
He appointed me high priest of Amun
for 27 years.[8]

I was a good father to my staff, nurturing their young,
offering my hand (to) the one in need,
sustaining the one in poverty,
and ⌜performing⌝ benefactions in his temple.

I was chief overseer of works in Thebes
for his (Amun's) son who came forth from his body,
Dual King, Usermaatre Setepenre,
son of Re, Ramesses Meryamun (Ramesses II), given life,
who makes monuments for his father Amun,
who had placed him on his throne;
made under the charge of the high priest of Amun,
Bakenkhons, true of voice.[9]

He says, as follows: I performed benefactions in the domain of
        Amun,
being overseer of works for my lord.
I made a temple for him,
(called) "Ramesses-Meryamun-who-hears-prayers"

in the upper portal of the domain of Amun.[10]

And I erected obelisks of granite in it,
whose tops approached the sky,
a stone terrace before it,
in front of Thebes,
the *bah*-land and gardens planted with trees.[11]

I made great and very mighty doors of electrum,
whose tops were united with the sky.
I carpentered great and very mighty flagstaffs
and I erected them on the noble court
in front of his temple.

I carpentered great rivergoing boats
for Amun, Mut, and Khonsu;
(all this) by the member of the *pat*, count,
high priest of Amun, Bakenkhons.

Around upper base:
    Member of the *pat*, count,
    high priest of Amun,
    Bakenkhons, ⌜true of voice,
    he says:⌝ I was one truly silent, effective for his god,
    who trusted himself to his every action.
    He placed charm [*ca. 6 groups lost with traces*],
    ⌜I was a humble man⌝ whose hands were ⌜together⌝ upon the
            steering oar,
    acting as a helmsman in life.

    I am happier today than yesterday,
    and at dawn he will increase my happiness;
    for I have been within the domain of Amun from youth to the
            ⌜onset⌝ of old age,
    following ⌜him in a truthful way,
    my eyes⌝ seeing his uraei.
    May he complete a good lifetime for me after 110 years.[12]

Around lower base:
    Made under the charge of the member of the *pat*, count,
    overseer of works on all monuments … [*rest of text lost*][13]

2B. CAIRO STATUE (FIG. 3)

Front of knees:
    An offering which the king gives to Amun-Re,
    the primordial one of the Two Lands, noble potentate,
    who prevails in majestic splendor, great of terror,
    to Mut the great, eye of Re,
    and to Khonsu, perfect of peace,
    that they may place my name enduringly in Thebes,
    established in Karnak,
    and all that goes forth from their offering tables before my statue,

    for the *ka* of the god's father, pure of hands,
    third priest of Amun,
    second priest of Amun,
    overseer of the priests of all the gods,
    high priest of Amun,
    Bakenkhons, true of voice;

    he says: I was the overseer of works in Thebes
    in all excellent works,
    for I was an excellent confidant of his lord,
    guiding all the craftsmanship in every monument
    which he made for his father Amun.

Back pillar:
    God's father of Amun,
    third priest of Amun,
    second priest of Amun,
    overseer of the priests of the gods, the lords of Thebes,
    high priest of Amun,
    Bakenkhons, true of voice;

    he says: I was a man of Thebes from my father and my mother,
    the son of the second priest of Amun in Karnak.
    I came out from the room of writing
    in the temple of the lady of the sky as an excellent youngster.[14]

    I was taught to be a *wab*-priest in the domain of Amun,
    as a son under the guidance of (his) father.
    He favored me; he perceived me because of my character.

Fig. 3. Cairo Block Statue of Bakenkhons (no. 2b: after Legrain 1909, pl. 18).

I followed him in a truthful way.
I was initiated to (the position of) god's father and I saw all his
    manifestations.[15]

I did what is beneficial in his temple,
consisting of all effective works.
I did not commit evil in his domain.
I did not neglect my duties at his side.
I stepped in humility upon his ground,
fearful of his awesomeness.

(I) did not become angry with his staff;
I was a father to them.
I judged the wretched with the powerful,
the strong with the weak.

I gave every man's possessions to him,
(for) greed is my abomination.
I made a burial for the one lacking an heir,
a coffin for the one who had none.

I defended the orphan [who appealed (?)] to me.
I cared for the widow.
I did not drive a son from the place of his father
and I did not take a nursling from his mother.

My arms were open and I gave to the one who had nothing,
my food offerings (given) to the one who is in need.
I stood [... ... ...]
[receiving (?)] the one who came to petition me.

I opened (my) ears to the one who spoke Maat
[and I cast out ... ... (the one) involved] in wrongdoing;
for the *ka* of the member of the *pat*, count, [...]
[*ca. 10 groups lost*]
⌜Ba⌝kenkhons, true of voice.

Around base:
    Member of the *pat*, count,
    god's father, beloved of the god,
    keeper of secrets in the sky, earth, and underworld,
    chief of seers of Re in Thebes,

sem-priest and chief controller of crafts of Ptah,[16]
overseer of all the priests of all the gods,
high priest of Amun,
Bakenkhons, <true of voice>;

he says: I was one silent, truly assiduous,
the possessor of graciousness among people,
who respected [his god], who magnified his renown,
who trusted himself to his every action,
being joined with the crew,[17]
favored of the Hidden-of-Name.

[I made (?)] [... ... ...]
[eating (?)] from his provisions.
May I receive an old age bearing the favors
which he gives in his temple.

3A–D. The Block Statues and Inscriptions of Roma from Karnak

Roma succeeded Bakenkhons as high priest in the reign of Ramesses II and may have been his brother. Roma also referred to himself as Roy, and his inscriptions use the two names interchangeably (Egyptological publications often refer to him as Roma-Roy). Roma held office through the reign of Merenptah and into the turbulent years at the end of the Nineteenth Dynasty.

Three Block Statues

Four statues of Roma are known from Karnak, three of which bear biographical phraseology. These three were found by Legrain in 1903–1904 among hundreds of statues buried in the court between the seventh and eighth pylons, probably as the result of temple clearance in Greco-Roman times; this find is termed the "Karnak cachette." The statues are now in the Cairo Museum. The fourth statue, not included here and now in the British Museum, was found in the temple of Mut and is inscribed with offering formulas addressed to Amun and Mut.

At 0.47 meters (1'5"), statue 3a is half the size of 3b and 3c. It may be the oldest of the group since it bears a cartouche of Merenptah across the knees:

Lord of the Two Lands, Baenre Meryamun, given life. *Six horizontal lines of text on the front of the knees relate Roma's loyalty to his king using phraseology very similar to that on the upper base of Bakenkhons's Munich statue (no. 2a). The name* Amun-Re *is inscribed on the right shoulder and* Mut, lady of the sky, *on the left.*

Statues 3b and 3c are similar in appearance and size—both are just over a meter (3') high—and each bears columns of biographical inscription on the sides of the body as well as the front of the knees, back pillar, and base. These complementary narratives are concerned with Roma's promotions, building works in the temple, and moral character. His dedication of two visually parallel biographical statues is also evocative of Bakenkhons's statues (no. 2). However, Roma's are made from different materials, one in black granodiorite and one in limestone. This may suggest that the statues were produced at different times or were set up in different areas of the temple. The erased cartouches on the shoulders of the granodiorite statue perhaps relate it to the dynastic crisis after the death of Merenptah. The limestone statue bears no cartouche.

3A. SMALL BLOCK STATUE

> *Front of knees:*
> An offering which the king gives to Amun-Re, king of the gods,
> lord of the sky, ruler of the Ennead,
> to Mut the great, lady of Asheru,
> and to Khonsu, perfect of peace,
> that they may place my name enduringly in Thebes,
> and established in Karnak,
>
> for the *ka* of the member of the *pat*, count,
> god's father, beloved of the god,
> keeper of secrets in the sky, earth, and underworld,
> overseer of the priests of the gods, the lords of Thebes,
> high priest of Amun,
> Roma, true of voice;
>
> he says: I was one who respected his Horus (the king), who
> magnified his plan,
> who trusted himself to (his) every action,
> whose hands were together upon the steering oar,
> acting as a helmsman in life.

3B. Granodiorite Statue

Front of knees:
An offering which the king gives to Amun-Re-Horakhty-Atum, lord
of Karnak,
that he may place ⌜the radiance of the sky⌝
and the might ⌜of the earth⌝ before Geb,
bread and beer,
beef and fowl,
libations, ⌜incense,
wine, milk, and everything good and pure
that comes forth⌝ daily ⌜from the offering tables⌝ of Amun,

for the *ka* of the one true of heart, free from evil,
⌜since he came forth from⌝ the womb,
favored one, member of the *pat*, count,
god's father, beloved of the god,
keeper of secrets in the sky, earth, and underworld,
sacrificer for Kamutef,

overseer of the ⌜treasury⌝ of Amun,
overseer of the granary of Amun,
overseer of the priests of all the gods,
high priest of Amun,
Roma, true of voice.

Right side:
He says: I grew up as a youth in the domain of Amun,
as an excellent *wab*-priest, being discerning of heart
and perfect in character,
my step at the (right) place.

I was chosen for my perfection in his temple.
I was initiated to (the position of) god's father,
in order to hear the summons of his noble *ka*, in order to satisfy his
wishes.
He recognized my perfection; he favored me on account of my
character.[18]

He placed me in the knowledge of the king,
and my name ⌜was⌝ called out in the presence of the courtiers.

He made a decree concerning my office,
[being distinguished at the side of (?)] the king himself,[19]
Usermaatre Setepenre (Ramesses II),
the son of Amun, of his body.

He favored me again for (my) excellence;
[he appointed me (?)] second priest.
His treasury and his granary
provided everything beneficial and strengthened his temple.
He increased the (number of) good things he did for me.
He placed me as chief spokesman in his temple,
as high priest [of Amun].

Left side:
High priest of Amun,
Roy, true of voice,
he says: I am effective, one excellent in the domain of his lord,
intelligent in (building) every monument.

I performed benefactions in the domain of Amun,
in the great name of the lord of the Two Lands,
[*erased cartouche*],
in (the form of) statues of silver and gold,
worked by beating.

[... ... ...] and noble [...] ⌜in⌝ every precious stone,
great doors of gold,
⌜adorned⌝ with every ⌜precious⌝ stone.
⌜I carpentered⌝ rivergoing boats
for Amun, Mut, and ⌜Khonsu⌝.

I built [... ...] ⌜in⌝ granite, and I widened its portico,
bearing the great name of the lord of appearances,[20]
[*erased cartouche*],
[who resides (?)] within it,[21]
his heart rejoicing.
I did not set aside any beneficial ⌜task⌝ which had not been done for
 his *ka*.

May he place ⌜my⌝ statue ⌜enduringly⌝ for eternity,
resting upon the earth of his domain perpetually,

that Amun may address it in his every festival,
my name enduring ⌐upon it perpetually⌐.

Back pillar:
An offering which the king gives to Amun-Re,
lord of the thrones of the Two Lands, foremost in Karnak,
that he may place my name enduringly for eternity,
(so that) it never has to be sought (in vain),
for the *ka* of the high priest of Amun,
⌐Roy, true of voice⌐;

he says: O priests, god's fathers, *wab*-priests,
the great ones of the domain of Amun,
the numerous generations who will come to be:
give ⌐garlands to my statue,
libations⌐ for my *ka*,
remember my name daily,
perform the offering ritual for my statue,
in as much as I exerted myself in doing what was beneficial
for Amun, Mut,
and Khonsu in ⌐Thebes, perfect of peace⌐.

Remains of text around base:
… like all the true ones who follow him …
… a perfect lifetime …

3C. Limestone Statue

Front of knees:
An offering which the king gives to Amun-Re, king of the gods,
to Amunet, who resides in Thebes,
to Mut, lady of the sky, mistress of the gods,
and to Khonsu in Thebes, perfect of peace,
that they may establish my statue enduringly,
resting in Karnak forever,
for the *ka* of the high priest of Amun,
Roy, true of voice;

he says: I have come before you, lord of the gods,
Amun, ruler of the Ennead,

so that I may praise your perfection every day, so that I may satisfy
    your desires.
Grant me (sight of) your perfect face, for I am your true servant.

May you favor your defender upon earth,
that I may follow you in a truthful way
and grow old in your domain, in possession of your favors,
my eyes seeing your uraeus;
for the *ka* of the overseer of the priests of all the gods,
high priest of Amun,
Roma, true of voice.

Right side:
    He says: I was strong, vigilant,
    one effective for his lord,
    who made monuments in his domain with a loving heart,
    my heart assessing every work,
    seeking out what is beneficial for my august god.

    He favored me for what I did, inasmuch as I am beneficial to him.
    He caused me to be supreme chief spokesman over his domain.
    I reached old age in his following, possessing his favor,
    my body provided with health,
    my eyes far-seeing,
    and the provisions of his temple firm in my mouth,
    the favors of the king with me as the gift of Amun.

    He placed my children in my presence as an entire future
        generation;
    they are priests shouldering his image.[22]
    I was high priest as the gift of Amun,[23]
    my (eldest) son established at my side as second priest,
    my second son as *sem*-priest
    in the royal (mortuary) temple on the west of Thebes,

    the son of my son as fourth priest
    shouldering Amun, lord of the gods,
    the son of my son as god's father
    and lector priest, pure of hands, of the Hidden-of-Name.

    May he cause my name to be established upon my statue,

at the side of this monument which I made in his domain,[24]
so that my name will be remembered upon (both of) them beyond
        eternity,
so that I may favor the generations who will come,
so that they may proclaim my goodness as well as my strength.

Left side:
High priest of Amun,
Roy, true of voice,
he says: I was the chief overseer of works in Karnak,
who gave every instruction to the craftsmen,
who assessed knowledge,
who was wise in skills.

There was no deed of which he (Roma) was ignorant,
all good qualities were foremost in his heart.
One was pleased with the counsels of his mouth,
the abundance of Amun was effective for his *ka*,
excellent confidant for His Person,
for he knew what was pleasing for his Horus.

One greatly favored by his god Amun,
who gave his possessions, who procured offerings,
sustenance and provisions (being) upon his every path,
whom the people loved, who mastered the heart,
content without a lustful heart.

That which is ordered to be done occurs immediately,
for he has trusted himself to the plan of his god.
The length of a lifetime is in the hands of Amun,
to bring to its end in perfection,
just like what is done for one who is truly assiduous,
effective in the domain of his lord.

Back pillar:
An offering which the king gives to Amun-Re, king of the gods,
to Mut the great, lady of Asheru,
Khonsu in Thebes, perfect of peace,

Thoth, lord of Upper Egyptian Heliopolis (Thebes),
Montu-Re, dwelling in Thebes,

Ptah, perfect of face, father of the gods,
Hathor, principal of Thebes,

Rettawy, mistress of the gods,
Maat, daughter of Re,
and to the gods and goddesses, the lords of Thebes,
the Ennead of Karnak,

that my statue be established on earth,
my name carved upon it for eternity,
bread and beer upon the offering table in front of it,
from the remainder of every offering service for those (the deities)
      who are in Thebes,[25]

that Amun may address it (the statue) each time he appears,
and Mut and Khonsu assent to him as (they do) to the great ones,[26]
inasmuch as I performed benefactions with a loving heart
in every effective ritual in Karnak,
being favored for what I have done as well as for my effectiveness,
being established in Karnak forever;

for the *ka* of the pure one before Amun,
god's father of Amun, third priest of Amun,
second priest of Amun,
overseer of the treasury of Amun,
overseer of the granary of Amun,
overseer of the priests of all the gods,
high priest of Amun,
Roma, true of voice.

Right half of base:
> For the *ka* of the high priest of Amun,
> Roma, true of voice;
> he says: [*ca. 6 groups lost with traces*]
> Amun favored me for my beneficent acts.
> I was given a good lifetime in his temple,
> the king's favor before me, being free from terror.

Left half of base:
> For the *ka* of the high priest of Amun,
> Roy, true of voice;

he says: I was high priest as the gift of Amun;
it was he who chose me himself, in front of his temple.
He gave me a venerable position shouldering his image,
all my limbs being strong,
my eyes far-seeing,
sustenance and provisions in my mouth perpetually.

3D. The Inscriptions of Roma on the Eighth Pylon in Karnak

The most fundamental departure from tradition in the Ramessid use of the biographical genre is the inscription of scenes and narrative texts on the walls of Karnak by Roma and, much later, by the high priest Amenhotep (nos. 5–9). The walls of state temple complexes such as Karnak were reserved for representing the relationship between gods and king through scenes of offering and ritual performance; images of nonroyal individuals were usually confined to lower registers, exterior walls, and scenes of festival and war. However, some factors may temper any claim to royal prerogative Roma might seem to make. His inscriptions are carved on the east massif of the eighth pylon, around and beside a doorway leading into the pylon. This is an exterior wall that has the appearance of spare and available space.

The lintel bears two figures of Roma, kneeling in adoration, framing six columns of text in the middle. The central two columns contain cartouches, probably of Amenmesse, which are now erased. These cartouches are flanked by epithets of Amun: Dual King, lord of the Two Lands, [*erased cartouche*], beloved of Amun-Re, king of the gods, lord of the sky, chief of the Ennead; son of Re, lord of appearances, [*erased cartouche*], beloved of Amun-Re, lord of the thrones of the Two Lands, foremost of Karnak. *The flanking columns record Roma's prayers. Those on the left read:* Giving adoration to Amun-Re, kissing the ground for Horus, powerful of arm, that they may give a perfect lifetime, for the *ka* of the high priest of Amun, Roy, true of voice. *Those on the right read:* Giving adoration to Amun-Re, kissing the ground for Horus, great of terror, that they may give life, prosperity, and health, for the *ka* of the high priest of Amun, Roma, true of voice. *Beneath the columns of text is a single line of inscription:* Made under the charge of one whom His Person taught, high priest of Amun, Roma, true of voice. *Above the lintel is a scene of Sety II making offerings to Amun; the cartouches here are intact. Three columns that fill each of the jambs consist of offering formulas and prayers to Amun and the king for the prosperity of the high priest; these are translated below.*

The long biographical inscription is in a demarcated rectangular zone to the right of the doorway. In the bottom right area of the scene, Roma stands with both arms raised in adoration. Behind him stands the slightly smaller figure of his elder son, Bakenkhons, the face and lower arms of which were deliberately damaged in antiquity. The text consists of nineteen vertical columns, artfully arranged, with new columns beginning at salient points of the narrative. The name of the son, inscribed between the figures, was erased in antiquity but can be deciphered from traces: His son, second priest of Amun, ⌜Bakenkhons, true of voice⌝. *The first column of the text abuts the texts on the jambs and lintel.*

It begins as a hymn to Amun and goes on to recount Roma's restoration of a particular type of service building (a "wabet" or preparation chamber). The east end of the eighth pylon looks out over what was probably the service area for Karnak, which would have included this building. The text is also addressed specifically to members of temple staff, while the "wabet" was probably used in the preparation of offerings for the temple. Therefore it had a different function from more "central" structures and cult objects, like the temple Bakenkhons built for his king (no. 2a) or the statues, vessels, and structure that Roma describes on the left side of his granodiorite statue (no. 3b).

> *Left jamb of doorway:*
> An offering which the king gives to Amun-Re, king of the gods,
> lord of the sky, ruler of the Ennead,
> and to the royal *ka* of the lord of the Two Lands,
> [*erased cartouche*],
>
> [that they may] grant me a long lifetime in victorious Thebes,
> shouldering Amun in Karnak,[27]
> his sustenance before me,
> without his being far from ⌜me⌝,
> his ⌜provisions⌝ being established in my mouth,
> coming and going in the domain of Amun,
> receiving the favors of his *ka*,
> in order to attain 110 years on earth like everyone justified;[28]
>
> for the *ka* of the member of the *pat*, count,
> ⌜overseer of the priests⌝ of all the gods,
> high priest of Amun,
> Roma, true of voice.
>
> *Right jamb of doorway:*
> An offering which the king gives to Amun-Re, lord of the thrones of
>   the Two Lands,
> foremost in Karnak, [*ca. 5 groups of deities' names and epithets lost*],

that they may give life, prosperity, and health,
a perfect lifetime in the domain of Amun,
my name being established ⌜in⌝ his ⌜temple⌝ forever.
May the ⌜coming⌝ generations laud me
for the benefactions ⌜which I performed⌝.
May they give bouquets to my likeness and pour forth libations;

for the *ka* of the ⌜member of the *pat*, count⌝,
god's father, beloved of the god,
third priest of Amun,
second priest of Amun,
⌜overseer of the treasury of⌝ Amun,
⌜overseer of the granary of Amun⌝,
overseer of the priests of all the gods,
high priest of Amun, Roma.

Main inscription to right of doorway:
Giving praise to Amun-Re,
kissing the ground before his perfect face,
by the high priest of Amun,
Roma, true of voice;

he says: I have come before you, lord of the gods, Amun,
who came into being first,
divine god, creator of what exists,
lord of gods and people, ruler of Heliopolis,
chief in Thebes,
great of appearances in the temple of *benben*.[29]

The eyes of everyone see because of you,
breath goes forth from your mouth to every nose,
great of majesty, [*ca. 6 groups of epithets lost with traces*],
lord of lords, ruler of the Ennead.

Gods and people exalt your *ka*,
life is in your hand, health belongs to you,
Shay and Renenet
united in your grasp.

May you guard your son, your beloved, lord of the Two Lands,
⌜Userkheperu⌝re Setepenre (Sety II)

in life, stability, and power ⌜forever⌝.
May you grant me a long lifetime shouldering your image,
my eyes seeing your uraeus daily,
my body equipped with health, without being lustful of heart,
free from terror.

O valiant king of perpetuity (Amun),
(may) your provisions be with me, your favors before me,
your name as protection for me.
May you lengthen my lifetime as a perfect life,
being established in your temple,
my body [...], serving your *ka*,
my eyes far-seeing,
until I reach the west of Thebes,
being sated with seeing Amun,

my son being in my place,
my office in his hand,
one ⌜son⌝ (after) the next for eternity,
as is done for one truly assiduous,
effective in the domain of his lord;

for the *ka* of the excellent individual, truly assiduous,
greatly favored one of his god Amun,
effective for Mut,
favorite of Khonsu,
confidant of the lord of the Two Lands,

member of the *pat*, count,
god's father, pure of hands,
keeper of secrets in the sky, earth, and underworld,
sacrificer for Kamutef, *sem*-priest of the horizon of eternity,
chief of seers of Re-Atum in Thebes,

third priest of Amun,
second priest of Amun,
high priest of Amun,
Roy, true of voice.

He says: O *wab*-priests, scribes of the domain of Amun,
good servants of the divine offerings,

butchers, brewers, overseers of confectionery,
bakers of *idenet*-bread, *bit*-loaves, and *pesen*-loaves,
who perform ⌈all their [...] for their lord⌉,
who will enter this preparation chamber,
which is within the [... ...] ⌈of Amun⌉:
⌈Proclaim my⌉ name daily as a good memory!
Celebrate me for my goodness as well as my strength!

I found this room entirely ruined,
its walls toppling,
the timbers ⌈thereof⌉ weakened,
the wooden door-frames decaying,
a smoothness upon the images.[30]

So I ⌈embellished it⌉ exceedingly throughout,
making (it) high and broad ⌈in excellent workmanship⌉,
and I (re)built its door frames in sandstone.
I established the doors within them in real pine,
(as) a place for the butchers and brewers who are within it.
I made it of perfect construction
from the back to the front, for the protection of [... ...],
for my god Amun, lord of the gods.

Pay attention and listen to what I say.
Do not transgress anything I have accomplished.
Cause my name to prosper, ⌈magnify⌉ my deed.
Speak favors for me in the presence of Amun,
for he will favor you [greatly],
as he does (for) [those who attain (?)] old age in his domain,
his provisions with you,
so that you may hand on (your offices) to your children,
one son to the next
in his domain forever.

Place offerings before my statue,
overflowing onto the ground in my name.
Place bouquets before me when you enter.
Say for me: "May he favor you,"
with a loving heart for my god
Amun, lord of the gods,
so that others who will [come (?)] will offer to you (?).

Cause the inscriptions to be read out [... ... ...]
to act according to my speech which is before you.
Place my good name in the mouths of (future) generations,
inasmuch as I performed benefactions in the temple of Amun,
consisting of every ⌈excellent⌉ deed ⌈in Karnak⌉.

May Amun favor me for my beneficent acts.
May he give me 110 years shouldering his image.
[*ca. 6 groups lost with traces*]
... magnified forever.
I have said in my heart,
[... ... ...] his *ka*,
for the *ka* of the high priest of Amun, Roy.

4–9. THE INSCRIPTIONS OF AMENHOTEP FROM KARNAK

Amenhotep was the son of the powerful high priest Ramessesnakht and a member of one of the most influential and well-connected families in Thebes in the late Twentieth Dynasty (Polz 1998). Ramessesnakht had included a biographical text on the walls of his own mortuary temple on the Theban West Bank, of which only fragments remain (Polz 1998, 268). He had also carved offering scenes to the Theban triad (Amun, Mut, and Khonsu) above the inscription of Roma on the eighth pylon (no. 3d), extending this zone of priestly display.

Amenhotep is the only other high priest of the Twentieth Dynasty for whom extensive biographical narratives are known. The majority of these were inscribed on the walls of the southern processional route in Karnak. He also built a portico or gateway for Ramesses IX, inscribed with his own images and short texts, on the south side of pylon eight (Habachi 1938, pl. IX, no. 1: not translated here). Amenhotep is first attested in the office of high priest in year 10 of this king, a date that occurs in one of his reward texts (no. 7). He may have held office into the reign of Ramesses XI but his career is poorly known. These were turbulent years in Thebes; later records of a "war of the high priest," as well as the presentation of his suppression from office in his own narrative (no. 8), indicate an upset in his position that may have resulted in his death. Both the dating of this suppression and whether Amenhotep survived are disputed (for discussion and references, see Morales 2001).

The extent to which Amenhotep used the temple walls as a medium for his own inscriptions is remarkable. For this reason I translate most of these texts here, despite the fact that some are not narrowly biographical. The translations are ordered spatially, beginning with a statue inscription from the interior of the southern processional route and moving to ones carved, from south to north, on exterior walls and in the northern part of the temple complex. Due to the large number of these inscriptions, I have assigned each a separate text number.

4. THE SCRIBE STATUE OF AMENHOTEP

In contrast to the block statues dedicated by Bakenkhons (no. 2) and Roma (nos. 3a–c), the only statue attested for Amenhotep is this figure of him as a scribe found on the south side of the seventh pylon, beside the central doorway, at the foot of a colossus of Thutmose III. It depicts Amenhotep seated cross-legged with a papyrus unrolled over his lap. The active writing pose of scribe statues contrasts with the passive, squatting posture of the block statue type and therefore seems to have a different range of associations, perhaps relating to official functions and actions within temples. The head and torso of this life-size statue are well-preserved, but the lower half is severely abraded and large sections of the inscriptions are lost. The papyrus was carved with vertical columns of text that are now almost entirely illegible. The text translated here wraps around the front and right side of the base in three horizontal lines and records Amenhotep's work in temple buildings and on cultic paraphernalia. The treatment of the statue's face suggests that it was carved in the late-Eighteenth or early-Nineteenth Dynasty and was then reused by Amenhotep (Scott 1989, III, 478). The decline in the production of statuary in the Twentieth Dynasty perhaps limited available options for fine work. A high-quality antique may have been a desirable vehicle for a leading official's self-presentation.

> [...], member of the *pat*, count,
> high priest of ⌜Amun-Re, king of the gods,
> Amenhotep⌝, true of voice;
>
> he says: O priests, *wab*-priests, [*ca. 4 groups lost*]
> I placed [*ca. 10 groups lost with traces*]
> ... [offerings (?)],
> guiding the craftmanship in every work,
> so that I could build the great southern place,[31]
> the ... [*rest of line lost, including the beginning of a title string*]

god's father, pure of hands,
high priest of Amun-Re, king of the gods,
⌐Amenhotep, true of voice¬;

he says: I ⌐established its¬ double-leafed door
with real cedar,
[bolts] in copper,
and images in fine gold,
bearing the ⌐great name¬ of the lord of the Two Lands.

I built this [double] terrace for the domain of Amun anew.
I made its double-leafed door in cedar,
the images in fine gold,
bearing the great name of ⌐His Person¬,
[*rest of line lost, including the beginning of a title string*]

[… high priest of Amun-Re], ⌐king¬ of the gods,
Amenhotep, true of voice,
son of the high priest of Amun,
Ramessesnakht, true of voice;

he says: [I carpentered (?)] 6 poles
[which carried] the image of Amun.[32]
I found the [*ca. 6 groups lost with traces*]
at the side of the [… … …]
and I built it in [addition (?)], in excellent work,
[making (?) …] [*end of text lost*]

5. THE INSCRIPTION OF AMENHOTEP IN THE TEMPLE INTERIOR

On the inside wall of the court of the seventh and eighth pylons, next to the side door, is this very worn inscription detailing Amenhotep's building works in Karnak. The inscription fills the lowest section of the wall between the doorway and the pylon, beneath an earlier relief of Ramesses III standing before an unidentified god. The narrative centers on Amenhotep's restoration of a preparation chamber ("wabet"), perhaps equivalent to the one built by the high priest Roma over 150 years earlier (no. 3d); Roma's inscription describing this chamber is less than 10 meters from this one.

Made under the charge of one whom His Person taught,
high priest of ⌜Amun-Re, king of the gods⌝,
Amenhotep, true of voice,
(saying) as follows: I found this preparation chamber
of the former high priests of Amun,
which is in the domain of Amun-Re, king of the gods,
⌜fallen⌝ into ruin.

It had been made in the time of King Kheperkare,
son of Re, Senwosret (Senwosret I).[33]
And I ⌜completed⌝ (it), having built it anew
as a perfect creation in excellent work.
I caused its walls to be strengthened,
from rear to front.

And I greatly extended it, making its columns and door frames
from great stones of excellent craftsmanship.
And I ⌜(re)established⌝ the great doorleaves with pine and cedar,
and I greatly enlarged its great doorway of stone,
which (now) appeared complete,
broadened and ⌜heightened anew⌝,
(by) the high priest of Amun, who is in the domain of Amun.

And I assembled its great door of [pine (?)],
bolts of copper,
and images of fine gold,
upon [... ...] [its strength (?)].

And I built its great terrace of stone
which opens out onto the southern lake,
the pure [lake (?)] of the domain of Amun.[34]
And I surrounded [it with a wall (?)] of brick,
and I set in place its great stone carvings on the door frames,
the door supports and doorleaves being of pine.

And I made the [... ... ...]
of great stones, dragged (into position),
carved with ochre within a border[35]
and [...] in the titulary
bearing the name of Pharaoh, ⌜my lord, l.p.h.

I⌐ built a treasury of brick anew
in the great court, whose name is ...
[*ca. 11 groups lost*]

[bolts of (?)] copper, door supports of stone,
doorleaves of pine, inscribed within the borders ...
[*the rest of this column and half of the next are lost*]
... as His Person.

It was behind the storehouse
for the taxes of the domain of Amun.[36]
... the great and noble court,
to distinguish the high priest of Amun.
... everything good and pure.

I placed its superiors and favored ones (?)
... when there was not ...
feet, seizing the ...
[door supports (?)] ⌐of stone, doorleaves⌐ of pine,
... ⌐Asheru, and they⌐ [planted (?)] trees (?) ...

As for the foremost one, Mut the great, ...
[*ca. 9 groups lost with traces*]
Pharaoh, my lord,
sacrificing for Mut the great, the [...]
and she received ⌐them⌐ in its ⌐court⌐,
and she ...[*ca. half a column lost*],
as something beneficial for Amun-Re, king of the gods, my lord,
for I know his greatness, his strength (?), his might,
saying: "you are the lord of every land."

May ⌐he⌐ grant ⌐life, prosperity, and health⌐,
a long lifetime, and a great kingship,
to the Dual King, Neferkare Setepenre,
son of Re, Ramesses Khaemwaset Meryamun (Ramesses IX),
and may he give to me life, prosperity and health,
a long lifetime, a great old age,
and favors in the presence of Pharaoh, my lord.

Made by the high priest of Amun-Re, king of the gods,
Amenhotep, true of ⌐voice⌐,

son of the high priest of Amun,
Ramessesnakht, ⌜true of voice⌝.

6. Inscriptions of Amenhotep on the Side Door to the Court of the Eighth Pylon

A set of texts relating to Amenhotep was carved on the north thickness, ceiling, and outer lintel and jambs of the side door leading from the court of the eighth pylon to the area of the sacred lake. The inner jambs of this doorway bear inscriptions of the Eighteenth Dynasty king Thutmose III, two columns on the left jamb and three on the right jamb. This lack of symmetry suggests that the doorway had been widened after the Eighteenth Dynasty texts were carved. The interior lintel above the door, which depicts an uncaptioned king offering to Amun in parallel scenes, was also oriented to the doorway's original, narrower, width. In contrast, Amenhotep's text on the ceiling and his scene on the outer lintel are oriented to the doorway's new width. The side door may therefore have been widened by him as part of the remodeling of temple structures in the southern part of the Amun precinct that is described in his other texts (nos. 4–5). The emphasis throughout the texts on the doorway that it was "made under the charge of one whom His Person taught" *supports this suggestion.*

The north thickness of the doorway bears an image of Amenhotep offering a bouquet, described as a bouquet of the god Montu, to Ramesses IX: ⌜Dual King⌝, lord of the Two Lands, ⌜Neferkare Setepenre⌝, son of Re, lord of appearances, Ramesses Khaemwaset Meryamun, given life and power forever like Re. *This is accompanied by a short text of praise for the king. The scene on the outer lintel shows Amenhotep kneeling in adoration of Amun, with cartouches of the king in the center of the tableau:* ⌜Horus⌝, strong bull, Khaemwaset, Neferkare Setepenre; ⌜Horus⌝, strong bull, Khaemwaset, Ramesses Khaemwaset Meryamun. *The scenes are accompanied by short, fragmentary hymns to the god. The southern external jamb bears three columns of offering formulas and titles. Two further columns of text that frame the southern jamb and lintel include some biographical phraseology. Matching texts on the northern jamb are lacking, giving a sense of incompletion to the whole doorway.*

North Thickness of the Side Door

Behind figure of king:
   The king, lord of the Two Lands, lord of cult action,

Neferkare Setepenre,
appears in the domain of his father Amun
for eternity and perpetuity,
his heart happy with his *ka*,
as he receives eternity and ⌜perpetuity⌝.

Above figure of Amenhotep:
   [... ... ...]
   ⌜Amun-Re⌝, lord of the thrones of the Two Lands,
   that he may favor you and love you.
   [May Amun (?)], lord of eternity, [grant (?)]
   sed-festivals on the throne of Horus.
   May he overthrow your enemies in death and in life,
   for Amun is the protection of ⌜your⌝ limbs, his Ennead
         overthrowing your enemies;
   every foreign land is beneath your sandals, without ⌜your⌝ being
         opposed.

   ⌜Made⌝ under the charge of one whom His Person taught,
   member of the *pat*, count,
   royal sealbearer, sole companion,
   effective confidant for his lord,
   god's father, beloved of the god,

   chief of seers of Re-Atum in Thebes,
   sem-priest in the horizon of eternity,
   who opened the doorleaves of the sky to see what is within,
   pure of hands when performing an incense offering
   to Amun in the Mansion of the Official,

   overseer of great works in the domain of Amun,
   high priest of Amun-Re, king of the gods,
   Amenhotep, true of voice,
   son of the high priest of Amun in Karnak,
   Ramessesnakht, true of voice.

Between figures of king and Amenhotep:
   <For> your *ka*, a bouquet of Montu,
   who resides in Thebes, lord of victory,
   ruler of the Nine Bows, chief, king of the gods,
   that he may give you bravery over the south

and victory over the ⌜north⌝.

Single line beneath scene:
    Made under the charge of one whom His Person taught,
    ⌜member⌝ of the *pat*, count,
    god's father, beloved of the god,
    excellent ⌜of⌝ hands when shouldering his lord (in procession),[37]
    who raises up the god in his appearances,
    [*rest lost*]

Single column on ceiling of side door
    Dual King, lord of the Two Lands,
    Neferkare Setepenre, given life.
    Made under the charge of one whom His Person taught,
    member of the *pat*, count,
    high priest of Amun,
    Amenhotep, true of voice.

The Outer Lintel and South Jamb of the Side Door

Above figure of Amun in south (left) scene:
    ⌜Words spoken by Amun⌝-Re,
    lord of the ⌜thrones of the Two Lands, foremost⌝ of ⌜Karnak⌝.

Above figure of Amenhotep in south (left) scene:
    ⌜Adoring Amun-Re⌝, lord of the thrones of the Two Lands,
    kissing the ground for the victorious [king],
    Horus, lord of *sed*-festivals,
    that they may cause his [... ...] to be established.

    For the *ka* of the member of the *pat*, count,
    god's father, beloved of the god,
    keeper of secrets [... ...] to see (the god?),
    pure of hands [... ...] for all the gods,
    ⌜high priest of Amun-Re, king of the gods,
    Amenhotep, true of⌝ voice.

Above figure of Amun in north (right) scene:
    ⌜Words spoken by Amun-Re⌝,
    lord ⌜of the sky, ruler of Thebes, primeval one of the⌝ Two Lands,
    [... ... ...]

Above the figure of the priest in the north (right) scene:
[... ...] ⌜favored one (?)⌝,
member of the *pat*, count,
effective confidant for his lord,
god's father, beloved of the god,
pure of hands [... ...] in Thebes,
high priest of Amun in Karnak,
Amenhotep, true of voice, in peace.

South (left) jamb of doorway:
⌜An offering which the king gives (to) Amun-Re, king of the gods⌝,
lord of the sky, ruler of the Ennead,
(for) the royal *ka* of the lord of the Two Lands,
Neferkare Setepenre, given life and power.

Made under the charge of one whom His Person taught,
⌜member of the *pat*⌝, count,
god's father, beloved of the god,
high priest of Amun-Re, king of the gods,
Amenhotep, true of voice.

⌜An offering which the king gives to Mut the great⌝, lady of Asheru,
(for) the royal *ka* of the lord of appearances,
Ramesses Khaemwaset Meryamun, (given life) like Re.

Made under the charge of one whom His Person taught,
member ⌜of the *pat*⌝, count, overseer of priests,
high priest of Amun-Re, king of the gods,
Amenhotep, true of voice.

⌜An offering which the king gives to Khonsu⌝ in Thebes, perfect of
        peace,
(for) the royal *ka* of the lord of the Two Lands,
Neferkare Setepenre, forever.

Made under the charge of one whom His Person taught,
member ⌜of the *pat*⌝, count,
god's father, <beloved of the god>, pure of hands,
high priest of Amun-Re, king of the gods,
Amenhotep, true of voice.

Framing columns beside the south (left) jamb:
[*ca. half a column lost: probably titles*]
he says: I was one who respected his god, who magnified his
        renown,
who went out upon his every path,
and who placed him in his heart.
I am ⌜happier⌝ today than yesterday,
and at dawn [...],[38]
whose hands were together upon the steering oar,
acting as a helmsman in life.

[*ca. half a column lost: probably titles*]
⌜Amenhotep, true of voice⌝;
he says: I was one who ⌜embellished⌝ the name of his lord in
        Karnak,
in order that his memory be established for eternity
in the sacred place, in the presence of the noble ⌜*ka*⌝ of the lord of
        the gods,
for I was the chief overseer of works in the domain of Amun,
guiding all craftsmanship ⌜according to⌝ my command.

7. The Reward Tableau of Amenhotep

*The two scenes depicting Amenhotep's reward by Ramesses IX form a tableau
along the eastern exterior wall of the court between the seventh and eighth pylons.
The scenes are separated by a central image of parallel, over-life-size figures of the
priest before offering tables. He wears a panther skin and holds a bouquet to his
nose with one hand, while a further bouquet with streamers is held to his side.
This scene is accompanied by offering formulas and declarations of Amenhotep's
moral standing and relationship to god and king. The reward scenes show him
standing before the king with his arms raised. In each the king stands on a plinth
with one arm raised toward the priest. Cartouches are inscribed above his head:
Dual King, Neferkare Setepenre, son of Re, Ramesses Khaemwaset Meryamun,
given life and power like Re. Tables between the figures of king and priest in
both scenes bear items of adornment, food, and vessels; these are depictions of the
rewards that are enumerated in the inscriptions. Two smaller figures attend to
the priest, their poses differing in each scene. These may be the individuals whose
speeches form the main body of the texts inscribed above Amenhotep.*

Although the sets of speeches accompanying both scenes are broadly similar in their praise for the building work and revenue Amenhotep had contributed to the temple, significant differences in structure and detail suggest that they may commemorate separate events. Amenhotep's reward scenes are striking in their formal display of priestly action and prestige within temple space, particularly in their use of the image of the king, perhaps as a way to legitimize their carving.

The northern reward scene is translated first because it is the better preserved of the two. Many of the notes to this text are also relevant to the southern scene.

North (Right) Reward Scene

Speech above the king's head:
> The king himself spoke
> to the nobles and companions who were at his side:
> "Give numerous favors and many rewards,
> in fine gold and silver,
> and millions of everything good
> to the high priest of Amun-Re, king of the gods,
> Amenhotep, true of voice,
> because of the effective and numerous monuments
> which he has made in the domain of Amun-Re, king of the gods,
> in the great name of the Perfect God (Ramesses IX)."

Titles framing Amenhotep's head:
> Member of the *pat*, count,
> high priest of Amun-Re, king of the gods,
> Amenhotep, true of voice, (who is now) at the seat (office) of his
> father,
> the high priest of Amun in Karnak,
> Ramessesnakht, true of voice.

Above figure of Amenhotep:
> Year 10, third month of *akhet*, day 19,
> in the domain of Amun-Re, king of the gods.
> The high priest of Amun-Re, king of the gods,
> Amenhotep, true of voice, was ushered
> into the great court of Amun.[39]
> A recital of his favors was pronounced to him,
> in order to proclaim him with choice, perfect words.

The nobles who were commanded to honor him (were):

the overseer of the treasury of Pharaoh and royal cupbearer,
Amenhotep, true of voice;[40]
the royal cupbearer, Nesamen,
scribe of Pharaoh;
the royal cupbearer, Neferkareemperamen,
herald of Pharaoh.[41]

(This is) what was said to him in favor and proclamation
on this day in the great court of Amun-Re, king of the gods,
saying: "May Montu favor you!
May the *ka* of Amun-Re, king of the gods,
Pre-Horakhty, Ptah the great,
South-of-his-Wall, lord of Memphis,
Thoth, lord of hieroglyphs,
the gods of the sky,
and the gods of the earth favor you!

May the *ka* of Neferkare Setepenre,
son of Re, Ramesses Khaemwaset Meryamun (Ramesses IX),
great ruler of Egypt,
beloved child of all the gods, favor you
for what you have accomplished,
(including) the harvests, taxes, and labor quotas
of the domain of Amun-Re, king of the gods, which were under
          your control.

And you have delivered them, heaped up in mounds.
For you had offered (all of) ⌜that⌝ which was made,
and you caused that they fill up the interior
of the treasuries, the magazines, and the granaries
of the domain of ⌜Amun⌝-Re, king of the gods.
And (there is) also the tribute and the office tax,[42]
(that is) the sustenance of Amun-Re, king of the gods,
which you ⌜had brought to⌝ Pharaoh, your lord.

(This is) what is done for a perfect servant
who is effective for Pharaoh, his lord,
and who has worked powerfully to act effectively
for Amun-Re, king of the gods, great god,
and to act effectively for Pharaoh, his lord,
your [... ...] which you made.

Look, this overseer of the treasury
and these two cupbearers of Pharaoh are instructed
⌜to favor⌝ you, to proclaim you,
to anoint you with sweet *qemy*-unguent,
and to give ⌜to you⌝ the basin of gold and silver
⌜as part of the customary allocation⌝ for this servant,
which Pharaoh, your lord, gives to you."

They gave (this) to him as a favor and as a ⌜reward
in⌝ the great court of Amun on this day,
and One (the king) caused that it be done as a favor each and every
  year.

Beneath scene:
Given as a favor from the king
to the great confidant of the lord of the Two Lands,
the high priest of Amun-Re, king of the gods,
Amenhotep, true of voice:

Fine gold in *seku*-work:[43]
1 *wesekh*-collar of an official,
supplemented with 2 *shebyu*-necklaces[44] as well as 1 pectoral,
1 garland for ⌜the head⌝ of an official,
and 2 gold knot amulets.
Total of fine gold in *seku*-work:
4 mixed pieces,
amounting to 10 *deben* of fine ⌜gold⌝.[45]

⌜Silver: 4⌝ *reheb*-vessels,
⌜4⌝ *wedjeh*-vessels, and 4 *sekhenek*-vessels.[46]
Total of silver (in) mixed vessels: 12,
amounting to 20 *deben* of silver.[47]
Total of fine gold and silver: 30 *deben*.

Good bread, meat, ...
[*5 groups lost*]
sweet *tjelek*-beer: 40 large *qeb*-vessels;[48]
sweet *qemy*-unguent: 2 *hin*-measures.[49]

(This is) what was said to him as royal words:
the document scribe ⌜of⌝ Pharaoh was made to come,

and One (the king) spoke ⌜to⌝ the overseers of the granaries ⌜of⌝
    Pharaoh:
"Give 20 arouras ⌜of⌝ grain-land[50]
as a favor for the high priest of Amun,
Amenhotep, true of voice;
they will be part of his customary allocation each and every year."[51]

South (Left) Reward Scene (fig. 4)

Speech above the king's head:
    ⌜The king himself spoke to the high priest of Amun,
Amenhotep, true of voice:
"May Montu favor you!⌝
May the *ka* of Amun-Re, king of the gods, favor you,
⌜because of the effective and numerous monuments which you
    made
in the domain of Amun-Re, king of the gods⌝,
in the great name of His Person."

Titles framing Amenhotep's head:
    Member of the *pat*, count,
great confidant of his lord,
high priest of Amun-Re, king of the gods,
Amenhotep, true of voice, (who is now) at the seat (office) of his
    father,
the high priest of Amun-Re, king of the gods,
Ramessesnakht, true of voice.

Above figure of Amenhotep:
    ⌜Year⌝ [… … … …]
⌜in the domain of Amun-Re, king of the gods.
The high priest of Amun-Re, king of the gods⌝,
Amenhotep, true of voice, ⌜was ushered⌝
into the ⌜great⌝ court ⌜of Amun.
A recital of his favors was pronounced to him,
in order to proclaim him with⌝ choice, perfect ⌜words⌝,
by the scribe Khons …
[*ca. 7 groups lost*]

⌜(This is) what was said to him⌝ in ⌜favor and proclamation
on this day in the great court of Amun-Re⌝, king of the gods,
⌜saying: "May Montu favor you!

Fig. 4. Reward Scene of Amenhotep, South Scene (no. 7: photographer unknown, ca. 1890; reproduced with permission of the Griffith Institute, Oxford).

May the *ka* of Amun-Re,
king of the gods, lord⌐ of the sky,
Thoth, lord of ⌐hieroglyphs, Pre-Horakhty,
the gods of the sky⌐,
and the gods of the earth favor you!

May the *ka* of ⌐Neferkare Setepenre,
son of Re, Ramesses Khaemwaset Meryamun (Ramesses IX),
the great ruler of Egypt⌐,
the beloved child of ⌐all the gods⌐, favor you

ᴦfor what you have accomplished
(including) the monuments ofᴦ fine gold, the altars, ...
[*ca. 9 groups lost*]
... of fine gold, this ...
[*ca. 9 groups lost*]

... ᴦAmun-Reᴦ, king of the gods,
[*ca. 6–7 groups lost*]
... the actions ᴦof a perfect and effectiveᴦ servant,
ᴦwho acts effectively for Pharaoh, hisᴦ lord.
And also the wall ...
[*ca. 6 groups lost*]
... for Pharaoh, your lord,
it being a work ᴦfor the domain of Amun.

And (there are) also your accomplishments, (including) theᴦ
        harvests and taxes
of the domain of Amun (which are) ᴦunder your authority;
you caused that they fill up the interiorᴦ
of his treasuries, storehouses, and ᴦgranariesᴦ,
[*ca. 7 groups lost*]
... your accomplishments ...
[*ca. 7 groups lost*]
every [...] which he did.

And he (the king?) filled the preparation chamber[52] with all his
        property,
for he is lord of totalities of possessions,
as well as what is presented ᴦas every perfect memorialᴦ.
Pharaoh, your lord, did these (things)
in the domain ᴦofᴦ this ᴦgreat god who knows youᴦ.

And (there is) also the tribute and the ᴦoffice taxᴦ,
(that is) the sustenance, which you had delivered to the halls of the
        palace,
and the very numerous exertions and effective acts
which you perform in this domain of this great god,
[... ... ...].

Beneath scene:
Moreover concerning your tasks,

the commissions of Pharaoh, your lord,
which were bestowed on you
with the instruction 'Do it!', you did them,
for everything you did was accomplished
for ⌜the gods⌝ and for Pharaoh, [your lord].
[*ca. 6 groups lost*]

[It was made to happen] in order to favor you, to proclaim ⌜you⌝,
to anoint you with *qemy*-unguent,
to delight you[53] with an allocation of silver
as [... ...]"
[*ca. 10 groups lost*]

Silver: ⌜4⌝ *reheb*-vessels,
4 *wedjeh*-vessels, and 4 *sekhenek*-vessels;
together a total of 4 allocations of silver,
amounting to 12 mixed vessels, making 20 *deben*.

Large baskets of provisions for this work: 22 well-provided units,
and 22 *qeb*-vessels of sweet beer,
[given as] his [reward] ⌜for⌝ [2 (?)] days of his [...].
⌜Large baskets of provisions for this⌝ work: 20 well-provided units,
and 20 *qeb*-vessels of beer.[54]

Total of silver: 4 complete allocations making 20 *deben*;
42 baskets of provisions, and 42 *qeb*-vessels of beer.

Central Scene of Parallel Figures of Amenhotep before Offering Tables

In front of figure on south (left):
    [*unknown amount lost, then traces*],
    having completed a perfect old age in Karnak;
    for the *ka* of [... ... ...]
    first of the companions,
    great confidant of his ⌜lord⌝,
    high priest of Amun-Re, king of the gods,
    Amenhotep, true of voice, before the lords of Thebes,
    Amun, Mut, and Khonsu.

Above figure on south (left):
    ⌜Member of the⌝ *pat*, count,

⌐great¬ confidant ⌐of his lord¬,
god's father, beloved of the god,
⌐chief of seers of Re¬-Atum ⌐in Thebes¬,
[…] who [… …] Amun […],

⌐high priest¬ of ⌐Amun-Re¬,
⌐Amen¬hotep, true of voice,
⌐son of the high priest of¬ Amun-Re,
Ramesses ⌐nakht, true of voice¬,
son of the royal scribe, high steward of the lord of the Two Lands,
Merybastet, true of voice.

Behind figure on south (left):
[*unknown amount lost*]
… no other apart from him,
that he may cause my name to exist, firmly established,
enduring beyond eternity;

for the *ka* of the member of the *pat*, count,
royal sealbearer, sole companion,
god's father, beloved of the god, lector priest,
skilled one (?), who knew his proper conduct,
who raised up the god at ⌐his¬ appearances,
high priest of Amun-Re, king of the gods,
Amenhotep, true of voice.

[*unknown amount lost*]
… in the brightness of his eyes (?),
that he may grant (me) a long lifetime seeing his uraei,
my mouth filled with the provisions of ⌐his¬ domain;

⌐for the *ka* of the member of the *pat*¬, count,
one effective of heart for this Perfect God,
who embellished monuments for his lord
to cause that his memory endure for eternity,
high priest of Amun-Re, king of the gods,
Amenhotep, true of voice.

In front of figure on north (right):
[*unknown amount lost*]
[…] and favor

established in Karnak forever;

for the *ka* ⌜of⌝ [the member of the *pat*, count (?)],
one greatly favored since he came forth from the womb,
high priest of Amun-Re, ⌜king⌝ of the gods,
Amenhotep, true of voice,
who […] every […]
in life and power.

Behind figure on north (right):
[*unknown amount lost*]
… on this day, better than yesterday;

for the *ka* of the member of the *pat*, count,
effective confidant of his lord,
god's father, beloved of the god,
keeper of secrets in the Mansion of the Official,
sem-priest and controller of the lord's kilt in the sacred place,[55]
high priest of Amun-Re, ⌜king⌝ of the gods,
⌜Amenhotep, true of voice⌝.

[*unknown amount lost*]
… perfect […] inside his temple;
for the *ka* of the member of the *pat*, count,
great companion of the king in his palace chamber,
god's father, pure of hands,
chief of seers of Re-Atum in Thebes,
overseer of the priests of Upper and Lower Egypt,
⌜high priest of⌝ Amun-Re, king of the gods,
Amenhotep, ⌜true of voice⌝.

8. The Inscription of Amenhotep on the Back of the Thutmosid Shrine

On the exterior west rear wall of a shrine built by the Eighteenth Dynasty king Thutmose III in the court between the seventh and eighth pylons are the remains of thirty-one columns of narrative text, as well as images of a priest and, possibly, a king. The dedicator's name has not survived, but Edward F.

Wente has convincingly attributed this text to Amenhotep (1966, 82; Polz 1998, 283; contra Helck 1984). Only the lower third of this inscription remains. Wente has restored the first three columns on the basis of close parallels with columns 1 and 2 on the back pillar of Bakenkhons's Munich statue (no. 2a). This may indicate that Bakenkhons's statue was still accessible or that the text was taken from stock phraseology recorded in temple archives. The remaining columns, although fragmentary, present Amenhotep's service to the temple of Amun and to mortuary temples on the West Bank of Thebes. In a remarkable mobilization of the untoward in the normally idealizing genre of biography, the text also records an act of suppression (see p. 59) and Amenhotep's successful appeal to Amun and the king for aid. The final section of the text returns Amenhotep to the "perfection" of the priestly life, teaching youngsters and planting gardens.

⌜Member of the *pat,* count,
high priest of Amun,
Amenhotep, true of voice,
he says: I was truly assiduous, effective for his lord,
who respected the renown of his god, who went forth upon⌝ his
          path,
who performed acts of beneficence within ⌜his temple
while I was chief overseer of works in the domain of Amun,
as an excellent confidant for his lord.

O all people who are discerning in their hearts,
who exist, who are upon earth,
and who will come after me,
for millions and millions (of years)⌝, after hoary old age,
whose hearts are ⌜skilled in recognizing worth,
I will cause you to know my character when I was upon earth,
in every office that I performed since my birth⌝.

... Amun-Re, king of the gods,
in the hall of the temple of millions of years
of the Dual King, Nebmaat[re] Mery[amun] (Ramesses VI),[56]
[*ca. two thirds of a column lost*]
⌜the temple of the Dual King,⌝ Usermaatre Meryamun (Ramesses
          III),
in the domain of Amun ⌜on the west of Thebes⌝.[57]

Again ...
⌜the temple of the Dual King, Nebmaatre Meryamun (Ramesses VI)⌝

in the domain of Amun on the west of Thebes.

Again His Person heard my speech concerning …
when my father went to rest on the west of Thebes,
in ⌈year⌉ […] of Pharaoh …[58]

⌈within⌉ the house with fine gold, true lapis lazuli,
turquoise, ⌈hard stone (?)⌉, and quartzite.
…
the great and costly pectorals which I made
for Amun-Re, king of the gods, [my lord].

…
likewise the name of Amun-Re, king of the gods, very exactly.
⌈and I⌉ caused …
⌈of⌉ great craftmanship;
I embellished them with […] forever.

…
I am one who gave barley, emmer,
incense, honey,
dates, ⌈vegetables⌉, bouquets,
…
upon an aroura [of inundated land] and his ⌈canal (?)⌉ of the temple,
… to please him, and I achieved it.
And I ⌈demolished (?)⌉ [… …]

…
[introduced (?)] to the House of Gold[59]
of Amun-Re, king of the gods,
to cause [him/it (?)] to be given [attention (?)]

… and I did them.
Never had the high priests of Amun,
whose ⌈duties⌉ I received, [achieved anything comparable (?)]
… which I [did], making five and a half years.

May Amun-Re, king of the gods, my lord,
give to me life, health,
a long lifetime, and a good old age,

... in the numerous effective acts and ordeals
which I undertook for him in ⌐his domain¬.

... seized it.
And he spent eight whole months in it,
and I suffered from it exceedingly,[60]
⌐and I¬ ...
⌐my¬ lord.
I am your servant who stood suffering for you (Amun or the king),
...

Amun-Re, king of the gods, heard my plea immediately,
for he did not permit delay ...
⌐and Amun-Re saw¬ me in this transgression against me,
and I appealed to Pharaoh, my lord,
⌐the one¬ who caused ...

⌐the temple of the Dual King, Usermaatre¬ Setepenre (Ramesses II),
in the domain of Amun,
the temple of the Dual King, Usermaatre Meryamun (Ramesses III),
in the domain of Amun on the west of Thebes,
to ⌐the place¬ ...

O high priests of Amun
who will come after me,
do not ⌐neglect¬ ...
I acted effectively for him,
(for) he had suppressed quickly the one who suppressed me,
without ⌐permitting delay¬.

... many youngsters in his domain.
I instructed them concerning their offices.
He caused (me/them) to control (?) ...
⌐I planted¬ many ⌐gardens¬
... within them.
⌐I¬ built ...
of perfection.

Behind figure of priest:
    ... in the domain of Amun,
    Merybastet, true of voice.[61]
    [*ca. 5 groups lost*]

... the temple of Ramesses Meryamun (Ramesses II),
(called) "Beloved-like-[Ptah]-at-Memphis,"[62]
the royal scribe and chief steward of the temple of millions (of
    years) ...
[*ca. 5 groups lost*]

9. An Inscription of Amenhotep from Karnak North

The large sandstone block (exact measurements not known) bearing this inscription was found in excavations in the complex of temples in the northern enclosure of Karnak and may show that Amenhotep dedicated a further structure in this area. Inscribed on both sides with texts pertaining to Amenhotep, including a building narrative, it is possible that this block was part of that structure. Alternatively, the crumbling portico, whose restoration he narrates in the text, may be the gateway he built for Ramesses IX on the south side of the eighth pylon. The block is a small section of what was originally a much larger scene and inscription and, therefore, could have formed part of a chapel wall or have been set up in a court, perhaps with other inscriptions belonging to Amenhotep. The front bears the remains of a scene of adoration before an ithyphallic Amun or Min. Before the god's face are traces of a bouquet offered to him, perhaps by a figure of a king. A lintel fragment with a scene of Amenhotep adoring Amun was also found in this area and may have come from a temple dedicated to the Eighteenth Dynasty king Amenhotep I with his mother Ahmose Nefertari (Jacquet 1999, 23, 470–73, no. 334).

Below scene on front surface:
    [*unknown amount lost*],
    member of the *pat*, count,
    high priest of Amun-Re, king of the gods,
    Amenhotep, [true of voice ... *rest lost*]

Behind image of god on front surface:
    [*unknown amount lost*] ⌜chief of seers of Re-Atum in Thebes,
    overseer of the priests of Upper⌝ and Lower Egypt,
    high ⌜priest of Amun-Re⌝, king of the gods,
    [Amenhotep, true of voice].

    [*unknown amount lost, then traces*]

member of the *pat*, count,
confidant of the lord of the Two Lands,
high priest of Amun- ⌜Re⌝, king of the gods,
Amenhotep, ⌜true of voice⌝.

Rear surface:
[*unknown number of columns lost, then traces*]
... a good burial inasmuch as we will be buried likewise.[63]

Now as for the one who will distort the words that I spoke
and who will ignore what I have done, and who comes ...
[*rest of this column and the beginning of the next lost*]
⌜he will not perform the⌝ office of high priest of Amun.
His son will not inherit from him.
He will not be buried on the west of Thebes, among its priests.

For I had extended ...
[... fallen (?)] into ruin
since the time of its construction;
the former high priests of Amun
having built it in the time of king Kheperkare,
son of Re, Senwosret (Senwosret I),[64]
the one who made ...
Amun-Re, king of the gods.

I came in order to reach out my hand to free it,
for its upper bricks in the chamber were crumbling,
and its wooden joinery, door supports,
frames, and doorleaves ...
making its ⌜entrance⌝.
I was the one who (re)built it in perfect construction,
making it greater in size
with perfect foundations upon its ground.

... and I (re)made ⌜its former wooden joinery⌝,
door supports, and frames
with great hard stones dragged (into position).
And I made its doorleaves ...
with ivory, [its base (?)] [... ...] ⌜with⌝ ebony.
And I had my name inscribed upon the bases (?),
...

As for the one who will remove my ⌐name⌐ in order to replace (it)
      with his (own) name,
Amun will reduce his lifetime throughout the land,
⌐for he (the transgressor) is⌐ [...] impure [...]
... ⌐since I was⌐ the one who (re)made this portico in stone,
this which I found ⌐fallen into ruin⌐.
...

⌐I was high priest of⌐ Amun-Re, king of the gods,
Amenhotep, true of voice,
son of the high priest ⌐of⌐ Amun-Re, king of the gods,
Ramessesnakht, [true of voice ... *rest of column lost*]

Part 2. Other Priesthood and Temple Staff in Thebes

10. The Statue Base of a *wab*-priest

This object, which seems to be the very damaged remains of a statue base, was found in the mortuary temple of the Eleventh Dynasty king Montuhotep II on the Theban West Bank and is now in Brussels. Much of the text, including the name of the owner is lost; I do not specify the extent of the lacunae. The remaining sections of five lines of inscription include traditional statements relating to moral character and social responsibility. The allusion to royal appointment to office can be compared with the divinely mediated promotions narrated by the high priesthood of Amun (nos. 2, 3b–c). This text indicates how such motifs, as well as ancient high elite phraseology, could be deployed at lower social levels.

> [*an unknown number of lines are lost from the beginning of the text, perhaps including a hymn or offering formula*]
> … [that] they [may place] my name upon …
> … [I gave bread to] the hungry, water to the thirsty …
> … [I ensured a man's inheritance, I did not deprive] another of his property,
> I did not speak [falsehood] …
> … for I knew his strength, after he had rescued me …
> … Usermaatre Setepenre (Ramesses II) [recognised me (?)].
> I was appointed *wab*-priest, scribe of the temple …
> [*the rest of the text, including at least one further line, is lost*]

11A–B. The Tomb of Samut, Assessor of Cattle of the Domain of Amun

Samut's tomb is one of at least three Ramessid tombs located off a court that probably belongs to a large, as yet unexcavated, Eighteenth Dynasty tomb in the Assasif necropolis on the Theban West Bank. Its transverse hall is decorated in the Ramessid parallel register style described in the introduction (3.3). The extensive biographical inscriptions, which dominate the west half of the hall, are in striking contrast to the more traditionally Ramessid scenes of the journey to the shrine and the next world, which dominate the east half. The text registers are complementary to these scenes, centering on Samut's relationship to the divine sphere.

The texts fill two of three registers that wrap around the walls of the west half of the transverse hall. The main biographical text (no. 11a) begins in the upper register of the south wall, beside the tomb entrance and in front of a figure of Samut, who stands with both arms raised in adoration. The text continues onto the west and north walls of the hall, closing before a figure of Mut, who is seated in a brightly painted and decorated kiosk. A second, more fragmentary inscription (no. 11b) begins at the same point in the register directly below 11a and ends on the right half of the west wall; extensive damage to this section of wall makes it difficult to establish its exact endpoint. The lowest register on these walls bears remains of offering and agricultural scenes.

The hieroglyphs of both inscriptions are written in retrograde to face toward the goddess. The images of Samut and Mut associated with both texts are largely parallel, but with a few key differences. In front of the surviving part of Samut's figure in the middle register is a brazier, an element not present next to his figure above. In the right half of the middle register on the west wall, traces of jars, lotus blooms, and offerings are visible between the end of the text and the image of Mut. Her pose and accoutrements match those in the register above, but the kiosk is plainer with a simple sloping roof and undecorated columns.

The uppermost text (no. 11a) is a distinctive mix of genres that departs explicitly from the traditional structures of biographical inscriptions. It begins as a "tale" of Samut's youth set in the third person and continues with a first person deposition of property to Mut, which is then followed by prayers and a hymn to her protective power. The text in the middle register (no. 11b) seems to be a copy of a legal document in which Samut bequeaths all his property to Mut in return for a "pension." The unusual predominance of text in the tomb prioritizes Samut's connection to the goddess. The legal document designates his tomb as part of Mut's domain, much as the biography dedicates his life and experience exclusively to her.

11A. BIOGRAPHY

South wall:
    There was a man of Southern Heliopolis (Thebes),
    a true scribe in Thebes,
    Samut was his name by his mother,
    called Kyky, true of voice.[65]

    Now his god instructed him,
    he taught him according to his teaching.
    He placed him upon the path of life,

in order to protect his body.

The god knew him as a youth,
decreeing for him rich provisions.
Then he (Samut) sought within himself,
in order to find a protector for himself,

and he found Mut at the head of the gods,
Shay and Renenet with her,
a lifetime of life and breath under her authority,
and all that occurs under her command.

He said: Look, I am giving to her
my property and all that (I have) accrued,
for I know that she is effective on my behalf,
that she is uniquely excellent.

She removed anguish for me;
she left me in a painful moment,[66]
(but) she came, the north wind before her,
after I called upon her by name.

I was a poor man of her town,
a vagrant in the vicinity of her city.[67]
I entered into her power in relation to my property,
in exchange for the breath of life.
Not one of (my) family shall divide it;
it is for her *ka* as offerings.

As for the robber who despoils,
the one who stands up to him will be under her authority.
I am speaking about an official in his moment (of success),
(for although) he is strong he will not attack, for that is with
          Sekhmet,
the great one whose sphere of action is unknown;[68]
there is no servant of hers who will fall into turmoil
forever and ever.

O Mut, mistress of the gods, hear my prayers:
(if) a servant testifies to the efficacy of his lord,
then ⌜his lord rewards⌝ him with a (long) lifetime.

I do not make a protector for myself among men.
I [do not attach] myself to the powerful, not even my son,
for I found that she [will provide for] the funeral.[69]
Burial, it is in your hand, unique one,
for you are the Meskhenet[70] [... ...]
that I may be assembled as an effective mummy,
after life has proceeded (to its end), being admitted [...]
[... ...] like me,
and they (followers of Mut?) will hand over their property to you.

May you keep me safe, until my end, from every evil.
Let my eyes see the rays, for you are the female sun.
(Let my) ears hear without deafness,
my nose inhaling the breezes,
the ⌜ways of⌝ life flowing without weariness,[71]
while my throat breathes, [my mouth] functions,
my lips are ready, my tongue distinguishing [taste (?)],
all my [limbs (?)] being complete as (in) life,
without the disappearance (loss of function) of my body,
and no [tongue (?)] having power over me,
or people harming me.

O Mut the great ⌜who made me (?)⌝,
act as protection (for me), unique one,
until your perpetual protection of me (in the next world) is
        acknowledged,
my name enduring in [...]

[...] to me protection in [seeing (?)]
(when) I [saw (?)] that she is powerful (?)
[in what the sun (?)] encircles ...
[ca. 7 groups lost]
... earth, seeing ...
[3 columns lost]

[ca. 10 groups lost from the next column, then traces]
... [Re (?)], the one who ...
[ca. 6 groups lost]
... upon [... ...] to judge testimony ...
[ca. 7 groups are lost, with traces, from the end of this column. There
is space for another column at this point although no traces remain]

West wall (this section is badly damaged and I do not specify the extent of the lacunae):
[*ca. 7 columns lost*]
... would that (?) ...
... evening in ...
... descending from the sky [...] in the ...
... to Mut,
that she may enable me to walk freely ⌜within⌝ ...
... of her provisions, that I may act ...
... love, while [... appeased/offerings (?)] ...
... (against) his raging, appeased ...
... my [...] in her presence.
It is good to be protected [from (?)] ...
... Mut (?) ...
... perfection, (for I) know that [you are (?)] powerful ...
... great in ...
... foremost of Memphis,
Sekhmet, beloved of Ptah, ...
... in the sky, appearing [... ...] at the beginning [of the year], ...
... the king, established [upon his head (?)], as Neith (?) the great ...
[*rest of column lost*]
... in every first-of-the-year-festival, when (you) appear ...
... from within it, living on ...
... mistress of [... ... ...] the West (?) ...
... as Mut [... ... ...] burial,
breath [of (?)] your mouth ...
... [you] make it, every [nose (?)] under your authority,
you open eyes ...
... your rays illuminate every path [of the sky (?)] ...
its [...], which your eye encircles (?).
I rejoice for [...] your power,
inasmuch as you are greater than any god.

My heart is filled with my[72] mistress.
I will not fear people when I lie down
for when I sleep, I have a defender.

As for the one who makes Mut a protector,
no god is able to harm him,
being favored by the king of his time,
as one who passes into veneration.

As for the one who makes Mut a protector,
evil will not assail him,
he will be protected every day until he joins the necropolis.

As for the one who makes Mut a protector,
how perfect is his lifetime and royal favor suffuses his body
—the one who places her in his heart.

As for the one who makes Mut a protector,
[he] came forth from the womb favored,
perfection destined for him
on the birthing brick;[73] he will achieve veneration.

As for the one who makes Mut a <protector>,
how fortunate is the one who longs for her,
the god will not overthrow him, as one ignorant of (proper) speech.

11B. LEGAL TEXT

*The text is largely lost from column 12; I do not indicate the extent of
the lacunae specifically.*

South wall:
[Year …], first month of *akhet*, day 19,
under the Person of the Dual King, lord of the Two Lands,
Usermaatre Setepenre,
son of Re, ⸢Ramesses Meryamun (Ramesses II)⸣,
given life, for eternity and perpetuity.

On this day the assessor of cattle
of the domain of Amun-Re, king of the gods,
Samut, ⸢called Kyky, true of voice⸣,
spoke thus: I give all my property and […
… … …] ⸢to⸣ Mut
and to the domain of Mut the great, lady of Asheru,
[… … …]

See, I have established it as an income for […
… …] my […] and (my) old age as my contract,[74]
without a ⸢son or daughter,

brother[1] or sister,
for I entrust myself to Mut,[75]
the [mistress who has given (me)] the breath (of life),
that she may ordain the West for me in old age,
[... ... ... the terror (?)] of the king.

As for servants who are brought ...
[*ca. 5 groups lost*]
... to Mut in the domain of administration (?)
and they ... [*ca. 7 groups lost*]
to the domain of Mut,
and they [*the twelfth column begins here and the text is very
　　　　fragmentary from this point*]
... songstress of Amun ...
... with the servants ...
... [of] Amun, in order to carry ...
[*1 column lost, with traces*]
... every [...] of the army ...
... who build (?) ...
[*2 columns lost, with traces*]
... domain of Mut ...
... under the authority of ...
... of life ...
... Mut ...
[*3 columns lost*]
... Mut, while the ...
[*3 columns lost, with traces*]
... all that I have done for Mut ...
... after resting (?) ...
... old age ...
... Mut ...
... domain of Mut ...
... she acted/will act for ...
... in front of ...

West wall:
[*1 column lost, with traces*]
... [Mut ... while the ... ...] upon ...
[*3 columns lost, with traces*]
... their [...] dwelling in my ...
... [As for] anyone who ⌜will interfere⌝ with the speech ...[76]

... the strong, which I made for myself ...
... made by the assessor of cattle, Kyky.
... which they will bear ...
... mistress of the gods, the lords of ...
[*1 column lost, with traces*]
... Mut ...
[*2 columns lost, with traces*]
... presented ...
... in front of ...
[*Columns 55–59 are lost, except for traces at the end of column 59. No more columns are visible*]

12A–B. The Tomb of Djehutyemheb, Overseer of Fieldworkers of the Domain of Amun

During the Nineteenth Dynasty, at least eight tombs of middle-level temple officials were hewn into the sides of the court of the large Eighteenth Dynasty tomb of the royal steward Kheruef in the Assasif area of the Theban necropolis. The tomb of Djehutyemheb is on the west side of the entrance to the court, in a position parallel to the tomb of Nakhtdjehuty, whose biography is translated in chapter II (no. 22). Both tombs can be dated to the reign of Ramesses II.

The decorative program of Djehutyemheb's tomb is unusual in its inclusion of a row of rock-cut stelae along the east wall and the south and north ends of the transverse hall. These stelae emphasize the intermediary role of a number of deities, particularly Hathor, thereby creating a virtual temple to her in which ritual performance and divine intercession are mobilized visually and textually. These themes culminate in the biographical text inscribed in the shrine, on the wall around the doorway to a sloping passage, which leads to Djehutyemheb's burial chamber. The first text (no. 12a) runs over the top of the doorway and continues down its right side, above a figure of Djehutyemheb, who stands, facing the entrance, with his arms raised in adoration. The text continues onto the west wall of the shrine, above the figure of Djehutyemheb's wife, ending by the entrance into the shrine. It begins as a hymn to Hathor and then continues with Djehutyemheb's narration of a dream in which the goddess foretold the location of his tomb. Her reply to his hymn (no. 12b) is inscribed on the other side of the entrance to the sloping passage, beginning above the door and continuing to the left to close before a now lost figure of the goddess. The very fragmentary text promises Hathor's continual protection of, and intercession for, Djehutyemheb in the next world. The two texts seem almost to represent a "conversation" between an individual and a deity, a motif almost unprecedented in the biographical tradition (compare no. 37). A dream of Hathor is also found in the stela of Ipuy from Deir el-Medina (no. 50).

12A. HYMN TO HATHOR

> *Shrine, north wall, left of doorway:*
> Adoring Gold, the eye of Re,[77]
> kissing the ground for ⌜her⌝ *ka*.
> ⌜Giving praise⌝ to her perfect face,
> paying her honor ⌜every day⌝,
> ⌜by the Osiris of the⌝ overseer of fieldworkers of the domain of
>   Amun,
> Djehuty ⌜emheb, true of voice;
>
> he says: I have come⌝ before you, O lady of the Two Lands,
> Hathor, great of love.
> ⌜Look, I am in adoration⌝ of your perfect face;
> I kiss the ground for your *ka*.
>
> I was your true servant,
> loyal to your command.
> I did not spurn the words of your mouth,
> I was not ignorant of your teaching.
> I was upon the path which you yourself set,
> upon the road which you made.
>
> How fortunate is the occasion for the one who knows you;
> everyone who sees you is favored.
> How joyful it is to rest by your side
> (for) the one who enters your shade.
>
> You are the one who foretold my tomb in the beginning,
> as it was ordained to be.
> That which you said happened, your plan is [established,
> sanctified] is the place for my body.
>
> You will give to me old age,
> that I may rest, being ⌜whole⌝,

and sated with life;
my eyes farseeing
and all my limbs complete.

You are the one who said to me with your own mouth:
"I am the perfect *hely,* my form is [the form (?)] of Mut,[78]
the one who comes to instruct you.
See your place, fill yourself with it,[79]
without going north, without going ⌐south¬,"

while I was in a dream and the earth was in silence,
in the depths of night.
At dawn, my heart rejoiced, I was in joy,
and I set (my) face to the West,
in order to do as you said.

You are the goddess who does what she says,
a noble one to whom one must listen.
I have not disregarded your speech nor transgressed your counsel.
I act according to what you say.

Shrine, west wall:
Set your face that I may worship it,
bestow your perfection that I may perceive your form in my tomb,[80]
in order to recount your strength, in order to cause generations to
        understand [...]
[... ... ...]

for the *ka* of the Osiris of the scribe of the offerings of the domain of
        Amun,
overseer of fieldworkers of the domain of Amun,
royal scribe, [... ... ...],
Djehutyheb, true of voice, in peace,
and his beloved sister, [*ca. 10 groups lost: probably her titles*],
Mut ⌐nedjmet, true of voice, on¬ the west of Thebes.

12B. HATHOR'S REPLY

Shrine, north wall, right of doorway:
Words spoken by Hathor, mistress of Thebes,

eye of Re, who resides in [Djesret]:
Welcome Djehutyemheb, true of voice,
the accurate, calm, ⌐silent one of Karnak⌐,
the discrete mouth of ⌐Thebes⌐.

[… … … …]
My heart mingles with your form.
I have ⌐made⌐ [a shrine (?)] for your mummy,
and I have sanctified a place for your body.
I will ⌐announce you⌐ to the great god
that he may say to you "Welcome."

I will commend ⌐you⌐ to Horakhty
that he may place you among his adorers.
I will hand ⌐you⌐ over to the lord of Heliopolis
that he may cause your offerings to endure.

I will commend you to [*rest of column lost*]
[I will hand you over] to Sokar and the *henu*-barque
that you may enter the *shetayt*-shrine.

I will hand you over to Nefertem
that you may go around Memphis with him.
I will commend ⌐you to⌐ [the one perfect of face],[81]
[*rest of column lost*]
[that he may place you among his (?)] favored ones.

I will commend you to Penpen[82]
that he may gather together your offerings.
⌐I will commend you to⌐ …
… ⌐as⌐ when you were upon earth.

May he favor you a million times
⌐that he may place you⌐ …
… your name, moment after moment,
your […] established forever.
…
that the sky may overflow for you [with birds (?)],
[fish (?)] coming from the river for [your *ka* (?)],
[*rest lost*]

13. THE TOMB OF TJANEFER, THIRD PRIEST OF AMUN

Family relationships indicate that Tjanefer held office from the end of the Nineteenth Dynasty into the reign of Ramesses III in the Twentieth. Inscriptions in the tomb of his son, Amenemopet, refer to events relating to reward or promotion in year 27 of Ramesses III (Gaballa and Kitchen 1981, 174–75, fig. 10). Tjanefer came from a very well-connected Theban priestly family. His son married the daughter of the powerful high priest Ramessesnakht, who dominated the middle years of the Twentieth Dynasty in Thebes (pp. 15, 59). Tjanefer himself was related by marriage to the high priest of Amun under Ramesses II, Bakenkhons (no. 2). His tomb was built in the exclusive necropolis of Dra Abu el-Naga, close to the tombs of Bakenkhons and Roma (no. 3) and at one of the highest points in the hill. Only sections of the decoration survive, but it seems have to consisted of standard religious scenes of the Ramessid period as well as more unusual elements, such as a statue of a king and a representation of the tomb owner raising a djed-pillar, a motif common in contemporary Memphite tombs, but rarely attested in Thebes (Kampp-Seyfried 1996, I, 450). Particularly striking is the use of raised relief, which demonstrates a large investment in the tomb's decoration. The plundering of Tjanefer's tomb in the late Twentieth Dynasty is vividly described in one of the tomb robbery papyri (Peet 1930, 60–61).

Tjanefer's short biographical text is inscribed on the local west (left) inner jamb of the entrance into the long hall of the tomb. No inscription survives on the parallel eastern jamb. The text consists of three columns above a figure of Tjanefer, who is depicted in undifferentiated bodily form squatting on a mat, his arms held to his chest, with a pile of offerings before him. His figure bears the caption: The Osiris of the god's father, pure of hands, the one who sees Re-Atum, priest of Amun, Tjanefer, true of voice. *The biography centers on generalized statements of proper behavior within the temple and includes some distinctive phrases, particularly concerning his relationship to Thebes.*

> [The Osiris of the priest] of Amun,
> Tjanefer, true of voice,
> he says: I was a priest, beloved of his lord,
> who did what he favored throughout every day,
> one weighty of counsel, effective of speech,
> discrete in relation to ⌈his plans⌉,
> the one for whom Thebes is his father and mother (?).
>
> I became a high official while I was a youth.
> I became powerful while I was fresh.
> I was one silent, temperate, patient,

one weighty in ⌜his⌝ projects, calm,
who spoke of matters [appropriately (?)], [... ...].

⌜I acted as⌝ the champion of the wretched,
who saved the fearful from his wrongdoing.
I was one approachable, who listened to concerns, accurate in
      judgment [...],
who (carefully) assessed [what was reported concerning his plans (?)].

Part 3: The Abydos Priesthood

14a–b. The Statue and Stela of Wenennefer, High Priest of Osiris

Wenennefer inherited the office of high priest of Osiris from his father Mery probably during the second decade of the reign of Ramesses II. Two inscriptions (including no. 14b translated here) show that he was still in office in the fourth decade of that reign. Wenennefer's family dominated the priesthood at Abydos from the beginning of the Nineteenth Dynasty, and his descendants continued to hold high priestly offices there until at least its end (see no. 17). Wenennefer also laid claim to collegial and family connections with influential members of the priesthoods and upper echelons of the court of Ramesses II, including the vizier Prehotep (no. 26), who is mentioned on a number of Wenennefer's monuments. The statue translated here (no. 14a) bears his name and that of Wenennefer's kinsman Minmose, the high priest of Onuris at Thinis. All Wenennefer's provenanced objects came from Abydos where he had a significant monumental presence.

14a. Standing Pillar Statue (fig. 1: frontispiece)

Although the provenance of this granodiorite statue is not known, it is almost certainly from Abydos and its exceptional form suggests that it was designed to be integrated into temple architecture. The standing figure of Wenennefer emerges frontally from a pillar almost two meters (6′6″) high. He stands on a small rectangular base and wears a kilt and panther skin. At his side he holds the Abydos standard. The stone pillar extends above his head, framing it in stone. On the left side of the block around the head is a figure of the king with arm raised toward the top of the standard. On the right side are inscribed cartouches of Ramesses II. Down the front and side of his body are inscribed his and his father's names and titles in hieroglyphs at a scale which resembles that of temple wall inscriptions. A flat band of text covers the front of Wenennefer's ankles. Beneath this, his schematically rendered toes are visible. The sides of his ankles and feet are shown in a similarly schematic way on the sides of the block. Wenennefer's body is, in some ways, an abstraction, dominated by the stone pillar and the hieroglyphs which bind it.

A faded column of text down the shaft of the standard gives royal cartouches and titles: Usermaatre Setepenre, son of Re, Ramesses Meryamun (Ramesses II); ⌜high priest of⌝ Osiris, Wenennefer, true of voice, [son of the high priest of Osiris, Mery (?)]. *On the right breast of the statue* Wenennefer *is inscribed without a determinative, so that the name captions the statue. Down the right arm is a further column*: High priest of Osiris, Wenennefer, true of voice. *Two columns of large hieroglyphs are inscribed on the front of the kilt*: High priest of Osiris, Wenennefer, true of voice, son of the high priest of Osiris, Mery, true of voice. *The band across the ankles also gives Wenennefer's title as high priest and his name. This is repeated immediately below, in a single line across the front of the base*: High priest of Osiris, Wenennefer, true of voice. *On the left side of the base are two lines giving the names of Wenennefer's mother and his wife*: His mother, songstress of Osiris, Maiany, true of voice; the lady of his house, songstress of Osiris, Tiy, true of voice. *On the right side of the base are two lines of inscription, setting out further kin relationships*: His brother, city governor, vizier, Prehotep, true of voice; his brother, high priest of Onuris, Minmose, true of voice. *Down the sides of the statue, where the kilt merges with the back pillar, are columns of large hieroglyphs giving cartouches and Wenennefer's name: on the right side,* Lord of the Two Lands, Usermaatre Setepenre; high priest of Osiris, Wenennefer, true of voice, *and on the left,* Usermaatre Setepenre Ramesses Meryamun; high priest of Osiris, Wenennefer, true of voice.

The biography, inscribed in four columns on the back pillar, presents Wenennefer's role in the key ritual event at Abydos, the "Osiris mysteries." The mysteries were performed as part of the annual festival that brought Osiris in procession from his temple, through the wadi, to his tomb in the ancient, originally royal, necropolis of Umm el-Qaab. The dramatic performance of the mysteries, which included acts of defense against the god's enemies, culminated with his "resurrection" in a series of secret rituals. Narration of an individual's role in the mysteries had been a key component of royal and nonroyal self-presentations since at least the Middle Kingdom (see Lichtheim 1988, 98–100; Simpson in Simpson [ed.] 2003, 339–44, 425–27). Wenennefer, who presents discrete stages of the performance in his narrative, elaborates traditional motifs by emphasizing his personal role in transfiguring the god through wielding potent, restricted ritual objects.

    Back pillar:
        High priest of Osiris,
        Wenennefer, true of voice,
        he says: Welcome, welcome, O victorious king,[83]
        who cleaves the sky with his plumes.
        You are welcome, being peaceful,
        coming in peace,
        your coming being for the span of eternity;

for the *ka* of the high priest of Osiris,
Wenennefer, true of voice,
and his sister, the lady of the house,
Tiy, true of voice,
who is called Nefertari, true of voice.

High priest of Osiris,
Wenennefer, true of voice,
he says: I was the sealbearer of the god, foremost one,
the priest of Horus-who-protects-his-father.

I brought the wreath of triumph[84]
and transfigured the god with it,
reciting acclamation in Ropoqer,
his effective place of the first time;

for the *ka* of the high priest of Osiris,
Wenennefer, true of voice,
son of the dignitary, high priest of Osiris,
Mery, true of voice.

High priest of Osiris,
Wenennefer, true of voice,
he says: I was a great priest in Abydos,[85]
the *weba*-servant of Wenennefer,[86]
firm of fingers in binding the diadem, who adorned the god,
who ferried the god to Ropoqer,
who overthrew the one who rebelled against the *neshmet*-barque;[87]

for the *ka* of the high priest of Osiris,
Wenennefer, true of voice,
born of Maiany, true of voice.

High priest of Osiris,
Wenennefer, true of voice,
he says: I ascended to Rosetjau.
I was equipped, bound in red linen,
the *ames*-club in my hand to smite the disaffected,
the *iaat*-weapon to smite the rebel.[88]
I read out the transfiguration spells performed for Isis.
I deposited offerings in the sacred land.

14B. STELA FROM THE SMALL WESTERN TEMPLE

This limestone stela (ca. 1.5 meters high, 4'9"), now in the Egyptian Museum, Cairo, was found in the mid-nineteenth century during Auguste Mariette's excavation (1880, 36–37) in a complex he termed "the small western temple," probably located in the wadi at Abydos, near the Osiris temple. At the top of the stela, outside the incised border, is the head of a falcon in raised relief. The scene in the lunette shows Ramesses II offering incense and pouring a libation before the figures of Osiris, Isis, and Horus who bears the epithet: Son of Osiris. *The caption before the king relates both to him and the figure of Osiris:* Lord of the Two Lands, Usermaatre Setepenre, lord of appearances, Ramesses Meryamun, given life, beloved of Osiris Khentimentu. *The middle register has a figure of Wenennefer in the center with a smaller figure of his wife behind him. Wenennefer's arms are raised in adoration of an unusual representation of Abydos that incorporates a shrine resting on a lion-footed chair that in turn rests on a sled with a uraeus. Behind the shrine, in an enclosed space, is a figure of a woman kneeling and holding the Abydos standard, which is embraced by a falcon. On top of the enclosure sits another falcon. The caption above reads:* Horus of the south side, *a form of Horus mentioned in the narrative. The short text inscribed in three lines in the lower register records Wenennefer's participation in a ritual event involving this form of Horus, perhaps as a component of the Osiris mysteries (see no. 14a).*

Behind figure of king:
> Year 42 of the Dual King,
> Usermaatre Setepenre,
> Ramesses Meryamun (Ramesses II).

Second register, beneath shrine:
> Praise to you Osiris, lord of people,
> rich in splendor, great of majesty,
> that you may cause that I exist like the divine *ba*s who see your
>   forms;
> for the *ka* of the high priest of Osiris,
> Wenennefer, true of voice,
> son of the dignitary, high priest of Osiris,
> Mery, true of voice.

Second register, above figures of Wenennefer and his wife:
> High priest of Osiris,
> Wenennefer, true of voice,

born of the songstress of Osiris,
Maiany, true of voice,
and his sister, lady of the house,
great one of the harem of Osiris,
Tiy, true of voice,
who is called Nefertari, true of voice,
daughter of the dignitary, overseer of the two granaries
of Upper and Lower Egypt,
Qeny, true of voice,
born of Uay, true of voice.

Lowest register, beneath scene:
High priest of Osiris,
Wenennefer, true of voice,
he says: I was a priest, skilled in his duty,
the great chief in Abydos.
I followed the god on his journey
on this his day of Horus of the south side,
spreading rejoicing at the entrance to Tawer,
(for) it is his day of judging matters;

for the *ka* of the high priest of Osiris, Wenennefer,
his brother, city governor, vizier,
Prehotep, true of voice,
and his brother, high priest of Onuris,
Minmose, true of voice.

15. THE STELA OF PASER, *WAB*-PRIEST OF OSIRIS

This small, roughly carved, limestone stela (50 centimeters high and 35 centimeters wide, 1'7" by 1'2") was purchased in a village near Abydos and is now in the Egyptian Museum, Cairo. The scene in the lunette depicts Paser with his arms raised in adoration before a barque held aloft by eight priests who stand in four pairs. A further figure of a priest wearing a panther skin stands at the center of the barque with one arm raised. This figure bears a caption and is also named in the text: The priest, Pairy, true of voice. The prow and stern of the barque bear royal aegises, each wearing a uraeus and an atef-crown. *A caption above the barque designates it as belonging to the deified king Ahmose,*

the founder of the Eighteenth Dynasty and owner of a vast mortuary complex
at Abydos, around three kilometers (two miles) south of the main Osiris temple
area: Perfect God, lord of the Two Lands, Nebpehtyre Ahmose. *A small figure*
of a queen holding sistra stands before the entrance to the central shrine on the
barque; she has the caption: God's wife, Ahmose Nefertari. *The adoring figure*
of Paser in front of the barque is captioned: *wab*-priest of Osiris, Paser, true
of voice. *A further two columns above his head record his speech to Ahmose*:
O vizier who judges justice for the just: how ⌜joyful⌝ is the one who fills
his heart with you! *On stelae from Thebes similar speeches are addressed to*
the deified Eighteenth Dynasty king Amenhotep I, Ahmose's son and also an
important oracular deity (Clère 1968b; KRI III, 464, n. 9a–10a). In the bottom
right of the stela is a standing figure with his arms raised in adoration. His
caption identifies him as Paser's father: *wab*-priest of Osiris, Mose, [...]. *The*
nine lines inscribed above and in front of this figure present details of an oracle
made to Paser by Ahmose concerning a dispute over fields. While not strictly a
biography, the motif of oracular action here can be compared with references
and allusions to oracles in other texts in this volume (e.g., nos. 1, 3b, 18, 37).
The stela also attests to the ongoing significance of the complex of Ahmose at
Abydos in the Ramessid period and the transformation of cult practice relating
to this king (Harvey 1998, esp. 121–22).

Year 14, second month of *akhet*, day 25,
under the Person of the Dual King, Usermaatre Setepenre,
son of Re, ⌜Ramesses⌝ Meryamun (Ramesses II), given life.
On this day, the *wab*-priest Paser, approached with the *wab*-priest
⠀⠀⠀⠀Tjay
to dispute ⌜before King⌝ Nebpehtyre (Ahmose).

The approach (to the god) made by the *wab*-priest Paser:
"As for this field, does it belong to <Tjay>, son of Sedjemenef (?),
[and] the children of Hay?"
(But) the god stopped.[89]
[He then] approached the god saying:
"Does it belong to the *wab*-priest Paser, son of Mose?"
[Then] the god assented emphatically
before the *wab*-priests of ⌜King⌝ Nebpehtyre:
the priest, Pairy,
the front *wab*-priest, Yandjabu,
the ⌜front⌝ *wab*-priest, Tjanefer,
the rear *wab*-priest, Nakht,
the rear *wab*-priest, Djehutymose.[90]

⌈Made⌉ by the *wab*-priest and draftsman
of the temple of Ramesses Meryamun in the domain of Osiris,
    Nebmehyt.

16. The Statue of Nebenmaat, Priest of Abydos (fig. 5)

Only the head and shoulders of this granodiorite statue survive. It was found by W. M. Flinders Petrie in or near the Osiris temple complex and is now in The Manchester Museum. Since the cartouche of Ramesses II is inscribed on the right shoulder, Nebenmaat may have served under the high priest of Osiris, Wenennefer (no. 14), or a member of his family. He is not known from any other monument. The half life-size statue wears a tripartite wig, and the face, although badly damaged, bears traces of cosmetic lines around the eyes. Both these features can be attributes of statues of gods in the New Kingdom. A further unusual element of the statue's iconography is the carving of the upper section of a pole over the statue's left shoulder. It is likely that this represents the top of an imiut-*fetish, the stuffed skin of an animal tied to a pole, which was one of the central symbols of Osiris and Anubis at Abydos. An* imiut *is also depicted between paired figures of recumbent jackals on the upper surface of the back pillar. The inclusion of this emblem seems visually to signal Nebenmaat's*

Fig. 5. Statue of Nebenmaat (no. 16; copyright The Manchester Museum, The University of Manchester).

involvement in cult performance, a theme that is also foregrounded in the
biographical statements inscribed on the surface and sides of the back pillar.

Rear surface of back pillar:
   Great administrator for the god of Thinite Abydos,
   god's sealbearer, of great returns (?),
   subordinate, who conducts the ritual in ⌐the mound of⌐ [...]⁹¹
   [*rest of column lost*]

   ... what he knew, being [foremost of the necropolis (?)],
   priest of Osiris,
   Nebenmaat, ⌐true of voice⌐,
   ...

   He says: I was a priest of Abydos,
   who embellished gold for [his] lord.
   ...

   I established the god upon his standard,
   I raised it upon his (the god's) side,
   the ⌐frame⌐ [being ...]⁹²
   ...

Right side of back pillar:
   Priest, Nebenmaat, true of voice,
   he says: I was a great *wab*-priest of Tawer,
   lector priest of the one (Osiris) who is in it,
   ...

Left side of back pillar:
   He says: As for what is [pleasing (?)],
   . (that is) performing what is effective and favored,
   I purified my god and I cleansed [...]
   ...

17. The Stela of Wenennefer, High Priest of Isis

This is one of two visually similar stelae owned by Wenennefer. The iconography

*and textual content indicate that both are from Abydos, but their findspots are
unknown. The stelae are now in the Musée du Louvre, Paris; the second stela,
not included here, bears a hymn to Osiris without a biographical narrative.
Wenennefer held office in the late Nineteenth Dynasty and was the grandson of
the prominent high priest of Osiris, Wenennefer (no. 14). The uppermost register
of this one-meter-high (3'3") stela depicts Wenennefer kneeling before Osiris and
Horus, who bear the captions:* Osiris, lord of eternity; Horus, son of Isis. *The
damaged inscription above Wenennefer begins as a short prayer:* Giving praise
to [Osiris, by the high priest of Isis, Wenennefer, son of the high priest of
Osiris], Yuyu, true of voice, son of the high priest of Osiris, Wenennefer, true
of voice. *The scene below shows Wenennefer before four goddesses each holding
was-scepters, the first three of whom are associated with birth: Isis of the birth-
house; Heqet, lady of the sky; and Nut, the beneficent one who bore the gods.
The last goddess in the row, Shenpet, lady of the sky, is a manifestation of Isis in
mourning. The caption inscribed above Wenennefer reads:* Giving praise to Isis
of the birth-house, kissing the ground for the great Ennead, for the *ka* of the
high priest of Isis, Wenennefer, true of voice.

*The epithet borne by Isis in these captions indicates that the stela was
associated with a birth-house, a type of subsidiary temple that thematized
the birth of a god as a dramatic performance. No archaeological evidence for
such a structure at Abydos has been identified predating the Thirtieth Dynasty,
but a group of late-New Kingdom stelae reveals that one existed in this period
(Sheikholeslami 2002, 1115–17). Themes of birth and childhood are central to
the biography of Wenennefer, which, although obscure in places, seems to narrate
his initiation into priestly office as a youth, as well as his symbolic assimilation to
the child form of the god Horus. The use of the third person to narrate this event
is particularly striking.*

> The high priest of Isis,
> Wenennefer, true of voice,
> son of the high priest of Osiris,
> Yuyu, true of voice,
> born of [Mutnefret], ⌜true of voice⌝,
>
> he says: O people of Tawer, I will cause you to hear something good
> concerning the plan of the god which he carried out
> for the servant of his domain,
> the one who made his offerings exist.
>
> The (high) priest of Horus and Isis,
> Wenennefer, son of Yuyu,[93]

began to carry this god while he was an exceptional youth,[94]
made stronger and more flourishing day by day,
like Ihy in the marsh,[95]
until the day of his favor came,
the god promoting his beloved (?).

[The musicians (?)] of Tawer
saw him like those who are children (?).
The youths [played sistra] as (his) companions,[96]
the youngsters ⌜drew near⌝ to him,
while others turned their faces to him,
facing him in order to [perform (?)].

The self-created goddess[97] [ordered]
that his (Wenennefer's?) form be revealed at once;
he became great as a royal acquaintance,
so that he mingled with the great ones of the palace,
his heart discerning the essence of Tawer.[98]

He was effective for those who are within it (Tawer),
its Ennead being content with his plan
—his efficacy suffusing (it)—
having appeared, [relying] on him,
in order to foretell perfection for him;[99]
for the *ka* of the high priest of Isis,
Wenennefer, true of voice.

PART 4: THE PRIESTHOOD OF ONURIS AT THINIS

18. THE TOMB OF THE HIGH PRIEST OF ONURIS, ANHURMOSE, AT EL-MASHAYIKH (FIG. 6)

At seventy-one columns, the biography of the high priest of Onuris, Anhurmose, is the longest known from the Ramessid period. Dated to the reign of Merenptah, it was inscribed in his tomb cut into the cliffs of el-Mashayikh approximately fifty kilometers north of Abydos. El-Mashayikh is one of the necropoleis of Thinis, the capital of the eighth Upper Egyptian nome, and an extension of the cemetery of Naga el-Deir, where First Intermediate period tombs had been cut into the lower areas of the escarpment. In selecting the site, Anhurmose broke radically with tradition: all known earlier New Kingdom high priests of Onuris had been buried at Abydos (Kees 1937, 79). His choice may be related to the temple of the goddess Mehit in the Nile Valley below. Anhurmose probably oversaw the restoration of this temple under Merenptah and he dedicated two statues within it. The connection to Mehit's temple inside his tomb is made principally through his wife, Sekhmetnefret, whose image is foregrounded in the decorative programme of the front chamber. She holds titles relating to temple performance and seems to be a representative of the divine female principle within the tomb.

Fig. 6. Scene of Anhurmose offering a bouquet to Sekhmetnefret (no. 18: line drawing after Ockinga and al-Masri 1988, pl. 18; reproduced courtesy of Boyo Ockinga).

Sekhmetnefret's image is also central to the biographical inscription, which begins on the east half of the south wall of the transverse hall to the left of the tomb entrance. It continues onto the east wall, filling the space on either side of a niche containing statues of Anhurmose flanked by his two wives. Unusually, the first part of the text wraps around a scene of Anhurmose offering a bouquet to Sekhmetnefret (fig. 6). A parallel scene is presented on the other side of the tomb entrance. The biography does not, however, express a connection with a female deity as do those in the tombs of the Theban temple staff Samut and Djehutyemheb, which have a similar emphasis on female presence in their decorative programs (nos. 11–12). Anhurmose's biography instead emphasizes his relationship to Shu, a god identified with Onuris, in some passages.

The text is an artful and detailed presentation of an individual's social responsibility, a theme not generally foregrounded in Ramessid biography, but one that explicitly mobilizes traditional Middle Kingdom models. The treatment in Anhurmose's text is considerably longer than most earlier examples, as well as being in part more elaborate in phraseology and metaphor. The loss to the latter parts of the inscription means that stanza breaks are approximate.

> *Between figures of Anhurmose and Sekhmetnefret:*
> The Osiris of the member of the *pat*, count,
> god's father, beloved of the god,
> pure of hands in adoring his horizon,
> who propitiated Shu and Tefnut with what came forth as his speech,
> who bound the amulet beneath the pendant upon the breast of Shu,
> who established the disc upon the head of Tefnut,
>
> chief of seers of Shu in Thinis,
> high priest of Onuris,
> Anhurmose, true of voice,
> in peace on the west of Behdet,[100]
> and his sister, lady of the house,
> songstress of Amun-Re, lord of the thrones of the Two Lands,
> Sekhmetnefret, true of voice, in peace.
>
> *South wall, east half, beginning around the figures:*
> Royal scribe, scribe of the elite troops of the lord of the Two
>   Lands,[101]
> chief of seers of Re in Thinis,
> councillor of Shu and Tefnut,
> high priest of Onuris,
> Anhurmose, true of voice,

who ⌜prayed⌝ for *sed*-festivals and health
for his Horus, lord of the Two Lands,
Baenre Meryamun,
lord of appearances, Merenptah Hetephermaat (Merenptah),
given life like Re forever;

he says: I was excellent as a weanling,
clever as a child,
discerning as a boy,
intelligent as a humble youth.

I was a humble youth who sat upright in the school room,
unwavering in it, who saw and found it.[102]
I was one beloved of his Horus, effective for his god,
without my heart being slack, being effective for their *ka*s.

I was wakeful in the boat, without slumber,
the crew of sleepers could rely on me.
I was strong upon land, without fatigue,
who saw many expeditions like the turning of a potter's wheel.

I was a scribe of the army and the chariotry,
(which are) numerous and great without limit,
an interpreter for every foreign land in the presence of ⌜his⌝ lord.
I was a strong scribe among his attendants.

My lord exalted me in the presence of everyone;
I was the possessor of favor in the presence of the king
because of (my) counsels every day, because of the exaltation of me,
all the attendants saying: "How greatly is he favored!"

I was a dancer for his people,[103]
the protector of his servants since the king strengthened (his) place
            as a companion.
I was a priest of Maat, whom Shu chose,[104]
who filled his treasury and his granaries (until) they overflowed.

I was effective in the temple, strong in the field.
I increased the number of workers who accrued to Shu,
my heart leading (me) every day, following my lord.
I was effective for the gods of ⌜the Two Lands⌝,

at the head of the southern ⌈council⌉.[105]

I was one who went forth upon the path of the god,
without transgressing the steps which he ordained.
I was one who bowed when he passed by the shrine,
in order to magnify the god a million [times].

I was a ⌈pure one⌉ with covered hands[106]
and clean [fingers], who propitiated the ⌈gods⌉.
I was one who gave … [ca. 6 groups lost]
… daily.

I was one who gave praise according to what is desired,
valiant in paying honor to the goddess.
I was one who performed great things for [everyone].

I was one who[107] [bestowed] his delight upon the offerings
for the akhs of [… …]
I was one who performed his voice-offering over the offering loaves,
[… … for] the [monuments (?)] of the lords of the underworld.

I was one who made ⌈Shu⌉ content, who did what was favored
for the gods, the lords, of his ⌈city⌉.
I was one who [worshipped] Re every day
when he shines and sets ⌈in⌉ the sky.

I was one who called ⌈upon⌉ all the names
of Amun-Re, king of the gods.
I was one who gave praise to Ptah
and who performed jubilations for Sekhmet the great.

I was one who administered offerings for the ka-chapel of ⌈Thinis⌉,
[… …] which is in it.
⌈I was⌉ knowledgeable in propitiating the god
at the courtyard of the sun-disc of Re.

I was one who offered many acclamations,
who kissed the ground in the stations of the great temple.
I was one who [served (?)] […] [of the temple (?)],
[paying honor (?)] to the lords of Thinis.

I was that man without fault,[108]
without dissembling among the council of thirty.
I was one who [... ... ...]
[passing upon (?)] his path.

I was one who [... ...], who loved his people [and dependants (?)],
a companion who honored his god.
I was excellent, free from [...] his voice (?);
violent words were an abomination (to me).

I was one who ... [*rest of column lost: probably the rest of this*
          couplet]
I was accurate of [heart], [... of truthful speech (?)],
without assenting to evil words.

I was silent, perfect of character, patient,
who loved ... [*rest of column lost: probably the rest of this verse and*
          the next]
... who associated with the one who had nothing.

I was ⌜friendly⌝ to the one of calm nature,
who hated the possessor of angry speech from a hot mouth.
I was one who ... [*rest of column lost: probably the rest of this*
          couplet]
... people.

I was one who expelled wrongdoing and [drove out] sorrow,
who ⌜paid attention to⌝ the voice of the widow.
I was one who rescued the drowning,
[... ...], giving sustenance ⌜to those who⌝ were lacking.

I was a protector of the indigent of arm,
who answered for the widow
robbed of her possessions.

I was a father for the one without [a father],
⌜a mother of children⌝, a champion of the small.
I was a nurse for his family,
who placed them on a good path.

I was a shepherd for his [followers],[109]

who defended them against every misfortune.
I was a captain ⌜for⌝ his dependants,
attentive and caring for their affairs.

I was one who rejoiced in [Maat],
[... ...] in appeasing disputants.
I was an intimate of the citizens,
who ⌜was concerned with⌝ the complaints of people.

⌜I was one who paid heed⌝ to the poor,
who acted according to the words of his mouth.
I was one who rejoiced at true speech;
heeding falsehood was an ⌜abomination⌝ (to me).

I was one who performed Maat upon earth,
more times than there are ⌜hairs⌝ on a head.
I was true of voice in all my places,
on the day of judging matters.

I was a scribe to be boasted of,
an official to be vaunted about.
I was effective, the possessor of a perfect name,
without fault in the palace.

I was beloved of the subjects,
over (whose) speech people delight.
I was open armed to the one who had nothing
in order to nourish the mourner.

I was one who wept over a case of misfortune,
who took thought for the one with downcast face.
I was attentive to the cry of an orphan girl,
who did all that is in her heart.

I was one who raised up the grieving child,
who put a stop to [...] and wiped away his tears.
I was one who put an end to lamentation
for that woman who was profuse in grief.

I was the possessor of a place in the West,
and in the [pillared hall (?)][110] [... ...]

[…] while I was in the womb.

I was the possessor of old age because of my character,
one who provided an example (even) when I was among those
          greater than me.
I was accurate, free from base action,
[… … …].

[I was] the balance of the lord of Busiris,[111]
for my desire was (to be) an example of the Filler.[112]
I was one who presented cattle to Atum,[113]
pomegranate wine ⌜being offered⌝ to his *ka*.

I was one who [… …],
[speaking (?)] in truth and not in falsehood.
I was one who anointed the widow who was destitute,
who gave clothing to the naked.

I was one who separated two men in a rage,
in order to cause them to [go forth] in peace.
I was one who appeased disputing kinsmen,
who drove out their anger through my advice.

I was one who drove out deficiency from the hearts of others,
who delighted the heart of ⌜one in suffering⌝.
I was a guardian who weaned the dependant,
until the day of his flying off came.

I was one who raised up the fallen
with this sustenance [which] the king [gave (?)].
I was one who [sheltered] the old woman,
in order to warm her limbs by the fire.

I was a possessor of sustenance, who poured forth ⌜provisions⌝,
who satisfied the one who wished to eat.
I was the lord of harvest in the field,
who nourished his workers as he desired.

I was one who … [*rest of column lost: probably the rest of this
          couplet*]
I was an official whose words were trusted,

free from indiscretion.

I was one who took ⌜his⌝ share in ⌜silence⌝,
[*rest of column lost: probably this verse and the beginning of the next*]
[I was one who ...] in all his words,
the standard for the scribes of the land.

I was one who performed invocations first,
without ⌜there being⌝ ... [*rest of column lost: probably the end of this
        verse and the next*]
[I was one who ...],
[who maintained (?)] their ⌜libations⌝, so that they relied upon me.

I was their support (?) [...],[114]
who drove out ... [*rest of column lost: probably the end of this verse
        and the next*]
[I was one who ...],
effective of heart, whose voice is free from fault.

I was a companion who had this burial,
the possessor of an interment within [...]
[*rest of column lost: probably one verse*],
who trusted ⌜in⌝ the path of my god.

I was one who went out in the service of his god,
without transgressing his [command (?)].
I was one who ... [*rest of column lost: probably the rest of this verse*],
who [...] the ordinary like the powerful.

I was one who trusted in Shu, son of Re,
without distancing ⌜myself⌝ from another god,
in order to [... ...],
[... a million times (?)], without any evil coming against me.[115]

All these things,
they are what (my) lord gave to me since my birth.
I sought [for (?)] my [heart (?)] so that [... ...] its time.
He achieved excellence for it.
It is he who is the lord of every heart,
gods as well as men.
My local god ⌜cares⌝ for them in the West.

[I prayed to Amun-Re, king of the (?)] gods,
for the health of Horus, the strong bull, who made me what I was;[116]
he (Amun) is his (the king's) protection until the time of rest in his ⌜shrine⌝.[117]
He caused me to follow him to [...
... ...] a perfect burial,
that I may proceed in peace to my temple,
his favors being established within me.

My lord says: "You will remain forever in Behdet."
[May he cause] my name to be [established] like the horizon;
it is day like the night of the divine children,
(for) my name is born when the children of Nut retreat.[118]

[... ... ...]
the *shetayt* of the temple of ⌜Sokar⌝,
that I may follow my lord in the great *neshmet*-barque
which was rescued from the reeds (?).[119]

May my name remain like the [...] mountain of Behdet,
that ⌜it⌝ may rest [there] for the future,
my statue in the following of my god,
just as one who is upon earth.

May he double benefits for me,
so that he may grant offerings to me
[which have come forth] from the following [of] my lord,
when it comes out from the tomb in all his perfect festivals.[120]

May I step in his presence as a living *ba*,
so that I may receive [offerings ... ...],
⌜which come forth⌝ [from all] his [altars (?)],
[being provided with] the cast-offs of his clothing.[121]

May he apportion [cakes, libations (?)], and breath,
so that I may join the underworld which is in the sacred land
and follow Osiris in [his ...] festival,
⌜in⌝ [...] ⌜with⌝ the ancestors,
so that it will be said in my city after (many) years:
"How fortunate he is!"

For the *ka* of the one favored by his god,
beloved of his lord, effective for his [god],
who prays for the health of his Horus,
one truly assiduous, complete in every aspect,
exceedingly [kind (?)] to people,
[for whom] his lord rejoices, [... ...],

overseer of the cities of the North and South,
who is at the great double gate of Shu, [son of Re],
[... ... ...] his [...] in his office,
[*rest of column lost*]
... of Shu and Tefnut,
high priest of Onuris,
Anhur ⌐mose, true of voice⌐,
[*rest of column lost: perhaps titles and name of Sekhmetnefret*]

II

ARTISTS

19A–B. THE MEMORIAL CHAPEL OF THE CHIEF SCULPTOR, USERHAT

The chief sculptor Userhat probably held office at the end of the Eighteenth Dynasty and perhaps into the early Nineteenth Dynasty: no royal name is inscribed on his stela and doorway presented here. Userhat may be depicted in the tomb of the overseer of the treasury Maya (van Dijk 1995, 31–32, fig. 1), which dates to the reign of Horemheb (the biography from Maya's tomb is translated in chapter III, no. 23), while certain features of Userhat's biography can be connected with events of the immediate post-Amarna period (van Dijk 1995; Willems 1998). A stela and shabti *bearing the names of Sety I and Ramesses II respectively were dedicated by an Userhat with similar titles, which could suggest that Userhat held office into at least the first quarter of the reign of Ramesses II (Guksch 1983, 23), meaning he would have had to have lived into his 70s or 80s. These later objects could, however, have belonged to a different man, perhaps an immediate descendant of the Userhat discussed here (von Beckerath 1995, 38–39).*

The stela, lintel, and jambs have no archaeological provenance, but motifs associated with Osiris and Abydos dominate their iconography and indicate that all three almost certainly came from that site. The lintel and jambs would have formed the doorway to a memorial chapel in which the stela was displayed. The visual parallels between the stela and doorway are matched by close textual associations: on the doorway Userhat bears titles that claim unrestricted access to cult images of gods, and this theme is the central motif in the biographical text, which narrates his initiation to divine presence and his role in creating and enlivening cult statues.

Userhat bears two other names in these texts: the abbreviated form Hatiay, and the patronymic, Penya, "he of Ya," the name of his father.

19A. LINTEL AND JAMBS

The lintel of the chapel doorway is arranged in two registers. In the corner of the lunette, paired figures of the jackal-form god Wepwawet lie on shrines with wedjat-eyes above them. Behind each figure is an offering stand bearing an incense vessel. The name and epithets of the god are arranged in large hieroglyphs to fill the rest of the sloping area behind the figures: Wepwawet of Upper Egypt, lord of Abydos, on the left and Wepwawet of Lower Egypt, lord of Abydos, on the right. These images frame six columns of offering formulas addressed to this god. The lower register of the lintel has the standard of Abydos in the center. A hymn in praise of Osiris, Wepwawet, and Thoth is inscribed on the left side. Verses from a hymn addressed to the lord of Abydos, also known from three other Ramessid monuments, are inscribed on the right (Clère 1959; Lichtheim 1992, 68–70). Adoring figures of Userhat frame both texts. The lintel is almost identical in layout, iconography, and textual content to one belonging to the table scribe Kha, which also probably came from Abydos (Clère 1959, 89–90). I restore damaged areas of Userhat's texts on the basis of Kha's lintel. A statue belonging to Kha that bears an inscription claiming a role in the Osiris mysteries is translated in chapter III (no. 30; see also no. 14a).

The jambs are almost two meters (6'6") high. Their faces are inscribed in four columns with hymns to Osiris and deities associated with Abydos. The lower section of each face bears a figure of Userhat seated before an offering table. The hymn on the right jamb requests offerings for the afterlife, while that on the left is concerned with judgment and includes a declaration of innocence, in which the emphasis on loyalty resonates with general themes of the biography on the stela. The thicknesses bear hymns to Re inscribed in three columns, accompanied by an image of Userhat kneeling in adoration. Both figures would originally have faced into the interior of the chapel. The hymns were compiled, in part, from various standard compositions (Assmann 1983).

> *Left side of lintel, upper register:*
>   An offering which the king gives to Wepwawet, lord of the sacred
>   land,
>   Anubis, foremost of the god's shrine,
>   and the gods, the lords of the necropolis,
>   that they may grant radiance and might in their temple,
>   justification in the place of performing Maat,
>   following Sokar when he goes around the walls
>   in all his annual festivals,
>   while I am first among those who sit before Wenennefer;
>   for the *ka* of the chief sculptor for the lord of the Two Lands, Userhat.

Right side of lintel, upper register:
> An offering which the king gives to Wepwawet, lord of Abydos,
> Anubis, who is in the embalming place,
> and the gods, the lords of Poqer,
> that they may cause you to be radiant in the sky,
> mighty in the earth (underworld),
> and justified in the necropolis,
> that you may receive the offerings which come forth from their
>> presence,
> with a bouquet from the remainder of the offering service;[1]
> for the *ka* of the one who enters before the lord of Hermopolis
>> (Thoth),
> keeper of secrets in the domain of Osiris,
> Userhat, true of voice.

Left side of lintel, lower register:
> Praise to Osiris inasmuch as his name is great,
> as His Person is more powerful than any god,
> by the keeper of secrets in the domain of Osiris, Userhat,
> begotten by the dignitary Ya, true of voice.
>
> Praise to Wenennefer in his sacred temple,
> while the Ennead who are in Tawer are rejoicing,
> by the one who enters into the secrets of the lord of Hermopolis,
> who fashioned their Persons, who concealed their bodies, Userhat.
>
> Praise to Khebesta,[2] with a loving heart,
> for he is the king of eternity, lord of perpetuity,
> who acted upon the seat of his father in the first time,
> by the one who enters before Wenennefer,
> who enters before his image,
> who was unrestricted in seeing (it), Hatiay.
>
> Praise to Wepwawet, to the height of the sky;
> the son of Isis is at peace, his heart happy,
> resting upon ⌐his throne, his attack having succeeded⌐.[3]
>
> Praise to Thoth a million times;
> his heart is content with ⌐Maat, (as) one successful of deeds⌐,
> who vindicated the weary-hearted[4] against his enemies,
> by the discreet one, without brashness,

who enters the Mansion of Gold, Userhat.

Right side of lintel, lower register:
Praise to the lord of Abydos,
as Isis rejoices on the day ⌜Horus⌝ was born
⌜as the strong bull⌝, protector of his father Osiris,
by the one who enters before the secrets of the lord of Hermopolis,
        Hatiay.

Praise to the lord of Abydos,
as Isis rejoices when her son Horus goes forth justified,
after overthrowing the disaffected as he had planned,
by the keeper of secrets in the domain of Osiris, Userhat.

Praise to the lord of Abydos,
as Isis rejoices when Thoth makes a testament for him (Horus)[5]
in the hall of Geb,[6] before the Sole Lord,
by the chief sculptor for the lord of the Two Lands, Userhat.

Praise to the lord of Abydos,
as Isis rejoices on the day Horus appears on the throne,
after receiving the double crown in life and power,
by the one who enters before the lords of Abydos,
chief sculptor for the lord of the Two Lands,
Hatiay Penya, true of voice, possessor of veneration.

Left jamb of doorway, front face, and above figure of Userhat:
An offering which the king gives to Osiris Khentimentu,
great god, lord of Abydos,
to Horus-who-protects-his-father,
the effective heir of Wenennefer,
and to Wepwawet, lord of the sacred land,

that they may give a voice offering of bread and beer,
beef and fowl,
libations, wine, and milk,
receiving oil, smelling incense;
by the keeper of secrets in the domain of Osiris,
one who enters before the lord of Hermopolis, Userhat,
called Hatiay Penya.

O gods who are in Tawer,
lords of life upon earth,
who hate falsehood and wrongdoing,
who live on Maat:

I was a righteous one, who was loyal to you,
my heart did not consort with the evil character.
ꜣI did not walkꜣ upon the path of the brawler;
I did not have words with the loud-voiced,
for the tumult of his words was an abomination to me.

Nor did I agree with any of his speech,
for I know what my god abhors and I am loyal to his command;
by the keeper of secrets in ꜣthe domain of Osirisꜣ,
Hatiay Penya.

Right jamb of doorway, front face, and above figure of Userhat:
An offering which the king gives to Osiris Khentimentu,
to Wenennefer, lord of the sacred land,
the gods who lead the underworld,
and to the Ennead who are within ꜣNut (?)ꜣ,[7] the gods who embrace
    their (proper) place,

that they may give duration upon earth before their Persons,
and justification in the perfect West;
for the *ka* of the one who enters before the lords of Tawer,
chief sculptor for the lord of the Two Lands,
Userhat, called Hatiay
Penya, true of voice.

May Hapy give you fresh water
from the water-vessel crafted for Ptah.
May Nepri give you his offerings
from [within] the field of reeds.[8]

May you be presented with ꜣofferingsꜣ,
the gifts of the lords of Maat.
May you adore Osiris, so that you may be pure (through) his efflux.[9]
May you ease the misery of those who are there.[10]

May your heart be yours as when (you) were on earth,

all your limbs [entirely complete (?)],
your clothing being fine linen and your anointing being (with) fine oils.

May your *ba* rest in the necropolis;
when one is invoked by name, may you be found.
May you cross over to the district of Poqer,
may you be purified in the pool of Maat,
and may Anubis himself mummify you;
by the chief sculptor for the lord of the gods,
Userhat Penya.

Thickness of left jamb of doorway:
Adoring Re-Horakhty by the keeper of secrets in the domain of
        Osiris,
Userhat, true of voice.
He says: O lord who travels through eternity,
whose existence is everlasting,
that disc, lord of rays,
who shines forth from his horizon;

(I) adore you, your perfection in my eyes,
your radiance suffusing my breast,
as you rise and set in the night-barque,
your heart joyful in the day-barque,
as you cross the sky in peace, all your enemies overthrown.

The unwearying stars acclaim you,
the imperishable stars adore you.
The baboons in the horizon announce you,
the chattering apes extol you
when they say to you what is in their mouths,
and ⌜they⌝ celebrate you with praise, praise!

Greetings to you, the one who made all this.
May you place me so that I can see your perfection, each time you
        appear,
and when you shine within the night-barque,
coming to rest in life;
by the one who enters before the lord of Hermopolis,
Userhat, true of voice.

Thickness of right jamb of doorway:
    Adoring Re when he rises
    in the eastern horizon of the sky,
    and Atum at his perfect setting;
    by the Osiris of the chief sculptor,
    Userhat, true of voice.

    He says: Greetings to you who comes as Khepri,
    having come into being as the one who created the gods.
    You will appear and rise on the back of your mother (Nut),
    having appeared as the king of the gods.

    All gods rejoice in you,
    the Ennead in adoration of your perfect face,
    the one who gives life to the humble (?);
    how perfect is your appearing in the sky!

    The gods are in acclamation at your rising;
    they live by seeing your perfection,
    their arms spread to (acknowledge) your power,
    all people kissing the ground;
    by the Osiris of Hatiay, true of voice.

    He says: Greetings to you, chief of the gods,
    who illuminates the underworld through what he has done.
    May your mother Nut extend her arms to you, performing *nini*,[11]
    until you set in the horizon of the western mountain.

19B. STELA (FIG. 7)

*Userhat's stela, a little over one meter high (3'3") and half a meter wide
(1'7"), is carved in sunk relief, with an incised border, and is divided into three
registers. The lunette depicts two recumbent jackals facing each another, their
hanging tails framing two wedjat-eyes. This composition is a visually condensed
version of the one in the upper register of the lintel. The same group of incense
burner, stand, and caption fills the sloping areas both on the lintel and on the
stela lunette.*

*   The main text in the middle register of the stela is inscribed in twenty-one
lines. On the left side, beneath the first seven lines of text, is a figure of Userhat
seated on a lion-footed chair, facing a further ten lines of text. He wears a long*

Fig. 7. Stela of Userhat (no. 19b; copyright Rijksmuseum van Oudheden, Leiden).

kilt and holds a lotus bloom to his nose in one hand. Beneath the chair is a squatting figure of one of Userhat's kinsmen, captioned: His brother, beloved of him, Yay, true of voice. *Beneath the large seated figure are three "boxes" containing four figures, facing the last four lines of the main text. The box on the left contains a man and woman seated on lion-footed chairs and identified as Userhat's parents:* His father, chief sculptor, Ya, true of voice; his mother, Wesey. *The two boxes in front of his parents contain kneeling figures of other kin of Userhat:* His brother, royal scribe, Hatiay; his sister, Iwy, true of voice.

Userhat's narrative centers on his initiation into the temple workshop and his fashioning of cult statues, which are incorporated into the text as a list of gods. The text closes with a description of cult performance and a claim of veracity. The list of deities is an innovative feature of the narrative, the rest of which is grounded in traditional biographical themes and phraseology. The list enumerates the statues of gods that Userhat was commissioned to produce for temples in Middle and Upper Egypt. This production may be connected with the restoration of temples in Middle Egypt that would have suffered most during the Amarna period (van Dijk 1995; Willems 1998). The creation of cult statues involved not only their physical production but also their activation and enlivening through a ceremony termed the "opening of the mouth"; in such a context artistic creation is inextricably linked with priestly performance (Kruchten 1992). The list of deities comes after the narration of Userhat's promotion, probably to the position of chief sculptor, and before the description of his performance of cult duties. It therefore mediates between his official role as an artist and his more specifically priestly duties, displaying his privileged access to restricted domains and perhaps acting as a catalyst for his own transformation of status and role in this world and the next.

The places and deities listed in this text are commented on stanza by stanza, each stanza approximately representing distinct geographic areas.

> Main text, mid section of stela:
> Praise to you Osiris Khentimentu,
> and Thoth, lord of Hermopolis,
> great god, foremost of Hesret, residing in Hutyebet,[12]
> divine leader when he appears in the crew of Re,
>
> one who is assiduous, who propitiates the two lords, the brothers,[13]
> who gives the *wedjat*-eye to its lord,
> possessor of splendor in (the presence of) the Ennead,
> who makes marvels in the secret shrine,
>
> great of journeys in the night-barque,
> glorious of appearances in the day-barque,
> great one in Busiris,
> who descends (the river) as a living *ba*,

guide of Re for his travels.

Greetings to you in all <your> names,
O Thoth, deputy of Re,
by the chief sculptor for the lord of the Two Lands,
Hatiay, true of voice,
son of the chief sculptor, Ya, true of voice.

He says: O nobles, great and small,
all the elite, all people, all sun-folk,
I will tell you (about) what has happened to me
—(for) I was distinguished above others—
so that you may report it from generation to generation,
elders teaching the young.

I was a minor one of his family,
a lesser one in his town.
The lord of the Two Lands knew me,
and I was greatly esteemed in his heart
when I saw the king in his aspect
of Re (and) in the seclusion of his palace,
so that he exalted me above the courtiers
and I mixed (with) the great ones of the palace.

My lord was pleased with my solutions,
ignoring ones from those greater than me.
Hidden things of the heart were told to me
while I was in the place of silence.
When One (the king) came out (from there),
the Two Lands said of me: "How great are his favors!"

He appointed me as director of works when I was a humble man,
for he found me estimable in his heart.
I was initiated into the Mansion of Gold,
in order to fashion the forms and images of all the gods,
none of them being hidden from me.

I was a keeper of secrets, who saw Re in his transformations,
and Atum in his manifestations,
Osiris, lord of Abydos, foremost of the lords of the sacred land,
and Thoth, lord of Hermopolis, who is in Kheritjehenu.[14]

I saw Shepses in his hidden sacredness,
and Wenut in her transformations,
Min who flaunts his potency,
and Horus residing in Hesret,[15]

Nehmetawy, daughter of Re,
Sekhmet, beloved of Ptah,
and the Ogdoad who are in Hermopolis, before Hutyebet,[16]

Khnum, lord of Herwer,
and the ruler-goddess Hathor,
Amun-Re residing in Wenu,
Hathor of Cusae,
daughter of Pre-who-protects-the-effective-One,[17]

the Ennead who are in Agenu,
Haroeris in Hutsnefru,
Hemen, lord of Hefat,
Montu residing in Tod,
and Anubis, lord of Tahedj,[18]

Horus, foremost in Hebenu,
Pakhet, mistress of Set,
and Thoth, bull in Roinet,[19]

Nemty in the district of Nemty,
Amun, who foretells victories,
the bull, lord of Saka,
the ruler-goddess, mistress of Gesy, and the two *herty* goddesses.[20]

I was one who caused them (the cult statues) to rest in their shrines
        perpetually
and I carried them as leader of the royal festival,
being the one charged with sailing the king in his barque;
I was in its prow, one who trod upon the place of electrum
in order to report on the state of the Two Lands,[21]

who ate bread from the royal meal,
who was quenched with his beer.
The gold of favor was given to me
by the king himself.

I do not speak falsehood concerning these things,
the Two Lands are my witnesses.
As Ptah, lord of truth, lord of Memphis, lives,
I have spoken these things truthfully.

He (the king) did it for me, for the sake of this (chapel),
—for one who is loyal to him—
with a duration of perfect life.
This servant was one who bore his lord, until the completion of
        (his) lifetime,
until the receipt of the prow-rope of his mooring,[22]
passing into veneration.

Lower register:
*The lower register contains two lines divided into ten boxes, each contain-
ing a kneeling figure. The figures alternate between men and women. These
are not all likely to be Userhat's siblings, as the Egyptian words generally
rendered "brother" and "sister" can refer to a number of relations of kinship
and collegiality. These figures are captioned in one vertical column and one
horizontal line above the head, and include both living and dead as identified by the epithet "true of voice." Arrows in the table below indicate which
direction each figure is facing.*

1	2	3	4	5	6	7	8	9	10
woman	man	woman	man	man	woman	man	woman	man	woman
→	→	→	→	←	←	←	←	←	←

11	12	13	14	15	16	17	18	19	20
woman	man	woman	man	man	woman	man	woman	man	woman
→	→	→	→	←	←	←	←	←	←

1	His sister, whom he loves, as his favorite, the lady of the house, Quny
2	His brother, chief sculptor, […], true of voice
3	His sister, whom he loves, Tel
4	His brother, chief sculptor, Se, true of voice
5	His brother, scribe, Horemheb, true of voice
6	His sister, Saty, true of voice
7	His brother, Neferrenpet
8	His sister, Mutemwia
9	His brother, Maya

10	His sister, Esenefret
11	His sister, Tanefret, true of voice
12	His brother, Ray, true of voice
13	His sister, Huy, true of voice
14	His brother, Ya, the younger
15	His brother, Ramose
16	His sister, Yy, true of voice
17	His brother, Ya, the younger
18	His sister, Yy, the younger, true of voice
19	His brother, Huy, the younger
20	His sister, Kakaya, true of voice

20A–B. The Saqqara Tomb of the Chief Goldsmith, Amenemone

The tomb of Amenemone at Saqqara can be dated stylistically to the end of the Eighteenth Dynasty. Like the chief sculptor Userhat (no. 19), Amenemone may be depicted in the tomb of the overseer of the treasury Maya (no. 23), where an Amenemone bearing the title "deputy of the craftsmen of the treasury of pharaoh" is present in a row of offering bearers (Ockinga 2004, 19–20). If this is the same Amenemone, he would have served under Tutankhamun, Ay, and possibly Horemheb.

Amenemone's tomb is located in the northern sector of the necropolis that centers on the pyramid of the Sixth Dynasty king Teti. A statue of a Fifth Dynasty king, Menkauhor, was depicted in the tomb's portico (relief now in the Louvre, Paris); both Menkauhor and Teti were the recipients of popular cults in the New Kingdom Teti pyramid cemetery (Malek 1992). Amenemone sought to participate in this cult through this representation and may also have been involved in the creation of the statue of Menkauhor (Ockinga 2004, 75–76).

In contrast to Userhat's detailed narrative with the lists of cult objects and temples that characterize his text (no. 19b) and the other biographies included in this chapter, Amenemone's two closely comparable biographical inscriptions draw on standard, generalizing epithets concerned with his moral character, particularly in relation to the king. His career as chief craftsman and goldsmith is not mentioned, although allusions to initiation and access to restricted knowledge in the text on the relief block resonate with Userhat's biography. Boyo Ockinga (2004, 20) suggests that reference to Amenemone's official role may also be found in the detailed depiction of the statue of Menkauhor, as well as in the highly elaborate renderings of ornamentation and jewelry both accompanying this image and throughout the tomb.

Amenemone's biographical texts are also paralleled in a section of inscription that follows a series of solar hymns on a stela from the tomb of an overseer of the king's private apartments, Pay (Raven 2005, 43–45, no. 70; frontispiece and pl. 75). Pay's tomb is also in Saqqara and dated to the late Eighteenth Dynasty. Points of comparison between the texts are included in the notes.

20A. PAIR STATUE

The 0.69-meter-high (2'3") statue of Amenemone and his wife was found by Victor Loret in the portico of the tomb during his excavations from 1897 to 1899, and is now in the Egyptian Museum in Cairo. The statue was positioned in front of the two inner columns that marked the entrance to the central chapel. This location would have made direct entry to the chapel difficult, and Ockinga (2004, 34) considers that the statue may have been moved to this position from elsewhere in the portico or from one of the side chapels. The statue depicts Amenemone and his wife seated on high-backed chairs. He wears a long wig, tunic, and kilt. She wears a tripartite wig and long robe. Both hold a folded cloth in the left hand and have bare feet. The statue was unfinished and is now quite damaged, especially in the head areas. The biographical elements are included in the twelve columns of text that cover the back area of the statue.

> An offering which the king gives to Ptah, South-of-his-Wall,
> to Osiris Khentimentu,
> Anubis upon his mountain,
> who is in the embalming place, lord of the sacred land,
> Wenennefer, lord of Rosetjau,
> Horus-who-protects-his-father,
> son of Isis, sweet of love,
> Sokar of the *henu*-barque, Nefertem,
> and to the tribunal who are in the necropolis,
>
> that they may give a voice offering of bread and beer,
> beef and fowl,
> libations of wine and milk,
> all *henkyt*-offerings and all vegetables,
> with all sweet-smelling flowers on which the gods live,
> for the *ka* of the Osiris of Amenemone, true of voice;

he says: O gods and goddesses who exist forever and eternity,
who are established in the sky of Re and the earth of Geb,
may the heart of Amenemone, true of voice, be established
in his body, just as Horus was established on the seat of his father,
just as Osiris was established on the throne of Geb.

The Osiris of Amenemone, he says: O Isis, lady of Hebit,[23]
the tribunal, who are in Busiris,
the Ennead, lords of the House of Regeneration,
Anubis, who is in the embalming place,
and Khentimentu, lord of the sacred land,

may you establish my heart in its proper place before the keeper of
        the balance,[24]
to follow Sokar on the day of his festival,
to be content (with) bread and beer
just as when in the body, receiving what is given,

for the *ka* of the one effective of understanding, perfect of speech,
true of heart, content to listen without anger,
overseer of craftsmen for the lord of the Two Lands,
Amenemone, true of voice,
begotten by the dignitary Kheruef,
born of Neferti, true of voice;

he says: I was a servant whom his lord favored,
whose *ka* the sovereign, l.p.h., made,
for (he) knew my character, being aware of my nature;
my skills were enduringly (present) to him,
as an excellent man without <fault>.

One who was discrete, reticent,
with access to knowledge, open of ears,[25]
skilled in all that is secret,
truly silent, who banished hot temper,
who did not associate with lowly people.

One effective, a possessor of (good) character, weighty of projects,
true of heart, who did not act duplicitously,
exact of tongue, precise of words when opening his mouth;[26]
for the *ka* of the overseer of craftsmen,
Amenemone, true of voice.

20B. A BLOCK FROM THE TOMB

The original position of this block is not known, although Ockinga (2004, 34) suggests that it was set up in the court. The scene depicts the first five of a procession of women wearing braided tripartite wigs and long robes. The remaining lower sections of six columns above the figures give the names and titles of the first three women: [His kinswoman], his beloved, songstress of [Amun (?), Khay]nesut, true of voice; his [kinswoman], one greatly favored of [Hathor, mistress] of the West, Nefertari; his [kinswoman], one greatly favored of [Hathor, mistress] of the West, Wiat.

The text that includes the biographical epithets, of which only the lower section of eight columns survives, is inscribed in sunk relief in front of the procession. These epithets occur in a more complete context on Amenemone's pair statue, translated above (no. 20a). Immediately preceding this text are the final three and one-third columns of a solar hymn carved in raised relief.

> [*ca. half a column lost*]
> ... ⌈a thousand of⌉ incense,
> a thousand of offerings and provisions,
> all *henkyt*-offerings and vegetables,
> and everything good and pure which comes forth [from the offering
>   table],
>
> ...
>
> ⌈the new moon festival⌉, the monthly festival,
> the festival of the sixth day of the month, the half-month festival,
> the calendar festivals of the sky,
> and all the festivals conducted in [Tawer,
> in *akhet* and *peret* ...][27]
> ... your [heart] joyful,
> walking freely to the sanctity of the Great Mansion,[28]
> being initiated before the god, without [...],
> ...
>
> [May you be content with] ⌈bread⌉ and beer,
> just as when you were in (your) body, receiving what is given,
> for the *ka* of one effective of understanding[29] ...
> he (the king) ⌈knew⌉ my character, being aware of my nature;
> my skills were enduringly (present) to him,
> ... ⌈who did not⌉ associate with lowly people.

One effective, a possessor of (good) character, weighty of projects,
true of ⌜heart⌝, …
effective concerning what was placed in his heart,
without a moment of hesitation,
who acted according to the plans […]
… in it in order to […][30]

21. THE BLOCK STATUE OF THE OVERSEER OF DRAFTSMEN OF AMUN, DIDIA, FROM KARNAK

Didia's name is known from a number of objects, including a wooden scribe's palette bearing the prenomen of Sety I, suggesting that he held office under that king (see Lowle 1976). His small granite statue, 0.5 meters (1'7") in height, was found in the Karnak cachette (see p. 46) and is now in the Egyptian Museum in Cairo. It is a plain block statue, with little indication of body shape beneath the garment, placed on a high plinth. An unusual and otherwise unattested feature is the offering basin set into the space on top of the knees. The top edge of the basin bears the cartouches Djeserkare (Amenhotep I) and Menkheperre (Thutmose III). The names of the gods Min and Amun are inscribed in a column down the basin's right side and the name of Khonsu down the left.

Each side of the statue bears eleven columns of inscription. The texts, which begin on the middle of the statue's front and close in front of the back pillar, include offering formulas, appeals to the living, and short biographical statements summarizing works Didia completed in a number of Theban temples. These temples are enumerated on the left side in a list that is poetically as well as geographically organized, being based in part on the way the name of each temple plays phonetically with that of the preceding one (N. de G. Davies 1922–1923, II, 82–83). Didia aligned himself not only with the Theban area, but also with the triad of gods associated with Elephantine through the offering formulas on the right side of the statue base, as well as with deities associated with Edfu, Hierakonpolis (ancient Nekhen), and Gebelein on the left side, perhaps indicating familial or official connections to these areas.

Right half:
An offering which the king gives to Amun, Amunet,
Mut, Khonsu, Maat,
Nefertari, Amenhotep (Amenhotep I), and Menkheperre
(Thutmose III),[31]

that they may grant a long life
and a perfect burial after old age,
interment on the west of Thebes,
my image enduring and flourishing
in the temple of the lord of the gods,
and that my name be pronounced and recognized in all the calendar
      festivals,
for the *ka* of the overseer of draftsmen of Amun, Didia;

he says: O priests, *wab*-priests,
lector priests, and every scribe who recites (these words),
may your gods favor you,
may your names pass down from mouth to mouth,
and may you hand over your offices to your children after
      prosperous old age,
inasmuch as you say "an offering which the king gives."

May you pour water for me,
and give me offerings before me (this statue) when offerings are
      made,
for I was the servant of the lord of joy,
Khonsu, perfect of peace.
May he rescue me and give me breath before the lord of the gods.

I was instructed by His Person
to work for Amun,
to restore monuments in Karnak
and on the great west of Thebes.
May he cause that I attain the west of his city (necropolis of Thebes),
the district of the just;

for the *ka* of the overseer of draftsmen of Amun, Didia,
son of Hatiay, born of Tel,
and his sister, the lady of the house,
songstress of Amun, Iuy.

Left half:
    An offering which the king gives to Re-Atum, Osiris,
    Ptah-Sokar, Isis, Horus,
    Min, Anubis,
    and Hathor, in the sanctuary of Nebhepetre (Montuhotep II),[32]

that they may grant radiance in the sky,
might in the earth (underworld),
and justification in the necropolis,
sailing downstream to Busiris as a living *ba*,
sailing upstream to Abydos as a phoenix.[33]

May a place be made for me in the *neshmet*-barque
at that festival of Wenennefer,
⌜with⌝ onions at my throat on the day of the *netjeryt*-festival.[34]
May you (the gods) give ⌜bread⌝ to me in the domain of Ptah,
libations and offerings in Heliopolis,
for the *ka* of the overseer of draftsmen of Amun,
Didia, true of voice;

he says: O every scribe
who is skilled in his office,
who will recite the name of this statue with a loving heart,
may the lords of eternity favor you,
and may you hand over the staff for the coffin after old age,[35]

for I was the overseer of works and overseer of crafts,
who directed every office for Amun,
in Akhmenu, in Menset,
in Akhset, in Djeserakhet,
in Djeserdjeseru, in Henketankh.[36]
May he (Amun) grant me veneration in peace,
⌜as is set down in writing (?)⌝ for his favored one;

for the *ka* of the one who honors his god,
whom everyone loves for his character,
the overseer of draftsmen of Amun, Didia,
and his sister, the lady of the house,
songstress of Amun for the second phyle,[37]
Iuy, born of Tjel.

Back pillar:
Overseer of draftsmen of Amun,
Mut, and Khonsu
in Opet and in the southern city (Thebes), Didia,
son of the dignitary, Hatiay, true of voice,
and his brother, the draftsman,

Samut, son of Hatiay.

Surface of plinth:
Overseer of draftsmen of Amun,
Didia, true of voice.

Right half of plinth:
An offering which the king gives to Khnum,
Satet, and Anukis, lady of Sehel,[38]
and to the lords of Elephantine residing in Biga,[39]
that they may give a perfect lifetime for the *ka* of Didia.

Left half of plinth:
An offering which the king gives to Horus of Behdet,
to Nekhbet, the white one of Nekhen,
Hathor, lady of Gebelein,
Sobek, lord of Sunu,[40]
and to Montu residing in Thebes,
that they may give the sweet breath of the north wind for the *ka* of
Didia.

22A–B. THE THEBAN TOMB OF NAKHTDJEHUTY, CHIEF OF CRAFTSMEN AND GOLD WORKERS OF THE DOMAIN OF AMUN

The tomb of Nakhtdjehuty is located on the east side of the entrance to the court of the Eighteenth Dynasty tomb of Kheruef in the Assasif in the Theban necropolis, in parallel position to the tomb of Djehutyemheb, the biographical text in which is translated in chapter I (no. 12). The structural correspondences between the two tombs, as well as correspondences between their texts, suggest they were planned and built in close association late in the reign of Ramesses II.

The facade of Nakhtdjehuty's tomb bears an appeal to the living (text unpublished) on one side of the tomb entrance and four registers of divine barques and temple doors on the other (no. 22b). These represent the products of Nakhtdjehuty's profession. The two lower registers of this scene (I–II) depict a series of temple doors, painted yellow. The upper two registers show two rows of portable barques of varying types on stands. Traces of other unidentified types of cult objects are preserved above these rows. This visual presentation corresponds with a list of divine barques included in the fragmentary biographical narrative in

*the hall of the tomb (no. 22a). This text begins on the northern half of the rear
(east) wall of the hall and continues onto the eastern half of the north end wall;
only the upper sections of the columns are preserved. The published summary
(PM I², 1, 295, (4)–(6)) indicates that the text is inscribed in the same registers
as underworld scenes.*

*The visual and narrative presentation of temple doorways and barques may
evoke a sense of processional space. The objects depicted and narrated are those
that govern transition and procession (doorways) and that were central components of cult and festival performance (barques). The priestly titles Nakhtdjehuty
bears at the beginning of the narrative are appropriate to this context, alluding to
the relationship between artistic creation and ritual action, which is mobilized
in some of the other biographies translated in this chapter.*

22A. BIOGRAPHY

⌜For⌝ the *ka* of the Osiris of the *wab*-priest,
lector priest ⌜of⌝ Amun,
[*over three-quarters of the column lost*]

They will come in order to walk about[41] …
⌜I was appointed⌝ as overseer of craftsmen, chief of gold workers,
(for) I had understanding (as) one who is skilled (?).
No ⌜craftsman was ignorant⌝ concerning ⌜my⌝ speech,

… of gold,
great doors in the […] of Karnak,
barques …
achieving perfect craftsmanship as one devoted to his ⌜skills⌝.
[… …] of his causing me to flourish on earth,
as one ⌜favored⌝ …
for his lord.

I am skilled in craftsmanship,
without their giving (me) instruction,
⌜I⌝ guided [work (?) …] …
their […] in gold, silver,
real lapis lazuli, ⌜turquoise⌝, […]
…

⌜I performed service⌝ for the barque[42]

of Isis ...
[*ca. 10 columns lost*]

⌜I performed service for the⌝ barque
⌜of⌝ [Isis, lady of Abydos (?)]
[... gold for (?) ...] West ...

⌜I performed⌝ service for the barque
of Khnum in Esna in year 55.
I performed service ⌜for the barque⌝
of Neb(etu)u[43] ... [*6–7 groups lost*]

I ⌜performed service⌝ for the barque
of Seth ... [of Upper Egypt (?)] in year 58.
I ⌜performed service⌝ for the barque
of Geb[44] ... [*ca. 6 groups lost*]

⌜I performed service⌝ for the barque
⌜of⌝ ... [*ca. 5 groups lost*]
I performed service for the barque
of ⌜Horus⌝ of Maaty[45] ... [*ca. 5 groups lost*]
[*up to 2 columns lost*]

22b. Captions to the Representations

*The lowest register (register I) bears images of thirteen doors with captions
above them:*
⌜Door⌝ of gold for the workshop of the ⌜domain (?) of Amun⌝.
[*captions for doors 2–4 lost*]
⌜Door of⌝ [...] for the House of Gold of Amun[-Re (?)].
⌜Door of⌝ [...] of Amun-Re.
[*caption for door 7 lost*]
Second ⌜door (?)⌝[...]
[*caption for door 9 lost*]
[First (?)] door of [... ... ...]
Second door of gold for the forecourt of Amun.
[Third (?)] door of gold for the forecourt of Amun.
The great door of [...]

Register II bears traces of images of nine doors (others are probably lost). Traces of captions to five of the doors survive:
> Great ⌜door of⌝ gold for the ⌜temple⌝ [... ...]
> [Door of (?)] Khonsu in Thebes, perfect of peace.
> Double door of gold of Mut.
> Door of gold of Mut.
> Door of gold of Mut.

Register III depicted a series of portable barques, of which only three images remain; all their names are lost. The remaining traces of a line of text running along the register line and interrupted by the bases of the barques gives the names and titles of craftsmen and a priest.

Below the first barque at the right of the register:
> [ca. 5 groups lost] ... her son, the sculptor, Nebwa ...

Between the last two barques to the left of the register:
> For the ka of the wab-priest of Khonsu, Shedsukhons.

Behind the last barque to the left of the register:
> Draftsman of the domain of Amun, Suty, true of voice, of Thebes.

A column to the right of registers I and II bears the following title and may be a continuation from the captions in register III:
> wab-priest and draftsman of the Mansions of Gold of Amun, [rest lost]

The top register (register IV) also showed a series of portable barques although all but three are lost. Nearly all the captions are lost. The remaining partial caption above the first image may represent part of the barque's name:
> [... ...] of victory (?).

III

CIVIL OFFICIALS

23. THE SAQQARA TOMB OF MAYA, OVERSEER
OF THE TREASURY

*Maya was overseer of the treasury in the reign of Tutankhamun but he must
have begun his career under Akhenaten or earlier. It is possible that he is the
same person as the military officer and steward May, who owned tomb no. 14 at
Akhenaten's capital, Amarna. A statue base, bearing biographical phraseology
relating to royal service (not translated here), belonging to an overseer of the
treasury May and datable early in the reign of Tutankhamun, strengthens the
evidence for the identification (van Dijk 1993, 71–76, fig. 11). Maya is last attested in year 8 or 9 of Horemheb (van Dijk 1993, 77–79).*

*Maya's tomb, which had been found by antiquities dealers in the early-nine-
teenth century and was rediscovered in 1986, was built adjacent to the nonroyal
tomb of the later king Horemheb in the New Kingdom necropolis southeast of
the pyramid of Unas at Saqqara. Inscriptions from the tomb suggest it was built
under Tutankhamun; although Maya lived at least another dozen years, it was
never completed. Maya is credited with coordinating the restoration of temples
in the immediate post-Amarna period, and phraseology concerning his fulfillment of this role, particularly in relation to cult statues, is a central theme of the
biographical narrative translated here. This motif also occurs in other texts and
titles from the tomb. Jacobus van Dijk (1995, 33) has suggested that the chief
sculptor Userhat, whose biography is translated in chapter II (no. 19), was part
of Maya's staff and was responsible for the creation of these statues.*

*Maya's main biographical text is inscribed around a raised relief scene on
the south reveal of the pylon gateway through which the tomb was entered. The
scene depicts Maya entering and being welcomed into the tomb by his wife,
Merit, and his father's wife, Henutiunu. Both women have their hands raised to
greet Maya who stands before them with a much smaller figure of his brother,
Nehuher, behind him. Maya wears numerous gold shebyu-necklaces and holds
a fan in his right hand. The register below shows nine men, led by a scribe, car-*

rying portable tables, most of which bear different types of gold collar. Captions with speeches of welcome are inscribed in front of both Merit and Henutiunu. Henutiunu's speech is largely lost, but was probably similar in theme to Merit's, which reads: Welcome, you who are adorned with the favors of Ptah, South-of-his-Wall! How well you deserve them, O favored one who comes forth before the favored ones, for you remain leader of the festival of the lord of the gods *(unpublished: translation and scene description from van Dijk in Martin et al. 1988, 11–12). The main text begins above the head of Henutiunu and wraps around all four figures to close with three columns behind Maya and Nehuher. A large block bearing approximately one-third of the text is missing and there are lacunae throughout the rest of the inscription.*

> Member of the *pat*, count,
> royal sealbearer, sole companion,
> fanbearer on the right of the king,
> festival leader of Amun,
> true royal scribe, beloved of him,
> overseer of the treasury of the lord of the Two Lands,
> Maya, true of voice;
>
> he says to the people who will come
> and who wish to take recreation in the West,
> to walk about in the district of ⌜eternity⌝:[1]
> [... ... ...] my tomb in [...]
> ⌜your⌝ [...] making [...] this speech of mine,
> rejoice [...] among them,
> [... ...] my name upon my monument,
> which [...] made for me.
> [*rest of this column and the next two largely lost*]
>
> [... ...] the state of affairs which came about through me,
> being what my god did for me since my youth.
> I grew up in the place where His Person was, while I was a child.
> I reached the end in happiness,
> in the favor of the lord of the Two Lands, countless times.
>
> I was one who [went forth in (?)] [...]
> [*nine columns lost*]
> [*ca. 7 groups lost*] [...] my actions (?) (in) making ⌜monuments (?)⌝
> ... in electrum.

I was one who was perfect in the beginning, bright at the end,
a possessor of veneration, in peace, in the temple of Ptah.
I was one who carried out the plans of the king of my time
and did not neglect what he had commanded.

... [to make splendid (?)] the temples,
in fashioning the images of the gods,
their ⌐rituals¬ being under my care.[2]

I entered before the ⌐august¬ image.
It was the eldest son who [...][3]
... in prosperity and health,
commanding a ⌐perfect¬ burial ⌐in Memphis¬;

[for the Osiris of ... ...,
true royal scribe, beloved of him],
⌐overseer of the treasury¬ of the lord of the Two Lands,
Maya, true of <voice>.

24. The Tomb of the High Steward, Nefersekheru, at Zawyet Sultan

Nefersekheru's tomb was cut into the upper slopes of the west side of the escarpment of Zawyet Sultan in Middle Egypt, the ancient Egyptian town of He-benu in the Oryx nome. Nefersekheru is not known from any other monuments but, since his career was probably in the north of Egypt where few monuments survive, evidence is likely to be scarce. Despite his biography's focus on palace life and royal favor, a king's name is not preserved in the tomb. The decorative program, particularly the inclusion of statues of deities and the use of raised relief, dates its creation to the early Nineteenth Dynasty, possibly the reign of Sety I. The badly damaged biographical inscription is carved on the west wall of the southern half of the hall of the tomb, next to the entrance. The text is accompanied by a figure of Nefersekheru at the bottom left corner of the inscription, wearing a number of gold shebyu-necklaces around his neck, signifying royal favor and reward. The text presents stages of his career in different administrative areas of the palace and culminates with his reward by the king, an episode that is also described in the harper's song inscribed in the tomb's shrine. The text closes with a distinctive claim of truthfulness, funerary wishes, and threat formulas.

Royal sealbearer, overseer of the granaries
in Upper and Lower Egypt,
high steward in the palace,
who was silent at the [right] ⌜time⌝...
[*rest of column lost*]

he is one who guards his heart,
all of whose words were exact,
the balance[4] ...
[*rest of column lost with traces*]

[who assessed (?)] an official on account of his speech.
He was benevolent without fault,
[*ca. 10 groups lost*]
... Nefersekheru;

he says: I will speak to you,
who exist upon earth and who will come to be,
to priests, royal nobles,
[*ca. 8 groups lost*]
[who understand the writing] in my tomb which is in the Oryx nome,[5]

so that your hearts may wonder (as you stand) in front of this
         writing,
so that you may speak with certainty (?),
in performing (?) before ...
[*ca. 8 groups lost*]
... that the ignorant may know as well as the skilled,
<all> ⌜that I say⌝ in my chapel.
I will speak of my character, my nature, and my ⌜plans⌝,[6]
so that my concerns and my [...] will be before you:

I have been a silent one since I descended from the womb,
one who came as a child in perfect form.
I [spent my youth of] ten years
as a child upon the arm of my father,
and I was taught to write.

After this, because of my wisdom,
I was (so) skilled that [I] went forth [from school] to the Mansion of
         Life.[7]

I purified myself there in order to serve His Person.
I wrote in the audience chamber,
the place where His Person was.

I was enclosed in the protected chamber of the outer palace,[8]
being a youth whom the palace staff loved,
because of the silence of my mouth;
there was no memorandum about me to a herald of the lord of the Two Lands.[9]

It was my good character which promoted me;
I was initiated into the [preparation chamber] in the hidden [horizon],[10]
beginning with the pronouncing of my name by His Person
to be the royal scribe of the meal for the king in his following.

⌜He⌝ recognized that I was effective,
my hand was firm because of [...].
[The actions] of (my) office are (fitting) for a man who does not stray.
Years passed by me in this commission.

I was promoted to high steward by the king,
being alert and not neglectful
concerning what was placed before me,
[when I performed] my [services] for my Horus.[11]

I was favored without ceasing every day.
I was rewarded very often for every task:
the gold thereof at my throat,
the myrrh upon my head,
real *iber*-balm from the beginning of the ⌜land
anointing⌝ my ⌜limbs⌝.[12]

When I went forth from the gates of the palace,
all my people were joyful
to the height of the sky.
Everyone who saw me (said):
"It is fitting for him, Nefersekheru, whose heart is true."
[... ... ...]

⌜Look⌝, I have reached old age without a falsehood within me,
there is no one who will report a misdeed of mine to him (the king).
I did not push aside the indigent one who has nothing in favor of
        one richer than him.
One who receives gifts ⌜in order to be partial⌝ is an abomination to
        me.
[I did not ... concerning] ⌜my possessions⌝ truly;
I did not think about (accruing) an abundance of millions of things.

Beware lest you say about it (the biography) that it is not the case
        (that is):
"Who saw it?
⌜Be indulgent⌝ when he tells it to us,
for every man boasts about himself in his own writing."
Believe my words; there is no falsehood therein—
a witness for the truthful one is his august tomb.[13]

As the king of eternity lives, foremost of Tawer,
the one to whom all people come without exception,[14]
everything which I said of my character,
⌜my⌝ nature, and every plan
was carried out when I was upon earth.

Bend the arm to me, invoke my name,
so you may act upon earth without loss of ⌜strength⌝,
and pass a lifetime in peace without the disfavor of the king,
a son-who-loves as the heir of every man [among you].[15]

[May you say an offering which the king gives to Osiris],
lord of Busiris, who is in Abydos,
to Horus, foremost of Hebenu,[16]
Sokar, lord of *shetayt*,
and to Anubis, foremost of the god's shrine,

that they may give [a thousand of bread and beer,
cattle and fowl,
and all good and pure things,
of alabaster and linen,

and the sweet breeze of the] north wind,
drinking at the eddy of the river,

[receiving the offerings which have come from the offering table of]
⌐Wenennefer⌐,
bread and provisions of Memphis,
libations and offerings in Heliopolis,

going forth as a living *ba*
in every form that he desires,
going around beside Orion, among the imperishable stars,
to see Re when he rises every day,
the great sun-disc which is in the zenith,
taking up (my) place in the divine barque, under the command of
the rejoicing crew.[17]

May my name be invoked and may I be recognized,
at the *wag*-festival and the Thoth festival,
[for the *ka* of the] ⌐royal scribe⌐,
Nefersekheru, true of <voice>.

He says: The one who stands among you is happy,
joyfully receiving what I have said [concerning my life on] earth,
all together;
if one pours water
for the honor of another, in accordance with the (venerated) state of
one who is there (?),[18]
he has no (evil) fate.[19]
(As for) the one whose heart is confused, who sees the dead as
negligible,
and destroys his tomb:
Stop yourself, you who are <before this place>, when you approach
my name.

(But) if you are here,
free from the like,
bear in mind that you have come to me
for millions of years,
so that I may be judged with you in the necropolis,
in the presence of the council, the lords of Maat,
before the keeper of the balance who is in the (Hall of) Two
Truths.[20]

I speak in order to let you know. It is good to listen.[21]

25A–C. THE THEBAN TOMB OF PASER, SOUTHERN VIZIER

Paser held the office of southern vizier under Sety I and Ramesses II. In contrast to the considerable number of monuments belonging to or associated with Paser that are datable to the reign of Ramesses II, only his tomb attests to his being vizier under Sety I, suggesting he received his appointment toward the end of that reign. His latest attestation as vizier is from year 21 of Ramesses II, and his successor Khay is named on an ostracon of year 30. A statue belonging to a high priest of Amun named Paser may indicate that he was appointed to that position later in his career; his father had also held this title.

Paser's tomb is located in a wadi between the hills of Qurna and Khokha in the Theban necropolis. Although it is unpublished, preliminary reports (Seyfried 1990; Hofmann 2004, 31–39) and early descriptions (PM I², 1, 219–24) indicate that much of its decorative program is in typical Ramessid style, incorporating images of Paser adoring the gods, funerary scenes, and rock-cut statues of deities in the shrine. Alongside these standard elements are others that present aspects of Paser's official role, centered in particular on his relationship to Sety I. These dominate the walls of the south half of the hall. Of particular note are the remains of scenes and texts on the west wall relating to Paser's installation, including traces of "the Duties of the Vizier," an instruction possibly composed in the early New Kingdom. This is the only known post-Eighteenth Dynasty redaction of the text (van den Boorn 1988, 365, 371).

A number of texts in the tomb incorporate biographical phraseology; I have selected the longest and most developed texts for translation, which are the two biographical texts on pillars on each side of the transverse hall that recount Paser's promotions, and the text accompanying a reward scene. In composition, phraseology, and theme, the biographies and the reward scene are aligned with Eighteenth Dynasty strategies of self-presentation.

25A–B. THE PAIR OF BIOGRAPHIES INSCRIBED ON PILLARS

These texts are on the east sides of the two pillars second from each end of a row of pillars in the hall (labeled B and G in PM I², 1, 222–24). The biography inscribed on the pillar in the south half of the hall is addressed to Sety I (no. 25a). An abbreviated version of this text, addressed to Ramesses II, is inscribed on the pillar in the north half (no. 25b). Both texts begin with eulogies of the king and follow with details of Paser's promotions to office. The version addressed to Ramesses presents shorter versions of the royal eulogy and omits Paser's closing speech to the companions. By dedicating parallel texts to the two kings, Paser seems to position himself as a key point of continuity and connection between them.

25A. BIOGRAPHY ADDRESSED TO SETY I

This text is inscribed in fifteen lines beneath a raised relief scene of Paser standing with his right arm raised in a gesture of address before the seated figure of the king, whose head and torso are now lost. The cartouche Menmaatre (Sety I) is visible in raised relief as is the location of his nomen, which is now lost. The cartouches are accompanied by traces of the phrase: Given life like Re forever. Eight columns of inscription begin before the king and continue over the figure of Paser, recording his address to Sety and the celebratory response of the court.

    Scene, above figure of Paser:
        Fanbearer on the ⌜right of the king⌝,
        city governor, vizier,
        festival leader of Amun,
        Paser, true of voice,

        he says: Greetings to you, Perfect God,
        Horus who appears in Thebes ⌜in⌝ ...
        [*ca. 8 groups lost with traces*],
        ... this his mountain of life
        being (where) Your Person will spend his lifetime (in the next
            world).
        May you may cause that this servant (Paser) rest there within it,
        like a servant who is effective for his lord.

        Let the courtiers and companions say:
        "How fortunate is that which has happened to him!"
        —a good occasion for one who follows Your Person is what you
            commanded for me.
        May you cause me to reach the west of Thebes like any of your
            favorites;
        for the *ka* of the city governor, vizier,
        Paser, true of voice.

    Biography:
        Given as a favor from the palace,
        to the member of the *pat*, count,

⌐dignitary⌐, he of the curtain, mouth of Nekhen,[22]
priest of Maat, fanbearer on the right of the king,
city governor, vizier,
Paser, true of voice;

he says: Greetings to you, king of Egypt,
Re of the nine bows.
You are a ⌐god⌐ who lives on Maat,
who perceives what is in hearts,
who judges bodies, who knows what is in them,
clever like the lord of Hermopolis,[23]
[... ... ...] in order to know,
like Ptah, who created workshops.

Now His Person, his heart happy,
was suffused with joy and ⌐exaltation
in⌐ his palace of delectation,
like Re within his horizon,

his mother Maat being the protection of his body,
having appeared as Great-of-Magic,
⌐taking⌐ her place between his eyebrows,
as the coiled one upon his head,[24]

having taken up the crook and flail,[25]
and the office of his father Geb,
[gods] jubilating in the sky,
the Mansion of the Official being in festival,
the lords of Heliopolis rejoicing.
Karnak was exulting and Amun-⌐Re⌐ very ⌐greatly⌐,
when he saw his son upon his throne.[26]

He (Amun) places him (Sety) before him,
happy to perform wonders for His Person.
He has caused the south, north,
west, and east,
⌐this⌐ entire ⌐land⌐ to flourish;
Dual King, Menmaatre, image of Re,
son of Re, Sety Merenptah (Sety I), given life.

My lord commanded that this servant (Paser) be promoted

to first companion of the palace;
he ⌜appointed⌝ him to be overseer of chamberlains,
and high priest of Great-of-Magic.

Then again he placed him as city governor,
and vizier who judges what is right,
who is charged to receive tribute
of the foreign lands of south and north
for the treasury of the victorious king.
He was sent [...] from it on account of his efficiency,
to calculate the revenue of the Two Lands throughout the districts
          of Upper and Lower Egypt.

(All this) by the true royal scribe whom he loves,
greatly favored one ⌜of⌝ the Perfect God,
overseer of works in the great monuments,
overseer of the overseers of all royal workshops,
festival leader of Amun,
city governor, vizier,
Paser, true of voice;

he says: [O ... ...],
companions and great ones of the palace,
the entourage who are in the king's house,
[...] for you in your faces,
as the counsels of the Perfect God,
ordained (?) [... ... ...] a good old age.

I have reached this (position) by performing Maat for my god, [...
          ...].
May he give (me) a place on the west side,
the West, [the necropolis (?)],
[... ... ...] under the command of Amun-Re,
the god who ordains [... ... ...]
attaining veneration, judging (?) [... ...].

25B. BIOGRAPHY ADDRESSED TO RAMESSES II

*The scene above this text has been erased or cut away. Ten lines of the biog-
raphy remain. It may be that no further lines are lost as the traces in the final line*

largely correspond with the final line of Sety's text (no. 25a). I follow Kitchen's
restorations of this text, which are based on that composed for Sety.

⌜Given as a favor⌝ from the palace,
to the Osiris of [27] the ⌜member of the *pat*⌝, count,
dignitary, he of the curtain, ⌜mouth of Nekhen,
priest of Maat, fanbearer on the right of the king,
city governor, vizier⌝,
Paser, true of voice;

he says: Greetings to you, King of ⌜Egypt,
Re of the nine bows⌝,
[… … … …]
Horus, beloved of Maat.

You are a god who lives on Maat,
⌜who perceives what is in hearts⌝,
a god [… … …]
[…] through his *ka.*

Now His Person, ⌜his heart happy,
was suffused with joy⌝ and exaltation
⌜in his palace of delectation,
like⌝ Re within his ⌜horizon,

his mother Maat being the protection for his body,
having appeared as Great-of-Magic⌝,
taking her place ⌜between his eyebrows,
as⌝ the coiled one upon his <head>,

⌜having taken up the crook and flail
and the office of his father Geb⌝;
Dual King, Usermaatre Setepenre (Ramesses II),
[… lord of (?) … …].

⌜My lord commanded that this servant (Paser) be promoted,
to first companion⌝ of the palace;
⌜he⌝ appointed him to be overseer of chamberlains,
and high priest of Great-of-Magic.

⌜Then again he⌝ placed ⌜him as city⌝ governor,

<and vizier> ⌜who judges what is right⌝,
who is charged ⌜to receive tribute⌝
of the foreign lands of south and north,
for the treasury of the victorious king.
⌜He was sent⌝ [...] ⌜from it on account of⌝ his efficiency.

May he give (me) ⌜a place on the West⌝,
⌜in⌝ the necropolis, in the endowed land of [...],
⌜Amun⌝-Re, the god ⌜who ordains⌝ [...]
[*ca. 6 groups lost*]

25C. PASER'S REWARD (FIG. 8)

This scene from the west wall of the south half of the hall, beside the tomb entrance, shows Paser standing rewarded before the figure of Sety I, who is seated in a baldachin with the goddess Maat standing behind him. Paser is depicted with his arms raised while courtiers adorn him with layers of gold collars and a robe. More collars are piled up on tables in front of him. A mid-nineteenth century drawing of the scene shows part of the text and only two courtiers (fig. 8). Three are named in the captions: Chamberlain, Patjuma; ⌜chamberlain, Ptahemay⌝; chamberlain, Meryre, who is called [Hel (?)]enre. *The fan that Paser holds over his head encloses a caption which gives his titles:* Member of the *pat,* count, dignitary, he of the curtain, mouth of Nekhen, priest of Maat, city governor, vizier of the (southern) city (Thebes), Paser, true of voice on the west of Thebes, favored one of the god who is in it.

Sety I wears the atef-crown, holds the crook and flail across his chest, and has an effigy-form body. The captions on either side of the winged disc above him read: Behdetite, great god, of dappled plumage, who gives life and power like Re; Behdetite, great god, lord of the sky, lord of Mesen (Edfu), who gives life and power. *The cartouches of the king are enclosed in a rectangle topped by a sky sign in the baldachin:* Dual King, Menmaatre, son of Re, ⌜Sety Meren⌝ptah, given life ⌜like Re⌝, beloved of Amun-Re, lord of the thrones of the Two Lands, lord of the sky. *The same cartouches and epithets are inscribed in rectangles on the columns of the baldachin. On two register lines facing the king are miniature groups of the royal ancestral souls of Pe (Buto: above) and Nekhen (Hierakonpolis: below), in gestures of acclamation; these figures are more usually depicted in scenes of royal ritual in temples or in royal tombs. Above their figures and running continuously, a caption reads:* Making jubilation by the souls of Pe and Nekhen. *A speech of Maat begins behind the king's head and continues above hers:* Words spoken by Maat, daughter of Re: "(My) arms are around ⌜you⌝

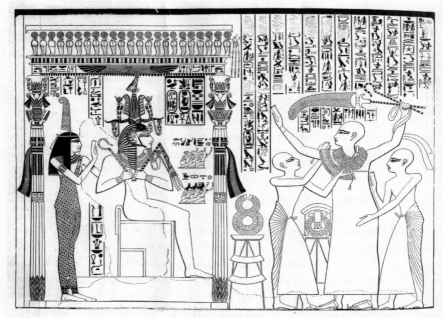

Fig. 8. Reward Scene of Paser (no. 25c: line drawing after Wilkinson 1878, III, pl. 64).

with life and power. I will cause that you be happy on the Great Throne forever and ever." *A single column behind the king's chair reads:* All stability, and power, all health, around him, like Re forever.

Vizieral installation scenes in Eighteenth Dynasty tombs, such as the tomb of Rekhmire who was vizier under Thutmose III and Amenhotep II (N. de G. Davies 1943, I, 15–16; II, pl. 13; compare Dziobek 1994, pls. 42, 72), provide earlier parallels for presentations of the king as an Osiris-like figure in nonroyal contexts. Paser may have drawn on such models. These representations partly deify the king, an implication that is strengthened by the inclusion of the souls of Pe and Nekhen. The accompanying text begins as a eulogy of Sety and then narrates Paser's entry to the palace and reward by Sety, which culminates with his mediation of Paser's transition to the afterlife. It is likely that Sety was dead when the scene was composed, which ideally placed him to welcome Paser to the next world.

> [... ... member of the *pat*, count],
> city ⌜governor⌝, vizier,
> Paser, true of voice;

he says: Greetings to you, [King] of Egypt,
Re of the nine bows,
Dual King, Menmaatre (Sety I),
Horus, who appears in Thebes,
[who penetrates minds (?)], who perceives hearts,
who knows what is in bodies.

He is a Khnum ⌐for people⌐,
who builds up the humble, who raises up the wretched, who [...] the
         high-ranking,
Hapy [for the entire land],
[the sun (?)] for the one who places him in his heart.[28]

May you cause that I pass by the council, [... ...] the ancestors,
that I may be told what is in the heart,
without [...] my [...] in the presence of the sovereign
in order to see His Person in the sanctuary,
[past the guardians (?)] of the hidden doors.[29]

The officials and companions were at the double gate,
[but I entered (?)] into the presence (of the king) without being
         announced.[30]
There was not [one who did (this)] before me.
The favors of the king are ⌐suffused⌐ through my flesh, because of
         my [character (?)].
He chose me ahead of millions,
for he comprehended my perfection in his heart.

I was a companion whom he raised,
his teaching was in my body,
all counsels were discerned in ⌐my⌐ heart,
(for) I was wise through these things he did for me,
admitted to [his presence in order to (?) ...]

[*7 columns lost with traces*]
... of his two uraei.
[His (?)] father [Amun (?)] extols [... ... ...],
son of Re, Sety Merenptah (Sety I),
alert one, who sees bodies,
wise [in the concerns] of this [servant].

May he cause that I spend my lifetime, rich in days (?),
[*ca. 6 groups lost with traces*]
... [to] perfection,
in the district [of the necropolis],
[... ... ...]
... in the necropolis at [your] side [every day],

so that I may mingle with the great ones, the ancestors, and the
     effective *akhs*,
and then those who are in the underworld will say to me:
"Welcome, welcome!
You have performed Maat for the lord of Thebes;
may he assign the West to you."

For the *ka* of the Osiris of the dignitary, he of the curtain,
mouth of Nekhen, priest of Maat,
city governor, vizier,
Paser, true of voice.

26A–B. Temple Monuments of Prehotep, Northern Vizier

Prehotep (or Rehotep as his name is commonly written) held the position of northern vizier during the reign of Ramesses II, probably taking up the position late in the second decade of that reign. His name is included on a stela of the high priest of Osiris, Wenennefer, dated to year 42 (translated here: no. 14b); in the king's sixth decade, Prehotep seems to have taken up the post of high priest of Memphis as the successor of the prince Khaemwaset (Raue 1998, 351). The inclusion of Prehotep on the stela as well as other objects belonging to Wenennefer (e.g., no. 14a) speaks to close collegial, and perhaps familial, connections between these powerful men and their families. Prehotep is attested on a number of objects from Saqqara, Memphis, Qantir (Piramesse), Abydos, Deir el-Medina, and Herakleopolis, the latter city probably being his city of origin; his tomb was at Sidmant, which was the necropolis of Herakleopolis. Scholars have long thought that there were two viziers under Ramesses II named Prehotep, thus termed Prehotep A (or: "the elder") and B (or: "the younger"), but Dietrich Raue (1998) has shown convincingly that there was only one.

26A. ABYDOS STATUE

Prehotep's block statue was found by Petrie in the Osiris temple complex. With a height of 0.68 meters (2'2"), it shows the vizier seated on a cushion with his arms folded over his knees, his right hand holding a fan. A pectoral bearing an image of Ptah in a shrine and the cartouche of Ramesses II is depicted hanging from his neck. Except at the front, the body is clearly modeled beneath the garment. Unusually for the New Kingdom, the statue has no back pillar. The upper right arm bears one column with Prehotep's titles and name: Royal sealbearer, god's father, (P)rehotep. *Two columns on the left arm, which include some cryptographic writings, read:* Keeper of secrets of hieroglyphs, who evokes Re at the beginning of the year, god's father, (P)rehotep, who follows Thoth. *A further line of titles runs across the front of the base:* Member of the pat, count, royal sealbearer, sole companion, dignitary before the name of the king, vizier, Prehotep. *The main texts on the statue are two sets of funerary wishes inscribed on the front of the knees, separated by a column of titles. The biographical statement describing Prehotep's temple upbringing—a motif found in a number of Ramessid biographies (e.g., nos. 2, 49; and see note 32 to this text)—and his appointment to office fills the front of the flat of the base, on either side of and between the feet. The texts on this statue are presented in full as an example of how short biographical phrases can be included on monuments whose textual content has a different emphasis.*

> *Front of knees, titles in the center column:*
> Keeper of secrets of the great place,
> who adores Ptah in the *shetayt*-shrine,
> royal sealbearer, [...],[31]
> subordinate of the god, (P)rehotep.

> *Front of knees, right of center column:*
> He says: O my lord, who protects me with perfection,
> let my *ba* see (?) and my corpse be sound.
> Make my body complete and my bones whole
> for the future because it (the body) acts;
> I am your (Ptah's) servant, truly beloved,
> vizier Prehotep, true of voice, so that I may be as a god.

> *Front of knees, left of center column:*
> He says: May you cause me to become like those in your following,
> who see your forms, may you exalt me among the *akh*s.
> May you cause me to be divine among the *ba*s,

that I may be summoned to your presence perpetually
so that I should not perish in the land.

   Top of base, around feet:
   My lord appointed me vizier,
   as one brought up in the temple of Ptah.[32]
   ⌜I became⌝ chief spokesman of the Two Banks,
   one who judges the land for the king.

26B. SAQQARA STELA

This large, free-standing square-topped stela probably came from a chapel Prehotep set up at Saqqara toward the end of his career. Made from pink granite, it has a height of 1.58 meters (5'2"), a width of ca. 0.82 meters (2'7") and a thickness of ca. 0.33 meters (1'), and is inscribed on both faces and both edges. For the purposes of description, I use Mohamed Moursi's (1981) designations of the faces and edges as faces A and B and edges C and D. The very worn scene on the upper register of face A depicts Prehotep on the right, wearing a long vizieral robe, with his right arm raised before figures of Ptah and Anubis. In his left hand he holds a fan. The text above him gives his name and titles: His ⌜favored and beloved one⌝, member of the ⌜pat, count⌝, city governor, vizier (P)rehotep, true of voice. *The gods bear the captions:* ⌜Ptah⌝, whose attention is on Memphis; Anubis upon his mountain. *The scene on face B shows Prehotep, in similar pose and costume to that on face A, facing right before figures of Osiris and Apis. The text above him gives his name and titles:* For the *ka* of the member of the *pat*, chief of the Two Lands, city governor, vizier, (P)rehotep, true of voice. *The effigy-form Osiris stands on a low pedestal with the bull-headed figure of Apis behind. The captions above them read:* Osiris, lord of eternity; the living Apis. *The inscription beneath the scene on face B aligns epithets of moral character with effective performance in office, from accounting for revenue collection to reports for administrative bureaus and the king. The texts on face A and in the columns on the edges of the stela provide examples of elaborate epithet formulations (for which see Rickal 2005) that crystalize key aspects of the role of vizier as second in command to the king. On this stela, Prehotep bears the high priestly titles of Re in Heliopolis and Ptah in Memphis, "chief of seers of Re-Atum" and "chief controller of crafts." Prehotep probably assumed these offices toward the end of his career, after leaving the position of vizier. Therefore this stela, and the chapel in which it was placed, may have been dedicated at the end of Prehotep's life or after his death, summarizing for posterity all the titles and offices he had held (Raedler 2004, 373).*

Face A:

Member of the *pat*, controller of the great ones,
city governor, vizier,
(P)rehotep, true of voice,
he says: I was vizier, curtain of the Two Banks,
[portal] of the sovereign,[33] high priest of Maat,
overseer of priests, controller of the lord's kilt,[34]
chief of seers of Re-Atum, chief controller of craftsmen,
setem-priest of Ptah, festival leader of South-of-his-Wall,

priest of the two *uraeus*-goddesses of Horus,
chief overseer of chamberlains of the lord of the Two Lands in the
   sed-festival hall,
who gave instruction to everyone,
overseer of works, controller of craftsmen,
overseer of the laws of the Perfect God
in the hall of judging Maat,

mouth of the King of Upper Egypt (*njsw*),
herald of the King of Lower Egypt (*bjty*),[35]
who contented His Person in the noble palace,
who presented Maat to his lord,
leader before the subjects,
who reckoned all the revenues in the entire land,
city governor, vizier (P)rehotep.

He says: O all lector priests, mourners of the living Apis,
the herald of Ptah,[36]
may you pay attention each time you come
before the tomb of Apis
and to the Mansion of Eternity of the city governor,[37]
vizier, (P)rehotep,
to perform censing and libation,
saying "for your *ka*, for your name,
vizier (P)rehotep," so you will say every day.

Face B:

The Osiris of the member of the *pat*, chief of the Two Lands,
god's father, beloved of the god,
keeper of secrets in the temple of Neith,
confidant of Horus in the horizon of eternity,

mouth of the king in the entire land,
curtain of the land, dignitary, mouth of Nekhen,
high priest of Maat,
fanbearer on the right of the king,
city governor—
(P)rehotep, true of voice—of Memphis,

he says: I was accurate, true of heart,
falsehood was my abomination,
one who lived every day performing Maat.

I was clever without equal,
skilled in all the works of the Filler-Thoth.[38]
I was one who entered when summoned, who tallied amounts,
who regulated the grain-measure,[39] who knew it in the documents.

I was one who examined the registers, knowledgable in advice,
who recited from the document without stumbling (?).
I was one honored, on whose plans one relied;
[people] did not bow to me without reason (?);[40]

for the *ka* of the Osiris of the member of the *pat*,
chief of the Two Lands, fanbearer on the right of the king,
city governor and vizier, (P)rehotep.

Edge C (to the left when before face A of the stela):
For the *ka* of the member of the *pat*, count,
god's father, beloved of the god,
keeper of secrets in the temple of Neith, curtain of the land,
dignitary, mouth of Nekhen, priest of Maat,
mouth of the King of Upper Egypt (*njsw*),
herald of the King of Lower Egypt (*bjty*),
confidant of the king, lord of the Two Lands,
who approached the king in his sacred presence,
who presented Maat before the palace,
fanbearer on the right of the king,
city governor, vizier,
(P)rehotep, true of voice, in peace.

For the *ka* of the member of the *pat*, chief of the Two Lands,
curtain of the sky, portal of the earth,

plumbline of the Two Banks.
He was the coffer of judging Maat,[41]
a shrine of the goddess (Maat),
great of speech of the council of thirty,
controller of the districts and the cities,
vizier who judged the Two Lands,
who saved the wretched (?),
city governor, vizier.[42]

For the *ka* of the member of the *pat*, count,
god's father, beloved of the god,
keeper of secrets of what is in the palace,
chief in the entire land,
vizier of the subjects,
he of the curtain of the sun-folk,
mouth of Nekhen, priest of Maat,
keeper of secrets in the Mansion of the Controllers,[43]
who has free access (in) the domain of Ptah,
fanbearer on the right of the king,
city governor, vizier (P)rehotep.

Edge D (to the right when before face B of the stela):
For the *ka* of the member of the *pat*, chief of the Two Lands,
god's father, beloved of the god,
dignitary for the subjects,
keeper of secrets in the mansion of the king of Lower Egypt,
confidant of the king in the horizon of eternity,
fanbearer on the right of the king,
mouth of the king in every foreign land,
city governor, vizier,
(P)rehotep, true of voice, in peace.

For the *ka* of the member of the *pat*, count,
god's father, beloved of the god,
keeper of secrets of the palace,
confidant of the king in truth,
he of the curtain, judge of the Two Lands,
eyes of the King of Upper Egypt (*njsw*),
ears of the King of Lower Egypt (*bjty*),
(so that) one can rely on all that he has done,
city governor, vizier,

(P)rehotep, true of voice.

For the *ka* of the member of the *pat*, chief of the Two Lands, leader
    of the Two Banks,
god's father, beloved of the god,
keeper of secrets in the shrine of Neith,
curtain and portal of the king,
plumbline of the Two Banks,
balance post of the Two Lands,[44]
mouth of the king in the entire land,
city governor, vizier,
(P)rehotep, true of voice.

27. THE FREESTANDING STELA OF THE OVERSEER OF THE TREASURY, TIA, FROM GIZA

*Tia was the husband of a sister of Ramesses II and a high ranking treasury
official; one of his main positions was overseer of the treasury of the mortuary
temple of this king (the Ramesseum). Tia and his wife, whose name was also
Tia, were the owners of a tomb at Saqqara, positioned in the relatively small
space between the tomb of Maya (see no. 23) and the nonroyal tomb of the later
king Horemheb, a location that associated them with the perceived founder of
the Nineteenth Dynasty. Fragments of a deliberately smashed stela bearing a
biographical inscription found within the cult chapel of this tomb may suggest
that Tia held offices under Sety I (van Dijk 1997, 51–52); otherwise, few details
of his career are known.*

*The monument presented here may have been set up in a shrine belonging
to Tia and his wife at Kafr el-Gebel, an area on the edge of the desert, south of
the Giza pyramid field (Martin 1997, 1). This area seems to have been particularly associated with Sokar in the New Kingdom (Edwards 1986). Its form, as
a four-sided pillar with a round-topped stela carved into each face, is unusual;
stelae are very rarely inscribed on four faces (compare no. 26b above). These
faces have a maximum height of 1.06 meters (3′5″) and width of just over 0.47
meters (1′5″). The curved upper surface of the object bears a large cartouche and
epithet of Ramesses II in the center:* Ramesses Meryamun, (given life) like Re,
flanked by two parallel columns bearing Tia's name and titles: The Osiris of the
royal scribe, overseer of the treasury in the temple of "Usermaatre-Setepenre-
of-the-domain-of-Amun," Tia, true of voice.

*Although the four faces differ in detail, they are largely parallel in arrange-
ment and iconography. The upper register of each face depicts Tia standing in
adoration of a standing figure of a deity. I translate the texts on the faces in an
order which I consider best reflects their content. The scenes on faces 1 and 2
show solar deities: Re-Horakhty, who is associated with the morning sun, and
Atum, who is associated with the evening sun. Faces 3 and 4 depict the mortuary
deities Sokar and Osiris. The cartouche on the top of the pillar is oriented to the
stela showing Osiris, indicating that this is the most important and culminating face. Between the figures in each scene is a stand bearing a vessel and lotus
bloom. Each deity holds a* was-*scepter in his right hand and an* ankh *in his left.
Tia wears a braided wig,* shebyu-*necklaces and broad collars, full pleated robe,
and sandals. In the scene on face 1, where Tia stands before Re-Horakhty, he
wears a fillet, and his robe is in a different style, incorporating a long, opaque
"apron." In that on face 2, the braids of his wig are more complex. Further details
of each scene are included with the translations below. The lower register of each
face bears eight lines of prayers addressed to, or associated with, the deity depicted in the scene above. These prayers integrate distinctive phraseology concerning
Tia's transition to the next world with ancient biographical statements of moral
character and successful fulfillment of social obligations.*

Face 1
*Re-Horakhty stands on the right, facing Tia on the left. Re-Horakhty is de-
picted as falcon-headed. He wears a sun-disc, feathered shirt, short kilt, and
bull's tail. His feet are bare. The caption above him reads:* Re-Horakhty,
great god, lord of the sky. *The four columns above Tia read:* Giving praise
to Re when he rises, by the royal scribe, chief overseer of cattle of Amun,
Tia, true of voice.

Lower register:
> Adoring Re in his sacred image,
> by the Osiris of the royal scribe, the effective one, true of heart,
> overseer of the treasury, Tia, true of voice:

> Greetings to you Re-Khepri-Atum,
> Horus who traverses the sky,
> divine falcon of the gods,
> perfect of face, with great double plumes.
> May he cause that I see the sun, behold the moon,
> and exalt the great god upon his Great Throne;[45]

> by the one greatly favored of the Perfect God,

true royal scribe, beloved of him,
overseer of the treasury of the lord of the Two Lands,
Tia, true of voice.

Face 2
Atum stands on the left, facing Tia on the right. He is depicted anthropo-
morphically with a sun-disc, feathered shirt, short kilt, and bull's tail. His
feet are bare. The caption above him reads: Atum, lord of the Two Lands
and of Heliopolis. *The four columns above Tia read:* Giving praise to Atum,
kissing the ground for his *ka*, for the Osiris of the overseer of the treasury,
Tia, true of voice.

Lower register:
Adoring Atum in all his names,
exalting his *ka* every day
(in) the place of supplication to the lord of *shetayt*, the divine
            precinct,
by the Osiris of the royal scribe, overseer of cattle of Amun,
Tia, true of voice;

he says: I was a unique excellent one, of perfect character,
who was patient in order to act justly,
one truly assiduous, who was not partial.

I have come in peace to the necropolis,
being free from the abomination that might be in it,[46]
resting in my tomb every day, beside the lord of *shetayt*.

Face 3
Sokar stands on the left, facing Tia on the right. He is falcon-headed and
wears the white crown with double plumes, relating to the plumes Osiris
wears on face 4. He also wears a feathered shirt, short kilt, and bull's tail.
His feet are bare. The caption above him reads: Sokar, lord of Rosetau.
Tia's name and titles have been erased from two of the five columns above
his head: ⌈Giving praise⌉ to Sokar, lord of Rosetau, by [... ... Tia], true of
voice.

Lower register:
Adoring Sokar in all his names,
Horus, lord of *shetayt*,
by the Osiris of Tia, true of voice;

he says: I have come from my town in the favor of the king,
having done what his *ka* desires,
for I know what the gods abominate and I have not committed evil.

I gave bread to the hungry,
water to the thirsty, and clothes to the naked.
[I] did not [disregard] the lowly in favor of the powerful;
[for my (?)] abomination is [... ...] necropolis.[47]

Face 4

Osiris stands on the left, facing Tia on the right. Unusually he is not depicted effigy-form, but anthropomorphically like the gods on the other faces. He wears two plumes on his head, banded shirt, short kilt, and bull's tail. He holds a flail as well as an ankh in his left hand. His feet are bare. The caption above him reads: Osiris, lord of Rosetau. *The five columns above Tia read:* Giving praise to Wenennefer, lord of the sacred land, by the royal scribe, overseer of the treasury of the lord of the Two Lands, Tia, true of voice.

Lower register:
The Osiris of[48] the true royal scribe, beloved of him,
overseer of the treasuries of silver and gold,
first dutiful one of His Person,
chief overseer of cattle of Amun,
Tia, true of voice, in peace;

he says: May you cause that I be effective through the work of
     Anubis,[49]
and that the necropolis be opened for me.
Cause that the youth of my time say:
"O may the lord of eternity, who is in the *tjenenet*-shrine,[50] order
     that he (Tia) be mourned."

Guide me to the perfect path.
Let me arrive there[51]
that I may see as Horus who is upon the ways;[52]
the Osiris of Tia.

28. The Naophorous Statue of Panehsy, Overseer of the Treasury (fig. 9)

This limestone statue entered the collections of the British Museum in London in 1833 and has no documented provenance. Panehsy was also the owner of a second unprovenanced naophorous statue now in Berlin and the author of a long letter, addressed to a priest of Amun, concerning temple estates in the north of Egypt. The two-thirds life-size London statue depicts Panehsy kneeling and holding a naos before him. He wears an archaizing amulet around his neck, a long, pleated robe, and sandals. Cartouches of Ramesses II are inscribed on both his shoulders. The naos bears standing figures of Osiris, Isis, and Horus. Horus and Osiris are both in effigy-form. Horus has his hands clenched in front of his body, as if holding a staff or scepter. Isis embraces Osiris with her right arm and holds her left across her body, as if supporting his elbow. The front of the vaulted roof of the naos bears an incised winged disc. The frame, top, and side exterior surfaces of the naos are inscribed with offering texts to a number of deities, particularly those associated with Abydos, as well as strings of Panehsy's titles.

Two columns on the back pillar include offering texts and funerary wishes. These texts and those on the naos incorporate elaborate epithets expressing Panehsy's duties to the gods and his kin relations. It is notable that the texts on the back pillar and the rear surface of the base include prestigious ranking titles which are absent from the arguably more visible front areas. The texts around the base are also striking in their address to the statue simultaneously as a separate being and as a fundamental component and extension of the self. Although not strictly biographical, these texts exemplify the range of textual material that could be present on statues. They also offer significant insight into the meanings that statues might have had in temple space. The inscription around the left side of the base is written in Late Egyptian (see Introduction: 3.2) indicating that this is a new style of text.

Right front edge of naos:[53]
    The venerated one before Horus,
    [son of Isis], who unites the Two Lands,
    Dual King, Horus-who-protects-his-father,
    for the *ka* of the overseer of the seals of south and north,
    who calculated the revenue of the lands and foreign lands,
    for the *ka* of the royal scribe, overseer of the treasury,
    Panehsy, true of voice.

Left front edge of naos:
    The venerated one before Horus

Fig. 9. Statue of Panehsy (no. 28; copyright the Trustees of the British Museum).

who is joyous among the gods,
and the Dual King, Osiris, lord of eternity,
for the *ka* of the overseer of the division of ⌜offerings⌝ for the god[s],
[who ensured (?)] the voice offerings for the *akh*s,
for the *ka* of the royal scribe, overseer of the treasury,

Panehsy, true of voice.

Over the upper edge of the naos:
An offering which the Dual King, Usermaatre Setepenre
(Ramesses II), gives
to the venerated one, enduring in favor,
royal scribe, overseer of the treasury,
Panehsy, true of voice,
son of the dignitary, Ramose, true of voice.

Right top and side of naos exterior:
ᒥAn offering given to Osirisᒧ, [ruler] of the West, lord of Abydos.
ᒥAn offering given to Horusᒧ-who-protects-his-father, son of Isis,
[sweet of love].
ᒥAn offering given toᒧ Upper Egyptian Wepwawet, controller of the
Two Lands,
ᒥgreat god, lord ofᒧ [Rosetjau (?)],
that they may ᒥgiveᒧ a gift of meat offerings from among the gods,
and to circle Ropoqer in the following (procession) of the god,
(for) the royal scribe, overseer of the treasury of the lord of the Two
Lands,
Panehsy, true of voice, possessor of veneration.

Left top and side of naos exterior:
ᒥAn offering given to Isis the greatᒧ, god's ᒥmotherᒧ,
lady of the sky, mistress of the Two Lands,
ᒥAn offering given to Anubis, before the god's shrine,
lord of ..., lord of theᒧ sacred ᒥlandᒧ,
that they may give a voice offering of bread and beer,
[beef and fowl,
incense, wine (?)], and milk,
for the *ka* of the royal scribe, overseer of the treasury of silver,
Panehsy, true of voice,
possessor of veneration, perfect in peace.

Left column of back pillar:
Venerated one before the great god,
who libates the *henu*-barque, who pours water for Rosetjau,
an intimate of Ptah,
chief *wab*-priest in the *tjenenet*-shrine,[54]
scribe ᒥof those assembled before the king (?)ᒧ,

the effective son of a justified man,
born of a justified woman;
for the *ka* of the fanbearer on the right of the king,
royal scribe, overseer of the treasury,
Panehsy, true of voice.

Right column of back pillar:
Venerated one, possessor of a perfect lifetime
in Memphis, the place of truth,[55]
one who has a burial, possessor of a perfect place next to the One-
upon-his-mountain (Anubis):
may Anubis place his hands (on) your body,
that he may [unite (?)] your bones perpetually;
for the *ka* of the fanbearer on the right of the king,
royal scribe, overseer of the treasury,
Panehsy, true of voice.

The texts on the base of the statue share the opening and closing couplet of Panehsy's principal titles and name. These verses are inscribed in single columns in the center front and center back of the base. I translate them for each half of the base inscription.

Right half of base:
Royal scribe, overseer of the treasury,
Panehsy, true of voice
he says: O my likeness, may you be firm for my name,
the favorite of everyone,
so that ⸢people⸣ will stretch out their hands to ⸢you⸣, bearing
splendid bouquets,
that you may be given libations and incense,
as the remainder of your lord,
and then my *ba* will come fluttering,
so that he may receive offerings ⸢with you⸣;
for the *ka* of the member of the *pat*, count,
confidant of the king ⸢throughout⸣ the Two Lands,
royal scribe, overseer of the treasury,
Panehsy, true of voice.

Left half of base:
Royal scribe, overseer of the treasury,
Panehsy, true of voice,

he says: O my statue, you are before the lords of the sacred land;
place yourself as the memory of my name in the domain of the lords
            of Tawer,
for you are here for me as an abode (?); you are my true body;
for the *ka* of the member of the *pat*, count,
royal sealbearer, sole companion,
keeper of secrets in the palace bureaus,
royal scribe, overseer of the treasury,
Panehsy, true of voice.

29. The Standing Statue of Huy, Great Mayor of Memphis

This fragment of a quartzite standing statue was found in the early 1940s in the ruins of the sanctuary of a small temple built for Ptah by Ramesses II in the southwest corner of the later enclosure of the main Ptah temple complex at Memphis. The current location of the statue is unknown. Huy's outer sarcophagus was also found during the same excavation, reused in a nearby Twenty-second Dynasty tomb (the inner sarcophagus had been removed some years earlier probably from the same tomb). Huy, who also used the full form of his name, Amenhotep, is also the owner of a pyramidion presumably from Memphis. The statue fragment, with a height of 0.70 meters (2'3"), consists of the mid-section of a standing figure, with highly modeled legs visible at the sides, wearing a long, flared, and pleated robe that covers the body. The hands are placed palm down on the front of the robe. A vertical band beneath the hands, running down the center front of the robe, bears a prayer and title string: May what reverts from Ptah be for the ⌈true⌉ royal scribe, ⌈beloved of him⌉, great mayor, steward, Huy, true of voice [*unknown amount lost*]. *Columns of text on the sides and rear surface of the back pillar vividly describe a temple called "Ramesses-Meryamun-Maat-is-united-with-Ptah," which Huy built for Ramesses II in Memphis. Huy also bears the title "steward in the temple of Ramesses-Meryamun-Maat-is-united-with-Ptah" on his outer sarcophagus (KRI III, 168, 2,7). Although it is tempting to equate this temple with the small temple in which the statue was found, later excavators found no evidence for the architectural features described in the text, such as the granite columns, and concluded that the statue's inscriptions must refer to another foundation of Ramesses II at the site (Anthes 1965, 9).*

Surface of back pillar:
   [... true royal scribe, beloved of him,

great mayor of Memphis, steward (?),
Huy, true of voice],[56]
he says: O all people who will come after millions of years,
I will speak to you that I may cause you to learn
about my excellence for the heart of His Person:

I made [this] ⌜temple⌝...
... (with) great pylons of limestone,
doorways of electrum,
a monumental hall extending before it[57]
(with) gateways of granite,
its [... ...] ...

[I made this temple (?)] for Memphis, as a monument
in the great name of His Person.
I planted its way with trees right up to this temple.
I dragged statues of granite ...

Left edge of back pillar:
    ... (the temple called)
    " ⌜Ra⌝messes-Mery ⌜amun⌝-Maat-is-united-with-Ptah;"
    its columns of granite,
    the bases in every kind of stone
    —a great open court before it—
    like the pillars of the sky.

    Its columns ...
    [Northerners (?)] were stupefied by the monument (?);[58]
    its door in real pine,
    the images thereof in gold and lapis lazuli;
    they are surrounded with copper ...

Right edge of back pillar:
    ... his [...],
    (I was one) free from tardiness in (doing) what he (Ptah?) desires,
    that he may cause his favors to endure in my house,
    (so) I may be endowed with his offerings;
    royal scribe, great mayor of ⌜Memphis⌝,
    [*rest lost: probably titles and name*]

30. The Naophorous Statue of Kha, Royal Table Scribe

Although the provenance of this statue is not known, the texts suggest that it was dedicated at Abydos, perhaps as a component of a memorial chapel belonging to Kha, who was also the owner of a lintel, perhaps from this chapel, which bears a version of the Ramessid "hymn to Abydos" (see no. 19a). The statue, which is of sandstone and relatively small (0.64 meters high and 0.24 meters wide, 2'1" by 8"), is now in the Louvre, in Paris. It depicts him seated on a cushion with his arms folded across the knees; in his right hand he holds a lettuce, a symbol of the god Min. In front of the knees is a naos containing a figure of Thoth as a baboon, wearing a heavy pectoral and seated above a laden offering table; both the image of the god and the offering table are in raised relief.

The statue is dated by cartouches of Ramesses II inscribed on both shoulders. The frame of the naos bears two inscriptions that fan out from the center top of the naos frame, sharing the opening word and continuing down each side. The inscription on the right of the frame reads: May all that goes forth from the offering table of Osiris, lord of Abydos, be for the *ka* of the table scribe of the lord of the Two Lands, Kha, ⌜true of voice⌝, son of the dignitary, Montuemmin, [true of voice (?)]. *That on the left reads:* May all that goes forth from the offering table of Anubis, lord of the sacred land, be for the *ka* of the table scribe of the lord of the Two Lands, Kha, true of voice, born of Eseemheb, true of voice. *A single line of inscription is carved beneath the depiction of the offering table:* For the *ka* of the Osiris of the royal table scribe of the lord of the Two Lands, Kha, true of voice. *Two offering formulas fan out around the statue base in a single line, sharing the opening word. That on the left reads:* An offering which the king gives to Anubis, foremost of the god's shrine, and to the great ⌜god⌝ (Osiris), lord of the sacred land, that they may give prosperity upon earth in the favor of the king, to be radiant in the sky, and mighty in the earth (underworld), for the *ka* of the royal table scribe of ⌜the lord of the Two Lands⌝ [*rest lost*]. *That on the right reads:* An offering which the king gives to Osiris Khentimentu, that he may give prosperity upon earth following the king [*rest lost*]. *The biographical text is inscribed in three columns on the statue's back pillar and centers on Kha's ritual adornment of the cult statue as part of the Osiris mysteries, the main annual festival at Abydos (see no. 14a). A contemporary parallel for Kha's text is that of the granary chief Siese translated below (no. 31). The existence of such a parallel points to the availability of stock phrases relating to this significant event.*

> Royal table scribe of the lord of the Two Lands,
> Kha, true of voice;
> he says: O my lord Osiris,

may you give to me the sweet breath which is in your nostrils,
because I was greatly favored in Abydos,[59]
a great *wab*-priest in the *tjenenet*-shrine,[60] who established the
    djam-scepter of the great one.[61]

I gave the *nemes* to the Hidden-of-Name.[62]
I caused the twin plumes to appear on the Abydos fetish,[63]
in the depths of the sarcophagus.
I fastened bindings upon the disaffected beneath (your: Osiris's)
    feet.[64]

I ferried the *neshmet*-barque to Ropoqer.
I brought it to the place-which-protects-its-lord (?),[65]
and I propitiated those in the underworld.

I inundated the sacred land with libations,
the return thereof being the stability of my corpse,
as one speaks to another (?) in perpetuity.[66]

31. THE STATUE OF TWO DEITIES DEDICATED BY THE OVERSEER OF THE TWO GRANARIES, SIESE, FROM ASYUT

Siese states in this text that he came from a long line of granary overseers. His genealogy stretches back to the late Eighteenth Dynasty (Satzinger 1978). He held office from the reign of Ramesses II into that of Merenptah, under whom he dedicated a statue bearing traces of biographical phraseology that are too fragmentary to present here. He was probably related by marriage to the high priest of Osiris, Wenennefer (see no. 14b), although his connection to the latter's influential family is not expressed on any of his monuments. All Siese's forebears claim a connection to Asyut, in Middle Egypt, and/or to its local god Wepwawet. Siese followed this tradition in his own self-presentation, commissioning a number of statues that depict Wepwawet, as well as a tomb in the local necropolis. The statue (1.3 meters [4'3"] high) that bears the text translated here is said to have been found in 1913 excavations at Asyut and may have come from Siese's tomb; statues of gods began to be included in nonroyal tombs in the Ramessid period (see Introduction: 3.3). It presents two striding figures of deities set against a broad pillar. The canid-headed Wepwawet stands on the group's left with the figure of Isis-Hathor, wearing a sun-disc and cow horns, on the right.

A central column of inscription gives a brief titulary of Ramesses II and the deities' names: Lord of the Two Lands, Usermaatre Setepenre, lord of appearances, Ramesses Meryamun, given life like Re, beloved of Wepwawet, lord of the sacred land, and Isis, god's mother, Hathor, lady of Medjedet (a cult place near Asyut), lady of the sky, mistress of the Two Lands. *On the right front and side of the base is an offering formula addressed to Isis-Hathor:* An offering which the king gives to Isis the great, lady of Medjedet, that she may give a voice-offering of bread and beer, beef and fowl, for the *ka* of the royal scribe, overseer of the two granaries, Siese, true of voice. *The left front and side are addressed to Wepwawet:* An offering which the king gives to Upper Egyptian Wepwawet, [who controls the Two Lands, that he may give … …], favors, and love, for the *ka* of the royal scribe, overseer of the two granaries, Siese, true of voice. *On the top of the base are three columns of text, one in front of Isis-Hathor's rear foot and two between the figures:* The servant of his (Wepwawet's?) *ka*, royal scribe, overseer of the two granaries, Siese, (grand)son of the dignitary, royal scribe, overseer of the two granaries ⌈of Upper and Lower Egypt⌉, Siese. *The text on the rear surface of the back pillar uses parallel phraseology to that on the statue of Kha, translated above (no. 30), in presenting aspects of Siese's role in the Osiris mysteries at Abydos (see no. 14a). The verses here are more funerary in focus, which is appropriate to the tomb setting. For explanatory notes to this text, see those for Kha above.*

       Royal scribe, overseer of the two granaries
       of Upper and Lower Egypt,
       Siese, true of voice;
       he says: O Osiris, Wenennefer, united *ba*,[67]
       lord of […], great of majesty,
       may you cause my *ba* to become divine in the necropolis,
       being divine in the land of the justified,
       because I was a servant of Abydos,
       a great ⌈*wab*-priest⌉ in the *tjenenet*-shrine.

       I established the twin plumes on the Abydos fetish,
       within the sarcophagus.
       I fastened bindings upon the disaffected beneath your (Osiris's) feet
       so that my *ba* may go forth to have its pleasure upon earth
       in any form that it desires,
       that I may go forth in the sky
       and descend to the earth,
       without my way being hindered;

for the *ka* of the royal scribe, overseer of the two granaries
of Upper and Lower Egypt,
Siese, true of voice,
son of the dignitary, royal scribe,
overseer of the two granaries of Upper and Lower Egypt,
Qeny, true of voice,
(grand)son of the dignitary, royal scribe,
overseer of the two granaries of Upper and Lower Egypt,
Siese, true of voice.

32. THE INSCRIPTION OF THE CHANCELLOR, BAY, AT THEBES

Bay, who may have been of Syrian origin, came to office under Sety II to-
ward the end of the Nineteenth Dynasty and is believed to have been the power
behind the throne during the reign of Siptah with the regent Tawosret, widow of
Sety II. Bay's positioning of himself as kingmaker is expressed through epithets
inscribed on some of his monuments: "one who placed the king on the throne of
his father" (KRI IV, 364,5; 371,8–9). The biographical text translated here, ad-
dressed to Siptah, further develops this theme by stressing actions undertaken
by Bay on the king's behalf. The close relationship between Siptah and Bay, as
expressed in this text, may have been short-lived; fragmentary sources indicate
that Bay may have been executed in that king's fifth year, shortly before his own
death (Grandet 2000; see Schneider 2003 for an alternative reconstruction of the
end of the Nineteenth Dynasty).

The text is inscribed in fourteen columns between figures of Siptah and Bay
on the west face of a rectangular structure, which formed the core of the front
area of the Eleventh Dynasty mortuary temple of Montuhotep II on the West
Bank of Thebes. Only the lower part of the structure is preserved and its origi-
nal form and purpose is debated; it has been identified as a pyramid or, more
recently, as a representation of the primeval mound (Arnold 2003, 150). The
surface that bears the surviving part of Bay's inscription (ca. 1.8 meters wide,
5'9") faces the rear of the temple. A section with a relief of the king's head is now
in the Royal Museum, Edinburgh. In the far right corner of the face is a kneeling
figure of Siptah wearing the atef-*crown and holding a crook and flail. The cap-*
tion to the figure reads: [... ... ...] whom Atum himself chose, ⌜Dual King,
lord of the Two Lands, Akhenre Setepenre⌝, son of ⌜Re⌝, lord of appearances,
Siptah Merenptah, given life. *The lower part of a figure of Bay, wearing a long*
robe and sandals, stands in the far left corner. About five groups are lost from

the beginning of each column. By displaying an inscription in this temple, Bay
may have been aligning himself, and his king, with ancient traditions of kingship,
including those of the oldest Theban Dynasty.

[*ca. 5 groups lost*]
kissing the ground before his perfect face,
divine one, beloved of …
[… by the member of the *pat*, count, …]
[effective (?)] for his ⌜lord⌝,
Bay, true of voice.

He says: Greetings to you, my [perfect (?)] lord,
…
[may you grant that I see (?)] your perfect face;
make me whole perpetually,
and may you give me …
and a perfect burial after old age,
following 110 years upon [earth (?)].[68]

…
I set my eyes upon you, in privacy,[69]
… [placing me (?)] foremost,
being at the head of the council of thirty, while on the path of …
[receiving a] perfect increase from your hand—
my lifetime in …

I defended all your people, acting [as? …] …
your [servants attended to (?)] my voice concerning your affairs,
…
I [know] that you are divine, being unique, more than all the gods,
…

I was a possessor of strength,
seeking out …
… that you may suffuse my limbs with health,
my perfection …

I was esteemed upon earth,
the chiefs and the great ones [extolling (?)] …
(I was one) truly assiduous, strong,
effective for his lord;

for the *ka* of the overseer of the ⌈great⌉ seal [of the entire land, Bay, true of voice].

33. The Stela from Bilgai

This stela was severely damaged by its use in modern times as a millstone, and the titles and name of its protagonist are lost. It is therefore referred to by its place of discovery, the village of Bilgai in the northern Delta. This location suggests that it may originally have been set up in a seaport or fortress at the mouth of one of the western branches of the Nile. The remaining fragment has a height of ca. 1.12 meters (3'7"), a width of ca. 1.07 meters (3'5"), and a depth of ca. 0.31 meters (1') and is inscribed on both surfaces; traces of paint and inscriptions visible down each side are now illegible. The front surface suffered the most damage with only small sections of the text remaining. The scene at the top is also partially destroyed. Gardiner (1912, 49) recorded that it represented a king offering wine to a triad of deities, perhaps Amun, Mut, and Khonsu. A goddess, very probably Seshat, is depicted standing behind the king recording his years of rule. Between the king and her are the remains of the phrase: [I give you innumerable] *sed-festivals. Part of the goddess's caption is also preserved behind her:* ⌈Daughter of⌉ Re, mistress of the gods.

The central concern of the inscription, which continues onto the rear surface, is a chapel which the protagonist made on behalf of the female king Tawosret for Amun-of-Usermaatre-Setepenre (Ramesses II), a form of Amun linked with the deified Ramesses II, who had temple estates in the area. The text on the rear surface includes extended threat formulas directed to future overseers of the fortress of the sea under whose jurisdiction the temple probably came. The protagonist probably also held this title. The enumeration of his actions focuses on the dramatic increases in wine, honey, and grain production that he managed to procure from the temple estates, perhaps partly to endow his own new chapel. These statements are specifically addressed to a named individual, a steward of temple estates in Thebes named Pabes, and include criticism of another high ranking official, Nedjem. The inclusion of these individuals is a remarkable feature of the text, seeming to orient it more toward the content of letters than biography. It is possible that the temple of Amun-of-Usermaatre-setepenre and its estates may have come under the jurisdiction of the main temple of Amun in Thebes, hence the address to Pabes. Alternatively, Ben Haring (1997, 153) suggests that the stela may have been an appeal to Pabes to act as a guarantor for the endowment of the new chapel.

Because the text is extensively damaged, I do not indicate the extent of the lacunae on the front of the stela specifically.

Front surface:
    Horus, strong bull ... the rebels ...
    ... son of Nut (Seth) ... who is born of ...
    ... son of Nut ...
    ... attending to [two cubits (?) of *bah*-land, new fields (?)] ...
    ... the eldest [daughter (?)] of Amun-of-Usermaatre-Setepenre
          (Ramesses II) ...
    ... attending ...
    ... the gods to rest upon their seats ...
    ... the town of [...],
    they being the gods, the great ones in the ⸢sky⸣, ...
    [... the royal scribe and steward
    of] ⸢the temple of millions⸣ of years
    of the Dual King, [*erased cartouche*],[70]
    ⸢of the domain of Amun⸣ on the west of Thebes,
    ⸢steward⸣ [of the estate of Sety Merenptah (Sety II)
    in the domain of Amun, Pabes].[71]
    ⸢This⸣ servant [made a chapel for (?)]
    ... [Amun-of-]Usermaatre-Setepenre ⸢which is⸣ [in]...
    ... forever in the name of ...
    ... [the great benefactress] of every land,[72]
    she [propitiates] him ...
    ... he will act ...
    ... in ⸢his⸣ granary.
    ⸢He⸣ will act ...
    [*rest of text lost*]

Rear surface:
    [*several lines lost*]
    [*ca. 12 groups lost*] ... Heliopolis,
    which is on the south of Heliopolis, exactly,
    [*ca. 15 groups lost*]
    ⸢furnished⸣ with a processional way,
    for Amun-of-Usermaatre-Setepenre (Ramesses II) forever,
    [*ca. 11 groups lost*]
    ... like the domain of Amun-of-Usermaatre-Setepenre,
    and no sibling and no one of my kin shall claim ⸢against⸣ [it
          forever].[73]

⌜As for any overseer of the fortress⌝ of the sea who will come to be,
and who will disregard the needs of this chapel
which the great [benefactress] ⌜of every land⌝ made
⌜for Amun-of-Usermaatre-Setepenre, her⌝ father,
in order to prevent Amun-of-Usermaatre-Setepenre resting in it
at the time of his appearance in any ritual,[74]
and who ⌜will take⌝ people ⌜away⌝ from it to involve them in other
        occupations
that are not part of the administration of (this) chapel,

he will be in the power of Amun-of-Usermaatre-Setepenre,
he will be hateful to the gods of the sky
and the gods of the earth,
he will be hateful to the reigning king.
None of his offerings will be accepted,
and he will not persist upon the lip, although brothers endure.[75]
His son will not stand in his place,
nothing that he does will succeed,
he will not keep charge of anything that he will do.

As for any overseer of the fortress of the sea who will come to be,
under whose control the domain of Amun-of-Usermaatre-
        Setepenre will be,
and who will pay attention to this chapel,
which the great [benefactress] of every land made
for her father Amun-of-Usermaatre-Setepenre,
and who will let Amun-of-Usermaatre-Setepenre rest in it
at the time of his appearance in any ritual of his,
and who will not take people away from it to involve them in other
        occupations
that are not part of the administration of this chapel,
which the great [benefactress] of every land made
for Amun-of-Usermaatre-Setepenre, her perfect father,

he will be in the favor of Amun-of-Usermaatre-Setepenre,
he will be in the favor of the gods of the sky,
and the gods of the earth,
he will be in the favor of the reigning king.
He will persist upon the lip, while brothers endure,
and keep charge of his office of overseer of the fortress,
so that his son will stand in his place.

When he is sent on a mission, he will give a report of it.[76]
His children will master all the education he provides.

I say to the royal scribe,
steward of the temple of millions of years
of the Dual King, [*erased cartouche*],
ᶠin the domain ofᶦ Amun on the west of Thebes,
steward of the estate of Sety Merenptah (Sety II)
in the domain of Amun, Pabes:

I am an effective official for his lord,
fulfilling harvest and tax obligations,
(such that) my excess of harvest and taxes
was ten times greater than my assessment of harvest and taxes:
4632 amphorae of wine was ᶠmyᶦ quota of people's labor,
(but) I had them (the amphorae) delivered as 30,000, an excess of
        25,638.[77]

Nedjem, who used to be high steward, did not [approach (?)] me at
        all[78]
in any task which I undertook:
70 amphorae of honey was my assessment of honey,
—I delivered them (the amphorae) as 700, ᶠan excessᶦ of 630;[79]
70,000 [sacks] of grain was my yearly harvest assessment,
—I delivered them (the sacks) as 140,000, an excess of 70,000.[80]

I am one vigilant among ᶠthe vigilantᶦ,[81]
[... ... ...]
all that I did succeeded.
I made a chapel for Amun-of-Usermaatre-Setepenre,
in the [eastern (?)] district, [making (?)] [... ... ...],
ᶠthe temple of millions of yearsᶦ,
of the Dual King [*erased cartouche*] in the domain of Amun
on the west of Thebes as a chapel in the ᶠwestern districtᶦ [...]
[*rest lost*]

34. THE STELA OF HORI, SCRIBE OF PHARAOH

*Probably from Abydos and now in the Staatliche Museen in Berlin, Hori's
stela (0.97 meters, 3'2" in height) records his mission to Abydos from his home-
town of Busiris to offer prayers on behalf of his king, Ramesses VIII. Abydos and
Busiris were the two ancient cities of Osiris, and the text probably mobilizes the
religious and ritual connections between them to reinforce the power of Hori's
requests to the god. The upper register depicts the king, who has disproportion-
ately large hands, presenting Maat to five deities. Cartouches of the king are
inscribed above him:* Lord of the Two Lands, Usermaatre Akhe<n>amun, lord
of appearances, Ramesses Atumherkhopshef (Ramesses VIII), given life like
Re. *A caption behind the king reads:* All protection and life around him, like
Re forever. *Onuris-Horus, a fusion of these two gods, is depicted first in the row
of deities. He wears a tall double-plumed crown and long robe, and bears the
caption:* Onuris-Horus, strong of arm, high of plumes. *Behind him stand two
forms of Osiris. The first is effigy-form, probably representing the god at Abydos.
His caption reads:* Words spoken by Osiris, lord of perpetuity, ruler of eternity.
*The second, identified in the caption as the local form of Osiris in Busiris, is an-
thropomorphic and wears an* atef-*crown:* Words spoken by Osiris, lord of Busiris, great god, lord of the sky, king of the gods. *Behind him stands Horus identified as:* Horus-who-protects-his-father; *and Isis:* Isis the great, god's mother.
*The lower register shows four men and three women, facing left, kneeling and
adoring. Hori is second in the row behind his father. His mother and maternal
grandmother are included in this row as well as being named in the main text
below:* Scribe of Pharaoh, Pakawet, true of voice; his son, scribe of Pharaoh,
Hori; priest of Isis, Paiabinher; priest of Onuris, [Hed]nakht; songstress of
Amun, Taweser; songstress of Amun, Nebkhaty, true of voice; songstress of
Amun, Helelmut.

An offering which the king gives to Osiris Khentimentu,
lord of Abydos, great god, ruler of eternity,
to Onuris-Horus, strong of arm,
high of plumes, who resides in Tawer,
Osiris, lord of Busiris,
great god, king of the gods,
Horus-who-protects-his-father, son of Osiris,
Isis the great, mistress of the gods,
and to Meskhenet, who is in Abydos,

that they may give millions of *sed*-festivals
and hundreds of thousands of years

of the kingship of Horus in happiness
to their son, their beloved,
Dual King, lord of the Two Lands,
Usermaatre Akhenamun,
son of Re, lord of appearances,
Ramesses Atumherkhopshef (Ramesses VIII), given life forever.[82]

Scribe of Pharaoh l.p.h., Hori, true of voice,
he says: I was a servant of your city, Busiris,
your district which is in Lower Egypt.
I was the son of a servant of your domain,
scribe of Pharaoh l.p.h.,
favored one of Abydos,
Pakawet, son of Seny, your servant.

I was brought from my city in Lower Egypt
as far as your city of Abydos,
being a messenger of Pharaoh l.p.h., your (the god's) servant,
for I had come to make praise before you,
in order to request *sed*-festivals for him (the king).

You will hear his (the king's) prayers,
inasmuch as he is effective for your *ka*s,
and you will rescue me together with Pharaoh l.p.h., my lord l.p.h.,
and you will give favor to me
in his presence every day.
Carry out your plans that I may act as a guardian,
so that one will say: "Who can reverse your plans?"

You are the lords of sky, earth, and underworld;
one acts according to that which you say.
You will give a voice offering of bread and beer,
and the sweet breath of the north wind
to my father, Pakawet,
and his son, scribe of Pharaoh,
Hori, true of voice,
son of the songstress of Amun, Taweser,
daughter of the songstress of Amun, Helelmut.

35A–B. Two Scribe Statues of Amenmose, High Steward
of the Western River

The mention of the mortuary temple of Ramesses III at Medinet Habu in the text of one of these statues of Amenmose suggests that he dedicated both in the later Twentieth Dynasty, at opposite ends of the country. The lack of a royal name on either monument means that the dating cannot be determined precisely; Amenmose is not known from any other monuments. The two statues, of granodiorite and both very damaged, are now in the Egyptian Museum, Cairo. Both relate aspects of Amenmose's involvement in the construction and elaboration of temples and temple equipment in Thebes and, in the case of the first statue translated here, in the Delta. The statues also document Amenmose's endowment of his own property to the temple of Amun.

35A. Delta Statue

Internal evidence indicates that this statue originated from the west Delta, perhaps set up in a temple in the town of Na-Amun-Re which is mentioned in the text. The figure is seated cross-legged in the traditional pose of a scribe. Of the body, only the lower area of the torso and legs remain, to a height of 0.53 meters (1'7"). The remaining shapes of the hands on the lap indicate that the left held the papyrus roll, while the right was poised to write. The text on the lap fills the area where a papyrus roll was traditionally laid out but breaks its boundaries, extending out to the edge of the kilt and running over both thighs and the shell palette that was originally shown on the knee. These erasures of iconographic elements may indicate that the statue was reused. The two lines of inscription around each side of the base are separated from each other by a single large ankh-*sign in the front center; two smaller* ankh-*signs separate the lines of inscription at the back center. The texts focus on detailed descriptions of works Amenmose undertook in temple foundations probably in Thebes, including the embellishment of portable shrines and statues; they also describe his construction of temples on reclaimed land in the Delta.*

On the papyrus roll, over the lap:
Royal fanbearer on the right of the king,[83]
document scribe of the lord of the Two Lands,
overseer of the treasury of Amun,
high steward of the Western River,
who gave his property to Amun-Re, king of the gods,
Amenmose, son of the dignitary, Paamun,

born of Nebetiunet, (of) Na-Amun-Re of the Western River;[84]

he says: I was overseer of works in the domain of Amun-Re, king of
     the gods,
in all the monuments of his domain
and in his House of Gold;[85]
its ceiling and its walls of gold,
its floor of pure silver,
doorleaves therein of hammered copper,
figured images in fine gold.

I performed service for the divine figures upon the Great Throne,[86]
being likewise of fine gold;
the shades, standards,
and protective equipment ⌜in⌝ gold.
I widened your great doorways of gold,
in the entrance of your great portable shrine with (its) seven
     carrying poles.

I was overseer of works for your Ogdoad of adoring baboons,[87]
which are in your forecourt.
I was overseer of works for your wooden columns (now covered
     with) gold,
which had been painted blue.

I was overseer of works for your portable shrine;
I placed it upon five carrying poles,
when it had been on three.
I created it again on seven,
established forever.[88]

I was overseer of works for your Ram sphinx,
the Great Protector of Thebes,
who is established in your open court
for eternity and perpetuity.
You (Amun) assented to him (the Ram sphinx) greatly
from your great portable shrine, with your Ennead.[89]

You favored me for it in the presence of the entire land,
and you caused me to be sated with [speech (?) … … …]
⌜established⌝ upon it (the statue?) forever upon the west of Thebes,[90]

Mut, Khonsu,
and Hathor being satisfied there.

Right half of base:
    I was the overseer of works for the noble staff
    of Amun-Re, king of the gods;
    I placed it upon a portable shrine with two poles[91]
    for the first time it was made (thus),
    for it used to be (upon) the shoulder of one *wab*-priest.

    I was overseer of works of Na-Amun-Re on the Western River.
    It had been a pool;
    I made for him chapels and shrines
    on its foundation in the domain of Amun.[92]

Left half of base:
    I was overseer of works in the temple of millions of years,
    "Imbued-with-Perpetuity," in the domain of Amun on the west of
        Thebes,[93]
    with its barques[94] and its Ennead
    resting within until eternity.

    I gave all my property to Amun-Re, king of the gods,
    consisting of male and female slaves,
    estates, vineyards,
    and cattle, (consisting) of all that I had accrued.
    It (the endowment) is established in every record office
    in documents of the palace and the domain of Amun likewise.[95]

35B. THEBAN STATUE (FIG. 10)

Amenmose's second scribe statue was found in 1897 in the Menset temple of Amun and the deified Eighteenth Dynasty queen Ahmose Nefertari in Qurna on the Theban West Bank. The head is missing but the remains of two long wig lappets are visible at the shoulder. It measures 0.82 meters (2'7") in height. The pose is similar to Amenmose's Delta statue (above, no. 35a), showing him holding a papyrus across his lap with his right hand poised to write. In contrast to his other statue, the borders of the papyrus roll set the boundaries for the text inscribed on it. Two lines of inscription wrap around the base, with two further lines on top of the base, one in front of the statue and one behind it. Despite the damage to the

Fig. 10. Theban Scribe Statue of Amenmose (no. 35b; after Borchardt 1934, pl. 170).

texts and the uncertainty of a number of readings, enough remains to indicate that they treat aspects of Amenmose's work in temples. These may have been some of the same buildings as those described in his Delta statue. The inscriptions also set out details of his property endowments to the estate of Amun.

On the papyrus roll, over the lap:
    [... ...], document scribe of the lord of the Two Lands,
    high steward of the Western River,
    overseer of the great treasury of Amun,
    Amen ⌜mose⌝, son of the dignitary, Paamun,
    born of Nebetiunet, of ⌜Na-Amun-Re on the⌝ <Western> ⌜River⌝;

    he says: I was overseer of works of Amun ...
    [*ca. 8 groups lost*]
    ⌜in his⌝ House of [Gold];
    ⌜its⌝ ceiling of [...]
    [... ...] its [...] in gold of [...]
    which is in gold, and in [...]
    [the brightness (?)] of his eyes.[96]

    I was (one who) [...] in the [...]
    [*rest lost*]

Around base:
    No priest, nor any deputy in the domain of Amun,
    nor any [...] of the West,
    acted (thus as) the servant of Ahmose Nefertari
    [since (?)] the primeval time on the west of Thebes,
    because of these servants whom I dismissed (?).[97]

    Moreover, as for my domain of authority,
    and my domain which is ...
    [*ca. 6 groups lost*]
    [singers, who sang for me (?) ... ...]
    each of them, whom I gave to the domain of Amun-Re, king of the
        gods;[98]
    it (Amenmose's endowment?) is established in ⌜the office of every
        domain⌝,
    in documents of the palace and of the domain of Amun,
    [being secured (?)] for [...] ⌜under the authority⌝ of the priest,
        Sa-[... ... ...][99]

Top of base:
    (in front of the statue) (This statue) which I placed (as) my [heir (?)]
        on the west of Thebes,[100]
    under the authority of Ahmose Nefertari,

in order that it be established for as long as eternity,
(behind the statue) whereas no priest, nor any ⌈deputy⌉ of the
    domain of Amun ⌈had acted⌉ (thus)
within (this temple?) for them (the deities) to the end of eternity
    and perpetuity.

IV

The Military

36. The Sistrophorous Statue of the Army Commander, Amenemone, from Thebes

Amenemone is known from a large number of monuments found through-out Egypt that attest to his considerable status and his influential family connec-tions. His father became high priest of Amun after the death of Nebwenenef (no. 1) and his elder brother Hori was a high priest of Onuris in Thinis. Other indi-viduals named on his monuments include high priests in Heliopolis and Coptos, the viceroy of Kush, Paser, and numerous other high-ranking priests and mili-tary men (e.g., KRI III, 272,1–274,6; Trapani 1995, 58–63).

This limestone statue, which is 0.69 meters high (2'3"), was found broken in several pieces in the northeast of the forecourt of Djeserakhet, the temple of Thutmose III at Deir el-Bahri. It is dedicated to Hathor and depicts the owner holding a Hathor-headed naos sistrum. The statue belongs to a new statue type that appeared in the Nineteenth Dynasty, which shows the protagonists bald and includes the title "bald one (js)" in the texts (Clère 1995). This designation, as well as the title "mediator (w̱ḥmw)" which is included in the text translated here, signal the statue's role as a priest of, and intermediary for, Hathor in the temple; neither is a title Amenemone held in life. Although the face and right hand of the statue were deliberately smashed, the line of the arm indicates that this hand was lifted and cupped in front of the mouth in a rare attitude that has been described as "begging." This gesture connects with the appeal to the living inscribed on the left side of the body in which the statue offers to perform its intermediary role in return for offerings.

Cartouches of Ramesses II are inscribed on the statue's shoulders and on the surfaces of the naos of the sistrum, which is set in front of the legs. A sin-gle column of inscription runs down the center of the sistrum's handle: Hathor, lady of Djesret, mistress of the West. The top of the naos bears a relief image of Hathor as a striding cow with a figure of a king, identified as Ramesses II by the cartouche Usermaatre Setepenre, kneeling beneath her muzzle. This image corresponds closely to the cult statue of Hathor and a king, which dominated the Hathor sanctuary in this temple complex (Romano 1979, 149). Thus Amenemone carries the most sacred elements in the sanctuary with him to the more accessible outer area of the temple where his statue stood, lending force to the text's claim that he was an intimate of the deity and intermediary for her.

The biography inscribed on the right side of the statue centers on Amenemone's career which began during Ramesses II's youth and culminated with high military positions and a role overseeing the construction of the king's "temple of millions of years," known now as the Ramesseum. His final appointment to the priesthood of the royal cult, a position attested for him only on this statue, complements that held in relation to Hathor, which is displayed by the statue's form and through the appeal to the living on the left side.

Right side:
>   Greatly favored of the Perfect God,
>   a confidant, excellent for his lord,
>   commander of the large army,
>   Amenemone, true of voice,
>   son of the dignitary, high priest of Amun,
>   Wenennefer, true of voice;

>   he says to this effect: I was a follower of His Person, when he was a
>   child.
>   He appointed me charioteer and overseer of horses, when he was
>   lord (king).
>   My lord favored me for my excellence,
>   and he appointed me commander of his army.

>   My lord favored me for my abilities,
>   and he sent me as a royal messenger to all foreign lands;
>   I reported to him concerning the lands in their every aspect.
>   He favored me again for my excellence
>   and he appointed me overseer of works in all his monuments.

>   He favored me again for my effectiveness
>   and he appointed me overseer of works
>   in his temple of millions of years
>   of the Dual King, Usermaatre Setepenre (Ramesses II), in the
>   domain of Amun.

>   I was one unique, excellent,

effective for his lord;
he appointed me *ka*-priest for his statue.
He made my property in all respects,
[... ... ...]

Commander of the large army,
Amenemone, true of voice,
born of ⌜the great one of the harem of⌝ Amun-Re in Karnak,
Ese, true of voice.

Left side:
Greatly favored of the Perfect God,
royal messenger to every foreign land,
commander of the large army,
Amenemone, true of voice,
son of the dignitary, high priest of Amun,
Wenennefer, true of voice;

he says: I am the bald one of the goddess,
the mediator for his mistress.
Anyone with petitions,
speak ⌜them to⌝ my ear,
so that I may repeat them to my mistress in her hour of indulgence.[1]

Give me beer upon my hand,
sermet-beer for my mouth,
sweet ointment for my bald head,
fresh garlands for my throat,
pour out wine and beer for me,
(for) I am a bald one of Gold.[2]

If there is no beer,
give me cool water,
because the mistress desires a bald one who is satisfied.
Flood water onto the ground for me,
for I was one prosperous on ⌜earth⌝.
I did not knowingly speak falsehood, (I) did not act duplicitously.
I reached this (place)[3] as one who acts truthfully;
I am in the position of a just man.

37. THE STELA OF THE OVERSEER OF WORKS AND CHIEF OF MEDJAY, [PENRE], FROM COPTOS (FIG. 11)

Although the term "Medjay" originally designated a nomadic people of the Eastern Desert who were deployed as mercenaries in the Egyptian army, by the early New Kingdom it was a general term for security patrols sometimes without any specific ethnic association. In the Nineteenth Dynasty, the title "chief of Medjay" was also often connected with the direction of building works; the overseer of building works in the mortuary temple of Ramesses II (the Ramesseum), Amenemone, whose biography is translated above (no. 36), held this title on some of his monuments. Although the protagonist's name is lost on the stela treated here, it probably belonged to Penre, whose title strings on a number of Theban monuments are similar to those it bears. These include his role as overseer of works in the Ramesseum and military titles, among which are troop commander, chief charioteer, and overseer of foreign lands (cf. KRI III, 269,5–6; Nims 1956, 146–47).

Two badly damaged statues belonging to Penre were found in the small mortuary chapel of Wadjmose, probably a son of Thutmose I, just south of the Ramesseum. One of these bears traces of a biographical text, part of which concerns Penre's work in the Ramesseum: "... I constructed works in his (the king's) temple of millions of years; I was rewarded with silver and gold of (royal) favor and every good thing of his giving ..." (KRI III, 269,16–270,1). The fragmentary text translated here narrates an oracle of Isis received by Penre that probably relates to his offices (the details are unclear). This biography is striking in including the direct speech of a goddess to a nonroyal person; in this it can be compared with the texts in the tomb of Djehutyemheb (no. 12).

The limestone stela fragment was found by Petrie at the rear of the temple of Thutmose III in Coptos and is now in the Ashmolean Museum, Oxford. Although the lower half of the stela is lost, consisting of approximately one half to two thirds of each of the eighteen text columns, the scene in the lunette and the upper sections of text in the lower register are well-preserved. The fragment is now 0.95 meters (3'1") high and may have originally been ca. 1.5 meters (4'11").

The scene shows a figure of Ramesses II censing before a barque held aloft by twelve priests. Another priest, wearing a panther skin, is depicted in the center of the barque carriers, beneath the shrine, with one arm raised in adoration. Three columns above the figure of the king read: Presenting incense to his mother Isis, by her son, Dual King, lord of the Two Lands, Usermaatre Setepenre, son of Re, lord of appearances, Ramesses Meryamun. *Above the king is a protective falcon with the hieroglyph of the* sed-*festival in its claws. Two columns beneath its wings read:* May he (Horus) give an eternity of sed-festivals. *Behind the king is a column of text:* All protection and life around him like Re forever. *The prow*

Fig. 11. Stela of Penre (no. 37; after Petrie 1896, pl. 19, upper; courtesy of the
Ashmolean Museum, Oxford).

*and stern of the barque bear aegises of a goddess wearing a crown of horns and
a disc. The column at the center of the lunette, above the prow of the barque,
identifies the barque's deity:* Isis the great, god's mother. *A vulture above the
barque, clutching a* shen-*ring signifying perpetual protection in its claws, has a
short caption beneath one outstretched wing:* May she give all life and power;
*this identifies the goddess as Nekhbet. Between the barque and the king is a col-
umn with a speech of its goddess:* I have given to you the years of Horus as ruler
of every land. *It is likely that an adoring figure of Penre was included in the lost
bottom right corner of the stela.*

Overseer of works in the temple of
Usermaatre Setepenre (Ramesses II)
[in the domain of Amun (?)],
[*one half to two thirds of column lost, giving titles*]
[Penre, true of voice],
ꜗborn of *x-*ꜗsakhmet, true of voice;

he says: Greetings to you, Isis [the great (?)],
[*rest of column of epithets lost*]
... his ꜗunique oneꜗ,[4]
perfect of face in the day-barque,
great of ꜗterrorꜗ [in the night-barque (?)],
...
[who abhors (?)] evil, who drives out uproar,[5]
who removes ...
who rescues the weak from the aggressive
... upon the ground of your (?) city,
invoking ...
[(so) you will not be] far [from me (?)]
...

... ꜗmeꜗ in Egypt.
I stood among ...
[taking my position among (?)] the companions as chief of Medjay.
[I was] appointed ...[6]
this servant (Penre) reached his city
in order to give praise to Isis,
in order to ꜗhonorꜗ [her perfection (?)]
... every day.

Then she stopped before this chief of Medjay,
[Bunakhtef (?)] ...
and she assented to him,[7] and she placed me at his side,
and I [kissed the ground before her (?)],
...
[She said]: "What I have done for Bunakhtef,[8]
I will do for you.
I will [appoint you (?) ...]"
...
saying: "yes!" emphatically.[9]

I made a stela accordingly ...
[... according] to her utterance,
and all her enduring and effective counsels for her action cannot be
        opposed.
How fortunate is the one who [places her in his heart (?)],
...
so that there will happen to him what happened to me.[10]

I acted as overseer of the foreign lands in the Northern lands.
I acted as ⌜chief of⌝ Medjay likewise,
charioteer of His Person,
royal messenger to every land,
overseer of works ⌜in the⌝ temple of
Usermaatre Setepenre (Ramesses II) in the domain of Amun,
as (would any) effective servant like me.
Isis granted me [... ...]

38. The Stela of the Marine Standard Bearer, Khetef

*No photograph or description of this stela has been published since Paul
Pierret's brief description and partial hand copy in 1878 (1–2). The stela's provenance is also unknown. Pierret's treatment indicates that the upper register bore
a representation of the protagonist and members of his family with the following
caption:* [Standard bearer] of the crew of (the ship) "(Ra)messes-Meryamun
(Ramesses II)-who-propitiates-the-sun-disc," Khetef, true of voice, possessor
of veneration, and his sister, lady of the house, his beloved, Taweret, true of
voice. *The short biographical text in the lower register narrates Khetef's leading
position in the army, in contrast with his relatively modest title, and a role in
ceremonial performance relating to his king, probably Ramesses II. These statements follow an offering formula addressed to Osiris, Isis, and Horus, the details
of which Pierret did not record.*

[An offering which the king gives to Osiris,
Isis, and Horus (?) ...]
for the *ka* of the standard bearer of the crew of (the ship)
        "Propitiating-the-sun-disc,"
Khetef, true of voice;

he says: I speak to you, everyone who lives upon earth:
I was leader of the king's army,
the first of his ranks.
I was announced in the presence of His Person
to [consult on] every plan of action (?).[11]

I sailed the king in the royal barque,
⌜commanding it (?)⌝ as the head of his ⌜crew⌝.
I called out before him, I proclaimed his name,
I extolled (?) (his) power in his presence, being favored (on account
    of it).[12]

39. The Stela of the Stablemaster, Bakaa (fig. 12)

The stablemaster Bakaa is known from two stelae of unknown provenance now in the British Museum, one of which may have been dedicated by him for his brother, the charioteer Huy (not presented here). Stablemasters were also connected with the army; introduced in the Second Intermediate period, horses were prestige military animals. The two stelae are similar in size and compositional features, including the dates of sed-festivals of Ramesses II in the lunettes. Only the stela treated here incorporates biographical material in its inscription.

This stela is 1.15 meters high (3'9") and is divided into three registers of scenes in the lunette with thirteen lines of text below. An inscription at the top of the lunette records the fifth sed-festival of Ramesses II: Year 37, being the fifth sed-festival ⌜on the⌝ throne of [his father Ptah-Tatenen (?)]. Ramesses II's third sed-festival, however, was held in year 37 and his fifth in year 42; it is possible that the number 3 was later changed to 5 as a way of updating the stela. Below is a pair of reclining figures of the jackal god Anubis with vessels above them. The figures are captioned: Anubis. Hieroglyphs inscribed behind them designate one as of Upper Egypt and the other of Lower Egypt. Each faces an imiut-fetish, a stuffed skin tied to a pole that was a symbol of Anubis and Osiris. Between the figures is a shen-ring and a water pot. This scene is separated from the one below by a long cartouche with much of the titulary of Ramesses II: Horus, strong bull, beloved of Maat, Dual King, Usermaatre Setepenre, son of Re, Ramesses Meryamun, beloved of Osiris Khentimentu, great god, lord of Abydos. The second register depicts Bakaa kneeling with his arms raised in adoration before Osiris, who is seated on a throne with a row of ten gods standing behind him. The caption above Bakaa reads: Adoring Osiris by the stablemaster Bakaa, true

Fig. 12. Stela of Bakaa (no. 39; copyright the Trustees of the British Museum).

of voice, possessor of veneration. *Osiris is captioned with his name. The other deities are not captioned but some can be recognized by their iconography as: Horus, Isis, two canid-headed gods (perhaps Anubis of South and North as in the lunette), Re-Horakhty, Onuris, Sekhmet, Thoth, and Khnum. The final deity is Hathor, who is represented as a cow emerging from a mountain.*

The third scene shows Bakaa standing offering incense and pouring a libation before eleven kneeling kin and colleagues; the women hold lotus blooms and the men scepters. Bakaa's caption reads: Stablemaster of the Residence, Bakaa. *The figures are captioned with their names and titles, beginning with Bakaa's parents:* ⌜His father⌝, god's father of Pre, Haunefer; his mother, Reiay; his brother, Panehsy, true of voice, possessor of veneration; his sister, Tepi, true of voice, possessor of veneration; his brother, scribe of the domain of Re, Iryiry; his sister, Maya, true of voice; his brother, the charioteer, Ptahmaya, true of voice; songstress of Pre, Puia, true of voice; his sister, Ti, true of voice; by the stablemaster, Bakaa, true of voice; the lady of the house, songstress of Pre, Nebttawy, true of voice. *The inclusion of the protagonist among figures receiving offerings from himself is striking and may be a way of representing all of the kin group together as well as laying particular claim to the stela. The figures in the scenes are carved in low relief with no internal detail; the scene and texts were originally painted yellow and must have had a striking, silhouette-like effect when complete. In the lower right corner of the stela is another figure of Bakaa kneeling with his arms raised in adoration; this figure is carved with slightly more internal detail than those in the upper register.*

The inscription in the lower register begins with a long hymn to Osiris; this is followed by statements relating to moral character that are oriented to judgment in the next world. The hymn and the passages concerning judgment before Osiris have parallels, with minor variations, on a stela belonging to an Amenmose who held the titles "royal table scribe" and "overseer of hunters of Amun-Re" in the reign of Ramesses II (KRI III, 218,12–219,8).

> Giving praise to Osiris,
> kissing the ground for Wenennefer,
> by the stablemaster Bakaa, true of voice;
>
> he says: O my lord, who traverses eternity,
> who will exist perpetually,
> sovereign of the gods, ruler of rulers,
> sovereign, Horus of the Horuses, whose paths exist always;
> you are known among gods and men,
> you designate their places in the necropolis,
> and they pray to your *ka*.

(For) those who come for millions and millions (of years),
the end (of life) is mooring with you.[13]
(For) those who are in the womb,
their faces are before you.
There can be no lingering in Egypt: they are (soon) with you.

All come to you,
great and small;
to you belong those who live upon earth,
everyone will reach you all together.
You are their lord, there being none other except you.
These (people) entirely, they are yours.
If one travels south or north within the span of a lifetime,
Your Person is tomorrow, as Re,[14]
and everyone is under your charge.

Bakaa, true of voice,
he says: I have come before you, knowing your ways:
you equip (yourself) with your forms in the underworld,
and you sit, Maat before you,
judging hearts upon the scale.[15]

I am before you, my heart bearing Maat,
and my breast without falsehood in it.
May I adore your power and your might,
propitiating the Ennead of the necropolis.
May I give you jubilation.
May I make acclamation for you, without wearying,
by the stablemaster Bakaa, true of voice.

He says: As for any people who live on earth,
all who will come after my lifetime,
and who will pass by my tomb,
every scribe who deciphers (documentary) writing,
who comprehends hieroglyphs,
may you listen without distaste;
delight (in it), take pleasure,
for this is no burden that would be heavy on your hearts.

Do not disregard my speech inasmuch as you are excellent,
(for) I was effective on earth and I have gathered up my goodness

before you;
I was truthful, the son of one true of heart,
loyal to his lord.
I did that which contents his *ka* and propitiates the gods,
following them, without a misdeed being mentioned,
presenting to his (Osiris's) *ka*, having performed every action
    perfectly.

I did not conceal anything from anyone.
I was one who raised up what was ruined, who eased distress,
being one confident,[16] free from vacillation,
content with any goodness, who masters (his) character,
whose words are in the place of what is true;
for the *ka* of the stablemaster, Bakaa, true of voice,
son of the dignitary, Haunefer, true of voice, <repeating> life.

40. THE DOOR JAMBS OF THE OVERSEER OF THE ARMY, NEHESY, FROM MEMPHIS

These two limestone jambs were found during 1956 excavations at Memphis (Mit Rahina). They had been reused as covering slabs for a Twenty-first Dynasty tomb outside the southern wall of the Ptah temple complex. Although it is possible that the jambs adorned the entrance to Nehesy's house, extended biographical material is rarely included on house doors and it seems more likely that they were a component of a tomb or memorial chapel (Budka 2001, 39–40, 239). An unnamed king is the central focus of the texts on the jambs; dating is consequently uncertain, but the forms of the hieroglyphs and features of text content point to the Nineteenth Dynasty.

Found in fragments and preserving only the upper sections, both jambs are of a similar size: the left jamb measures 1.6 meters (5'3") high and 0.52 meters (1'8") wide while the right measures 1.66 meters (5'5") by 0.45 meters (1'5"). Each jamb bears three columns of inscription presenting complementary aspects of the same key event, namely, Nehesy's elevation to the council of thirty, the core group of the highest officials. The left inscription provides necessary background concerning Nehesy's performance of his duties and the resulting royal recognition. The text on the right narrates episodes in the ceremonial surrounding Nehesy's induction, including extracts of speeches probably voiced by the king. The inclusion of these statements and their lack of introductory formulas is striking, especially in comparison with the formal royal speeches to the high priests of Amun, Nebwenenef (no. 1) and Amenhotep (no. 7). The treatment in Nehesy's texts may generate an intimacy and immediacy of setting and expresses the closeness of his relationship to the king.

Left jamb:
> Giving praise to your *ka*, O perfect sovereign,
> kissing the ground for the lord of the Two Lands,
> the god who nourishes people and who propitiates the gods,
> by the true royal scribe, beloved of him,
> overseer of the army of the lord of the Two Lands,
> Nehesy, true of voice.

> ⌜He says⌝: [*rest of column lost, including the beginning of an appeal to the living*]
> to every scribe who deciphers (documentary) writing,
> who comprehends hieroglyphs:
> I will cause to be known what happened to me
> —the beneficient acts my lord did for me—
> (for) I was a follower who followed his lord,
> a scribe of the troops,
> my command being [...], [my] instruction being [...],
> [*rest of column lost*]

> ... who guides a man on his journeys.
> My lord perceived me for my excellence
> and he appointed me to the position of a (royal) confidant,
> magnifying me among the officials;
> I was promoted to the council of thirty;
> for the *ka* of the true royal scribe, beloved of him,
> overseer of ⌜the army of the lord of the Two Lands,
> Nehesy, true of voice ... (?)⌝.

Right jamb:
> Giving praise to the victorious king.
> I adore his *ka* and Re-Atum,
> the sole god without equal,
> in whose possession are health and life,
> by the true royal scribe, beloved of him,
> overseer of the army of the lord of the Two Lands,
> Nehesy, true of voice.

He says: I was a scribe, truly precise,
effective [for his lord …]
[*rest of column lost*]
My reputation was made in the midst of the great ones,
having joined the council of thirty:

"Your step is as a count of the companions,[17]
your nobility (comes) through the *ka* of the king.
One (the king) is content with your speech."
[…] prayed […]
[*rest of column lost*]
"he is truly a man (of standing)."

He assessed me before millions,
for I am estimable in his heart:
"He is great," he (the king) said to me,
"when he offers and presents offerings."[18]

I have not left his side:
"my arms are together, bearing your *ka*;"[19]
for the *ka* of the ⌜true⌝ royal scribe, ⌜beloved of him,
overseer of the army of the lord of the Two Lands,
Nehesy, true of voice … (?)⌝.

V

Administering Nubia

Nubia is the stretch of the Nile Valley upstream from Egypt to the confluence of the Atbara and the Nile. The term Lower Nubia is used to designate the area between the first and second cataracts, known in the New Kingdom as Wawat. Upper Nubia, termed Kush in Egyptian sources, begins at the second cataract and continues to the ancient frontier at Kurgus. Nubia was rich in mineral resources, notably gold, and was also the main trading link for exotic commodities from further south in Africa. Military and economic control of part or all of Nubia had therefore been a priority for Egyptian kings since the Old Kingdom.

All the texts translated in this chapter concern or make reference to viceroys of Nubia. This post, which was created in the New Kingdom, concentrated administrative control of the area in the hands of one individual. The viceroy also governed the first three Upper Egyptian nomes, almost as far north as Thebes. Thus, alongside the position of vizier, that of viceroy was one of the most powerful and influential offices; its close relationship to the king is indicated by the literal meaning of the title as "king's son of Kush."

41A–B. The Inscriptions of Setau, Viceroy of Kush

Setau is first attested as viceroy of Kush on a double rock-cut stela that he dedicated at the temple of Abu Simbel in year 38 of Ramesses II. He was viceroy for at least twenty-five years, the longest known tenure of the office; the date when he left office is not known. The details of Setau's early career, which are narrated in his Wadi el-Sebua stela (no. 41b), indicate that he came from a civic rather than military background, in contrast to most of his predecessors in office. Setau is attested in at least one hundred sources distributed across Egypt and Nubia (see Raedler 2003, 140–45, fig. 8), and the range and scale of these dedications emphasize his status and influence. His now badly damaged tomb is in the high-status necropolis of Dra Abu el-Naga in Thebes. Architectural elements found at Abydos and Memphis indicate that he established commemorative chapels in those places. He also set up rock-cut chapels at Elkab in southern Upper Egypt which was in his own territory, and in Nubia at the sites of Qasr Ibrim and Faras. However, the majority of his known monuments come from the temple of Wadi el-Sebua. This temple, one of two he built for Ramesses II as new foundations, can therefore be seen as the central, culminating achievement of Setau's career and biography, and it forms the core element of the narrative on his stela translated below (no. 41b).

41A. INSCRIPTIONS FROM A CHAPEL AT ELKAB

Setau dedicated a number of monuments at Elkab including a rock-cut chapel and a small free-standing structure known as the "Thoth chapel" or "Hammam." Badly damaged scenes belonging to Setau in the entrance of the "Thoth chapel" include some biographical statements. Scenes on the side walls show Ramesses offering before various deities. An unusual scene on the rear wall seems to allude to the myth of the merging of the solar eye with the sun-god through the mediation of Thoth and Onuris (Derchain 1971, 72–73; Raedler 2003, 147–49). A statue of the king probably stood inside the chapel, linking the cult of the king with that of the sun-god. For scenes of a nonroyal person to be included with scenes showing the king before gods, in a chapel dedicated to a god, is exceptional.

Setau is depicted adoring Thoth on the thicknesses of the chapel doorway. On the interior wall to the left and right of the entrance he is shown presenting eulogies of the king. These eulogies may have been addressed to the deities depicted on the right and left interior walls. Nine columns of the eulogy on the left of the entrance wrap around a figure of Setau who stands, facing right, with his right arm raised in a gesture of address. In his left hand he holds a fan with streamers. A similar image is carved on the right of the entrance, also with nine columns of text. Here Setau holds a fan across his body with his left hand. The phrases and epithets in these texts can perhaps be seen as condensed formulations of the theme of the long narrative set up at Wadi el-Sebua (no. 41b).

> *Left thickness of doorway, above figure of baboon:*
> ⌜Words spoken by⌝ Thoth,
> who resides in ⌜Roinet⌝,[1] great god.
> May ⌜he⌝ give life, prosperity, and health.

> *Left thickness of doorway, above figure of Setau:*
> Giving ⌜praise to Thoth⌝,

[…], lord of hieroglyphs, […];
made by the viceroy of Kush, Setau.

Right thickness of doorway, above figure of baboon:
Thoth, lord of hieroglyphs in <Ro>inet.

Right thickness of doorway, above figure of Setau:
Adoring ⌐Thoth⌐, lord of hieroglyphs,
[…] giving […]
[*final column lost, with traces*]

Interior wall, left of entrance, before figure of Setau:
[… …] ⌐Nekhbet⌐,
⌐lady⌐ of …
[*ca. 6 groups lost, with traces*]
⌐she of⌐ the upper district,[2]
[… … …]

⌐that they may protect the king⌐, lord of the Two Lands,
Usermaatre Setepenre (Ramesses II),
and that they may give to him valor and ⌐victory⌐,
[all flat-lands (?)] and all hill-countries [having fallen (?)] beneath
          his sandals,
for eternity ⌐and perpetuity⌐.

⌐By⌐ [one greatly favored (?)] ⌐by⌐ His Person,
overseer of [… … …],
leader of all festivals in ⌐Thebes⌐,
⌐steward⌐ of ⌐Amun-Re⌐,
overseer of the ⌐southern⌐ foreign lands,
[… … …], ⌐Setau⌐;

⌐he says⌐: I was a servant, [effective for his lord],
[the overseer of] his double treasury […],
favored by ⌐his lord⌐,
[who rejoiced (?)] because of my perfection,
placing me at the head of his courtiers,
[…] on account of what I said.

Interior wall, right of entrance, before figure of Setau:
[*ca. three-quarters of column lost with traces*]
… Horus of Nekhen.[3]

[*ca. three-quarters of column lost*]
ˈthat they may protectˈ the king, lord of the Two Lands,
Usermaatre ˈSetepenˈre
ˈlord of appearances, Ramesses Meryamun,
who givesˈ [...] ˈto (?)ˈ [*ca. 8 groups lost*]

This servant (Setau) was [... ...]
one uniquely excellent, truly assiduous.
[*ca. 6 groups lost*]
[effective with] words, ˈpatientˈ,
[*1 column lost with traces*]
[... in the morning (?)] in order to consult with him,
viceroy of Kush,
Setau, [true of voice].

41B. STELA FROM WADI EL-SEBUA

The range of concerns encompassed by the role of viceroy is demonstrated by this biographical stela dedicated by Setau in the temple of Wadi el-Sebua. This temple, named "the temple of Ramesses-Meryamun-in-the-domain-of-Amun," was built by Setau on behalf of Ramesses II and dedicated to Amun-Re, Re-Horakhty, and the deified king. The second court of the temple seems to have been the central zone for displaying Setau's administrative and cult responsibilities and for presenting his role as intermediary for other individuals associated with the temple. Setau's biographical stela was found in situ against the north wall of this court, set up in a row with six other stelae. Setau's stela, at almost twice the height of the others, dominated the group. The others belonged to soldiers, and their surviving inscriptions state that they were dedicated for Setau. A further eight visually similar stelae dedicated by Setau and his staff were found in disturbed contexts elsewhere in the temple and probably belonged with or were related to this group. That these small stelae establish Setau as a patron for his client soldiers and staff is clear from their visual similarity to his stela, the dedicatory setting within the temple, and the inscriptions that mention Setau. Two stelae from this group also bear narrative texts relating to Setau's; the most complete of these is translated below (no. 42).

Setau's stela is 1.9 meters (6'2") in height and was carved from poor quality sandstone. It is framed on either side with jambs each bearing a single column of inscription. That on the left reads: [unknown amount lost], ˈDual Kingˈ, lord of the Two Lands, Usermaatre Setepenre, given life; one greatly favored, beloved of his lord, viceroy of Kush, overseer of the gold lands of Amun, fanbearer on the right of the king, overseer of the double treasury, festival leader of Amun, royal scribe, Setau, true of voice. *The right jamb bears a similar inscription:* [*unknown amount lost*], son of Re, lord of appearances, Ramesses Meryamun, given life; one greatly favored of the Perfect God, viceroy of Kush, overseer of the southern lands, fanbearer on the right of the king, high steward of Amun, royal scribe, Setau, true of voice, in peace. *The stela was probably topped by a lintel (the lintel displayed above the stela in the Egyptian Museum in Cairo, was probably a door lintel rather than part of this monument).*

The scene in the upper register of the stela depicts Ramesses II on the left kneeling and offering vessels of wine before four seated deities, including the deified Ramesses II. His figure is captioned: Perfect God, lord of the Two Lands, lord of cult action, Usermaatre Setepenre, Ramesses Meryamun. Offering wine to his father Amun. *Captions above each deity give their name and epithets:* Amun-Re, lord of the thrones of the Two Lands; lord of appearances, Ra⌈messes⌉ Meryamun; Mut, lady of the sky; ⌈Maat⌉, daughter of Re. *In the bottom left corner of the stela, adjacent to the last nine lines of text, are traces of a kneeling figure, presumably Setau, raising his arms in adoration.*

The biography, consisting of twenty-four lines of horizontal text, narrates Setau's career prior to becoming viceroy as well as his key activities in that position. These achievements include one of the very few nonroyal narrations of a military action known from the Ramessid period.

The surface of the stela is badly degraded and many readings are uncertain. I have drawn on the editions of Wolfgang Helck (1975) and Edward F. Wente (1985) for my translation; some but not all problems of reading are noted.

> Year ⌈44⌉, first month of *peret*, day 2,
> under the Person of Horus, strong bull, beloved of Maat,
> possessor of *sed*-festivals like his father Ptah-Tatenen;
> Two Ladies, protector of Egypt, who curbs foreign lands,
> the Re who fashions the gods ⌈and who founds the Two Lands,
>
> Golden Horus, mighty in years⌉ and great of victories;
> Dual King, lord of the Two Lands,
> Usermaatre Setepenre,
> son of Re, lord of ⌈appearances⌉,
> ⌈Ramesses Meryamun⌉ (Ramesses II)
> living for eternity and perpetuity.[4]
>
> Viceroy of Kush, overseer of the gold lands,
> fanbearer on the right of the king, royal scribe,
> Setau, true of voice,

says, in extolling this Perfect God,
Horus, beloved of Maat:

[I was a servant] whom His Person [himself] taught,
in the [majesty of the (?)] palace,
for I grew up in the palace when I was a youth,
[... ...] speechless in the affairs of the [one who is in the palace (?)].⁵
I was provided with ⌜complete⌝ rations from [the meal for the king],
while [I was in the room of writing and] in school.⁶
I was recognized [as one who performs beneficent acts for (?)] his
          lord,
while I was the [great (?) ...] of His Person.

I was recognized while I was a youth,
and I was appointed as chief scribe of the vizier.
I assessed the entire land with my great pen,
just as a venerated one of the king, truly unique and assiduous.
Fault ⌜was not⌝ found with me in anything that I did,
for I acted in every beneficent way
for my lord, since he recognized me.

I instituted divine offerings for all the gods,
and I increased the [regular offerings] for every day
through perfect action.
Their treasuries were overflowing,
filled with produce,
their granaries approached the sky,
with heaps of emmer
and goods as apportioned.
They were established as many [... ...],
[grain (?)] being under my control.

My lord recognized me as effective,
in delivering ⌜the grain of⌝ the granaries—
winnowed grain by the million.
I caused the granaries to be pregnant with the harvest,⁷
and I measured it (?) [...]
[... in order to nourish (?)] all lands.
[This land did not oppose me (?) ... ...]
[and I caused their] children to extol His Person.⁸

˹He˺ promoted ˹me˺ to high steward
of Amun[-Re, king of the gods, (?)]
and [I performed (?)] my [functions (?)] while I was overseer of the
        double treasury,
and festival leader of Amun.
The braziers of gold were in my hands,
presenting before him, exalting His ˹Person˺,
˹honoring˺ the lord of the Two Lands, ˹each time he appeared˺,
[adoring Amun on behalf of] the sovereign,
my god who built me up through his ˹guidance (?)˺,
that he (Amun) might grant him eternity as king of the Two Lands.[9]

Again my lord recognized my name because of the greatness of my
        excellence;
I was appointed as viceroy
of [this] land [of Kush (?)], [overseer of the (?)] gold [lands].
Northerners presented to him (the king),
in tens of thousands and thousands,
Nubians by the hundreds of thousands without limit.

I brought in all the assessments of this land
of Kush, in double measure.
I caused ˹the tribute˺ of this land of Kush
to be ˹like˺ the sand of the shore,
for no viceroy of Kush had done it
since the time of the god.

The powerful forearm of Pharaoh, (my) perfect lord, plundered
the land of ˹wretched˺ Irem.
[He captured the] chief of Akerty,[10]
together with his wife, child, and all his staff;
I was the army commander leading the way at the head of his army,
for no [viceroy of] Kush had (previously) trod this path (?).
I stepped out (with) all those who were captured through my action
and brought together in one place.
I informed one (the king) of them, and they were taken to Egypt.

Then ˹I built the temple˺
of "Ramesses-Meryamun-in-the-domain-of-Amun,"[11]
carved from the [western] mountain as a construction of eternity,[12]
filled with numerous people of the plundering of His Person,

its storehouses being filled with goods approaching ⌜the sky⌝,
[barley (?)], emmer, and many grains,
while he (the king?) is within the shrine of Amun-of-Ramesses-
        Meryamun,
lord of the ways,[13]
Horus of Quban with him,[14]
[... ... ...]
great [...] of/from the south.

I (re)built all the temples of this land of Kush,
all of which had previously fallen into ruin,
made anew in the great name of ⌜His⌝ Person,
his ⌜cartouche⌝ being established upon them perpetually.

My lord favored me on account of what I had done
and he made me exalted.
He caused me to sit in the court in order to judge the Two Lands,
being foremost [of the companions], at the head of the courtiers.
My response made the lead for them
when judging cases, and they concurred with me,
(agreeing) entirely with my [counsel (?)],
[after my (?)] speaking Maat, without doing anything false,
for I know that His Person loves Maat.

She is the one who [protects (?)] him.
And I am the servant of Maat, great [...];[15]
⌜she⌝ instructed [my lord and she caused] him to recognize me,
as I sought to perform beneficent acts for him with a loving [heart].
He placed (me) at the head of the courtiers, so that I might mingle
        with the favored ones.

Let every noble do what I have done for my lord,
since he recognized my form and my character entirely,
so that their names (also) [be recognized (?)];
for the *ka* of the viceroy of Kush, overseer of the gold lands,
fanbearer on the right of the king, ⌜royal⌝ scribe,
Setau, true of voice.

42. The Stela of the *sek*-officer, Ramose, from Wadi el-Sebua

Ramose's stela was found in four pieces north of the row of sphinxes that lines the axis of the temple of Wadi el-Sebua in its first court (Barsanti and Gauthier 1911, 83). It belongs to the group of "client" stelae which were dedicated in association with the biographical stela of the viceroy Setau (above, no. 41b). Ramose's is a small, rectangular stela (68 centimeters high by 53 centimeters wide, 2'2" by 1'7") with framing texts on either side, mimicking the jambs which flank Setau's larger stela. The framing texts on the left read: An offering which the king gives to the royal *ka*, lord of appearances, Ramesses-Meryamun-in-the-domain-of-Amun, that he may give ⸢life, prosperity, and health for the *ka* of⸣ the viceroy of Kush, Setau, true of voice. Made by the *sek*-officer Ramose. *Those on the right are dedicated to a form of Amun who, in Setau's biography, is said to be present in the temple at Wadi el-Sebua:* An offering which the king gives to Amun, lord of the ways, that he may give favors [... ...] of the king for the *ka* of the viceroy of Kush, Setau, true of voice. Made by the *sek*-officer, Ramose.*

The upper register of the stela shows Ramesses II offering incense and libations to Amun, the deified Ramesses II, and two goddesses (possibly Anat and Hathor). Cartouches of the king are inscribed above him: Usermaatre Setepenre, Ramesses Meryamun, given life. *The deities are depicted within a portable shrine on a pedestal. A rampant lion is shown on the side. The shrine is captioned:* Ramesses-Meryamun-in-the-domain-of-Amun. *In the lower register a figure, probably Ramose, kneels with his arms raised in adoration and a stick or club tucked beneath his left arm. The text records, in eight lines, Setau's receipt of a royal command to recruit for a military action. This action, against different groups of people from those mentioned in Setau's stela, was intended to provide a work force to complete the temple of Wadi el-Sebua. Ramose's stela is one of two within the group of client stelae on which a narrative text survives. Traces of narrative, including the date "year 44, first month of peret," are also visible on the heavily damaged stela of a man called Paheripedjet (not translated here).*

Year 44: His Person commanded ⸢(his) confidant (?)⸣,
the viceroy of Kush, Setau, <true of> voice,
and the soldiers of the company of Ramesses Meryamun
(called) "Amun-is-the-protector-of-(his)-son,"
that he should plunder the land of Libya in order to build in the temple
of "Ramesses-Meryamun-in-the-domain-of-Amun,"[16]
as well as commanding the *sek*-officer Ramose

to muster from the company;[17]
by the *sek*-officer Ramose.

43. THE STELA OF THE FANBEARER, ⌜HOR/MUT⌝EMHEB, FROM SAI ISLAND

This fragment of the mid-section of a stela was found in the late 1950s during excavations in the extensive fortress on Sai Island in Upper Nubia, between the second and third cataracts. Traces of a recumbent animal on a pedestal are visible in the upper register, while the lower register bears the remains of nine columns of a longer inscription. Much of the text is lost and I do not specify the extent of the lacunae. It records the protagonist's service under the viceroy of Kush, Setau, as well as his predecessors in office, Paser and possibly Huy. In biography, such enumeration of actions had traditionally been oriented to the king. This stela therefore presents Setau and his predecessors in a quasi-pharaonic role.

[*unknown number of columns lost*]
... [the fanbearer] ⌜Hor/Mut⌝emheb;
⌜he⌝ says: [I performed *x* office for ...]
the steward of <Amun-Re (?)>
and viceroy Setau ...
[...] of/for Amun.

I acted as a scribe [...] in ...
[years that I spent for my Horus (?)],
(as) overseer of cattle of Amun ⌜in⌝ ...

I acted as account scribe of gold
(for) the overseer of the gold lands of Kush,
for [the king (?)] ...
[...umaat (?)] .[18]

I put them [in] writing ...
[for] the viceroy Paser.
I made ...

... [for the viceroy Huy (?)], while ...

[... ...] them, [in order to (?)] ...
[*rest lost*]

44A–B. The Tomb of the Deputy of Wawat, Penniut, at Aniba

Aniba (Miam in Egyptian) was the administrative center of Lower Nubia (Wawat). Penniut held the position of deputy of Wawat during the reign of Ramesses VI and his tomb was constructed in the necropolis at Aniba. It was dismantled and reassembled upstream near Amada during the salvage of monuments in Nubia in the 1960s, at the time of the construction of the Aswan High Dam. The tomb's hall is vividly decorated with scenes of Penniut and his family before various deities, offering scenes, and others that relate to his judgment and transition to the next world. In the shrine are three unfinished rock-cut statues, of which the central figure, with a cow's head, probably represents Hathor. Although the texts translated here, which relate a land donation and Penniut's reward by Ramesses VI, are not biographical in a narrow sense, they are a striking example of an alternative stategy for displaying events relating to an individual's biography within the tomb.

44A. Endowment Text (Fig. 13)

This inscription, probably a copy or adaptation of an original papyrus document, records an endowment made by Penniut for a statue of the king. It is inscribed in twenty lines in a rectangular area next to the entrance to the tomb, in the east (right) half of the hall. The inscription fills the whole of this area of the wall. The upper section of the text is flanked by figures of gods who perhaps ratify the endowment. On the right are standing figures of Amun, Mut, and Khonsu, who face left toward the text. An offering formula begins in a column in front of Amun and continues beneath the figures: An offering which the king gives to Amun-Re, king of the gods, to Mut the great, lady of Asheru, and to Khonsu in Thebes, lord of happiness, for the *ka* of the Osiris of the deputy, Penniut, true of voice, son of Heru<nefer>. *On the left are figures of Ptah and Thoth. The caption before them reads:* An offering which the king gives to Ptah, lord of Maat, king of the Two Lands, perfect of face upon the great throne, and to Thoth, lord of hieroglyphs, scribe of the Ennead. *The text in the line below them is the final part of an offering formula and prayer, which runs through all three walls in this half of the hall, dividing upper and lower registers. To the right*

Fig. 13. Endowment Text of Penniut (no. 44a: Breasted Expedition photograph, 1905–1907; courtesy of the Oriental Institute of the University of Chicago).

of the lower part of the endowment inscription, beneath the depiction of the Theban triad, are standing figures of two men. Penniut is depicted in front, wearing a long robe and holding a large lotus bloom in his left hand. His right hand is raised in adoration. The figure behind has both hands raised in adoration. The captions above them read: The Osiris of the deputy, Penniut; overseer of the granary, Penre. *Penre is not named in other published texts from the tomb, and his relationship to Penniut cannot be determined. In the lower register to the left of the inscription, beneath Ptah and Thoth, are two figures of women who belong with the offering scenes on the adjacent wall.*

The text sets out the areas of fields rented to endow the statue-cult, the total surface of which amounted to 15 khet *(a little over 10 acres). At the end of the document, Penniut added a further parcel of land, perhaps from his own property, to ensure provision of a regular sacrifice.*

Endowment for the statue
of Ramesses Amunherkhopshef, god ruler of Heliopolis (Ramesses VI),
which rests in Miam.

District north of "Ramesses-meryamun-in-the-domain-of-Re,"[19]
the town(-district), opposite the domain of Pre, lord of the eastern
　　　　district:
(Boundaries:) south at the endowed lands
of (the statue of) the royal wife, Nefertari,[20]
which rests in Miam;
east at the great desert;
north at the ⌜fodder⌝-fields of ⌜Pharaoh⌝, l.p.h.;
west at the river.
Area: 3 *khet*.[21]

District of ⌜Ruha (?)⌝ at the head (south) of Miu[22]
on the fields of the deputy of Wawat:
(Boundaries:) south at the endowed fields of the statue
under the authority of the priest Amenemope;
east at the great desert;
north at the fodder-fields of Pharaoh, l.p.h.,
which had been fields of the deputy of Wawat;
west at the river.
Area: 2 *khet*.

District of the domain of the goddess,[23]
on the east at the land which has no heir,[24]
and (its) east at the great desert:
(Boundaries:) south at the endowed fields of the statue
under the authority of the deputy of Wawat, Mery;[25]
east at the great desert;
north at the fields of the herdsman, Bahu;
west at the river.
Area: 4 *khet*.

District of the upper part of Tekhkhet[26]
on the western edge of the gardens (?) of Tekhkhet,
on the fodder-fields of Pharaoh, l.p.h.,
and the fields which have no heir,
(its) east at the great desert:
(Boundaries:) south at the fodder-fields of Pharaoh, l.p.h.,
east at the great desert;
north at the fields of "that (land) of Irsa (?)";[27]
west at the river.
Area: 6 *khet*.

Total (area) of land endowed to it (the statue): 15 *khet*,
which is calculated at ⌜a quarter⌝ of arable land (?),[28]
valid, recorded, and fixed.[29]

Its administrator: the deputy, Penniut,
son of Herunefer of Wawat,
with leased-fields for it (the statue) to supply one ox to it
from what is slaughtered for it annually:
the district on the *pat*-fields,[30]
which had been in the possession of the deputy of Wawat,
and are not included in the document (inscribed above):
its western (border) is at the beginning of the *khelel*[31] of the deputy,
        Penniut;
the southern (border) at the *khelel*-land of the deputy, Penniut,
the northern (border) at the *pat*-fields,
which are in the estate of Pharaoh, l.p.h.;
the eastern (border) is ⌜at the end⌝ of the *khelel* of the deputy,
        Penniut.
Area: 6 *khet*.

As for anyone who will dispute it (the endowment),
Amun-Re, king of the gods, will pursue him to expel him,
Mut will pursue his wife,
and Khonsu will pursue his children.
He will hunger and thirst,
he will weaken and sicken.

44B. PENNIUT'S REWARD

These scenes are located in the upper register on the east end wall of the hall. The lower register is filled with offering scenes showing many people, presumably Penniut's kin. At the left end of the upper register is a figure of a king, possibly a statue, seated in a baldachin, facing right. Cartouches in front of him read: Nebmaatre Meryamun, Ramesses Amunherkhopshef, god ruler of Heliopolis (Ramesses VI). *Before him, a bowing figure, probably the viceroy of Kush, stretches his left arm toward the king in a gesture of address. In his right he holds a fan. Five columns above the viceroy record the king's speech to him:* His Person said to the viceroy of Kush: "Give two silver vessels of *qemy*-unguent to the deputy." *The viceroy's reply is inscribed in a single column behind him:* He says: I will do it, I will do it. O a happy day is for every land! *It is noteworthy that the viceroy is not named in these texts despite the importance of his role.*

The column with the viceroy's speech separates this scene from the next, which depicts the viceroy and another official standing before a standing statue of a king on a stand. The statue bears two standards. One has a falcon's head, representing Horus, and the other has a ram's head, representing Amun. Beyond the statue is an offering stand bearing a vessel of unguent. The first of the two figures holds a staff in his left hand and stretches his right hand toward the statue in a gesture of address. The second figure has both hands raised, the right in adoration, and the left holding a papyrus roll, perhaps the deed of the endowment. The viceroy is captioned only with his title: The viceroy of Kush. *The figure behind him bears the caption:* The overseer of the ⌜treasury (?)⌝, Mery.

Twenty columns of inscription separate this scene from a depiction of the rewarded Penniut on the far right. This text, the speech the viceroy addresses to Penniut, is translated below. Penniut is shown with his arms raised and holding a vessel in each hand, probably the unguent vessels referred to as gifts. Two smaller figures clothe him and he is flanked by stands bearing vessels. The depiction of the statue and the reference to it in the viceroy's speech indicate that in some unspecified way the reward followed the endowment and related to the statue.

Viceroy's speech:
    May Amun-Re, king of the gods, favor you.
    May Montu, lord of Armant,[32] favor you.
    May the *ka* of Pharaoh l.p.h., your perfect lord, favor you,
    the one who caused to be fashioned the statue
    of Ramesses Amunherkhopshef, god ruler of Heliopolis,
    son of Amun, favorite like Horus,
    lord of Miam …
    [*ca. 8 groups of epithets painted only and now lost*]
    … who slaughters the rebellious.

    Listen, deputy of Wawat, Penniut,
    to Amun in Karnak.
    These things were spoken by Pharaoh l.p.h., your perfect lord:
    "May Amun-Re, king of the gods, favor you.
    May Re-Horakhty favor you.
    May Montu favor you.

    May the *ka* of Pharaoh l.p.h., your lord, favor you,
    the one who is confident with what you do

in the lands of the Nubians and the land of Akuyata;[33]
you had them brought as plunder
before Pharaoh, l.p.h., your perfect lord,
with your tribute, in ⌜thousands (?)⌝."

Look, one (the king) has given you your 2 vessels of silver,
and you are (now) anointed with *qemy*-unguent.
Increase the fulfillment of (your) commitments (?)
in the land of Pharaoh, l.p.h., in which you are!

Penniut's reply:
The deputy, Penniut, says:
"Numerous [people and property (?)]
are what Pharaoh l.p.h., my perfect lord, has given.
May Pre give to you all flat-lands
and all hill-countries under your sandals!"

VI

Texts From Deir el-Medina

Deir el-Medina is the modern name of the village associated with the construction and decoration of the royal tombs in the Valley of the Kings ("the Place of Truth") and the Valley of the Queens ("the Place of Perfection") during the New Kingdom. The walled village, with its neighboring cemeteries and chapels, is located at the foot of the cliffs of the Theban West Bank, about two miles from the modern riverbank and within walking distance of the royal cemeteries. Deir el-Medina is best known for the quantity and diversity of textual and material sources that illuminate the lives of the workmen and their families who formed the community from its inception in the early Eighteenth Dynasty until its dissolution at the end of the New Kingdom. These sources include tomb goods such as furniture and personal objects as well as innumerable ostraca and papyri (see Andreu [ed.] 2002). The texts in particular document an extraordinary range of activities and concerns: accounts, legal testimonies, records of deliveries, love songs, medical treatments, and letters, to name but a few (see McDowell 1999). The workmen also dedicated many votive monuments, especially stelae, in local chapels to the north of the village proper, as well as in other temples and sacred areas on the West Bank. Among these objects, the few that bear biographical texts attest to innovative forms of display deployed by the workmen. In particular, the theme of wrongdoing and divine response voiced in some of these texts presents a striking contrast to the positive and idealizing content of the biographies of elite individuals set out in the preceding chapters.

45. The Stela of the Draftsman, Nebre

Nebre and his family are well attested in documents from Deir el-Medina dating throughout the first part of the Nineteenth Dynasty. Nebre himself prob-

ably worked as a draftsman from early in the reign of Ramesses II. He is depicted in the tombs of a number of his contemporaries in the community, including that of the sculptor Qen (B. G. Davies 1999, 149, 153), the owner of a stela translated below (no. 47).

Nebre's stela, which is 0.67 meters high and 0.39 meters wide (2'1" by 1'3"), was found during Berlin Museum excavations in one of a group of small brick buildings located near the mortuary temple of Ramesses II (the Ramesseum) on the Theban West Bank. Three other fragments of votive stelae were found in the building, one of which belonged to a Deir el-Medina crew member. Nebre's stela is divided into two registers. The scene in the upper register depicts Nebre kneeling with arms raised in adoration before the figure of Amun. The god, who holds a was-*scepter and* ankh *in his hands, is seated in front of a temple pylon. This may be a representation of Karnak temple since Amun bears the epithet "foremost of Karnak" in the texts on the stela. The plumes of the god's crown and the flagstaffs of the pylon break through the incised line which frames the scene. In the bottom right corner of the lower register is an uncaptioned group of four kneeling, adoring figures in two rows. The forward figure at the rear of the group holds a bouquet in his right hand. The people depicted may include Nebre and his sons Nakhtamun and Khay, all of whom are named in the text.*

The hymn to Amun fills fifteen columns in front of and around the figures. It is the longest-known expression of individual wrongdoing, divine punishment, and forgiveness, a motif which is found on a number of stelae from the village. Nebre begs forgiveness on behalf of his son Nakhtamun who is said to be close to death after committing a misdeed against the god. This action seems to have been connected with a cow, perhaps misappropriated temple property, but the reading of the text is uncertain at this point.

Upper register, above and behind figure of Amun:
Amun-Re, lord of the thrones of the Two Lands,
great god, foremost of Karnak,
<noble> god who hears prayers,
who comes at the call of the afflicted individual,
who gives breath to the one who is wretched.

Upper register, above figure of Nebre:
Giving praise to Amun-Re,
lord of the thrones of the Two Lands, foremost of Karnak,
kissing the ground for Amun of Thebes,
great god, the lord of this court,[1]
great and beautiful,
that he may allow my eyes to see his perfection;

for the *ka* of the draftsman of Amun,
Nebre, true of voice.

Lower register:
> Giving praise to Amun.
> Let me perform adorations to him, for his name.
> Let me give him adorations
> to the height of the sky and across the breadth of the earth.
> May I recount the […] of his power to those who travel north and
>   south.

> Guard yourselves against him!
> Proclaim him to son and daughter,
> to great and small.
> Speak of him to generations who do not yet exist.
> Speak of him to fish in the deep
> and to birds in the sky.
> Proclaim him to those who do not know him and those who do.
> Guard yourselves against him!

> You are Amun, the lord of the silent one,
> who comes at the cry of the individual;
> when I cry out to you in affliction,
> you come and I am rescued.
> May you give breath to the one who is wretched,
> and rescue me (as) one who is imprisoned.

> You are Amun-Re, lord of Thebes,
> who rescues the one who is in the underworld, because you are
>   [merciful].
> And when one appeals to you,
> you are the one who comes from afar;

> made by the draftsman of Amun in the Place of Truth,
> Nebre, true of voice,
> son of the draftsman in the Place of Truth,
> Pay, [true of voice],
> in the name of his lord Amun, lord of Thebes,
> who comes at the call of the individual.

Adorations were performed for him, for his name,[2]

through the greatness of his strength.
Humble supplications were made for him,
before his face and in the presence of the entire land,
on behalf of the draftsman Nakhtamun, true of voice,
who lay sick, approaching death,
in the power of Amun because of his (Amun's (?)) ⌜cow (?)⌝.3

I found that the lord of the gods came as the northwind,
with sweet breezes before him.
He rescued the draftsman of Amun,
Nakhtamun, true of voice,
son of the draftsman of Amun in the Place of Truth,
Nebre, true of voice,
born of the lady of the house,
Pashed, true of voice.

He says: Just as the servant is sure to act wrongfully,
the lord is sure to forgive.
The lord of Thebes does not spend a whole day angered;
his anger ends in a moment and nothing remains.
Breath returns to us in peace,
(as) Amun circulates upon his breeze.
As your *ka* endures, you will be merciful;
what was averted is not repeated.4

It is the draftsman in the Place of Truth,
Nebre, true of voice,
who says: I will make this stela in your name,
and I will establish this hymn for you
in writing upon its surface,
for you rescued the draftsman Nakhtamun for me.
I spoke to you and you listened to me.
Now see, I have done what I said.

You are the lord for the one who calls to him,
content with Maat,
the lord of Thebes.
Made by the draughtsman Nebre
(and) his son, the scribe, Khay.

46A–B. Two Stelae of the Workman, Neferabu

Neferabu is attested on two ostraca from the village that bear dates in years 36 and 40 (B. G. Davies 1999, 158), indicating that he was active in the middle of the 66-year reign of Ramesses II. His title "servant in the Place of Truth" designates him as a workman. Neferabu owned a finely decorated tomb in the Deir el-Medina necropolis. He also dedicated a number of votive objects in local chapels, including the two stelae translated here. Neither stela has an archaeological findspot, but their dedications to Ptah and Meretseger suggest that they were set up in the cave sanctuaries for these deities located on the path running southwest from the village to the Valley of the Queens. Their texts center on his admission of misdeeds committed against the deities.

46A. Stela Dedicated to Ptah (fig. 14)

This small, round-topped stela (0.39 meters high and 0.28 meters wide, 1′3″ by 9″) is inscribed on both surfaces. The front surface is divided into two registers. The upper register shows Ptah seated under a canopy before a large offering table laden with food and a bouquet of flowers. Ptah is depicted in his standard form with an undifferentiated body, skullcap, and holding a djed-*pillar and was-scepter in his hands. He bears the caption:* Ptah, lord of truth, king of the Two Lands, perfect of face upon his sacred throne. *Inscribed above the scene is the hieroglyphic sign of two outstretched arms with a loaf of bread resting between them, which writes the Egyptian word* ka, *"life-force," and may represent this aspect of the god. The sign is flanked by four ears on the left and two eyes on the right; these probably symbolize Ptah's capacity to see and hear (Pinch 1993, 246–64, esp. 258). In the lower register, Neferabu is depicted kneeling with his arms raised in adoration, facing toward the god. Before him is a hymn to Ptah in nine short columns. The ten columns that fill the reverse side of the stela present a tale of Ptah's power centered on his reaction to Neferabu's misuse of his name in an oath.*

> *Front surface, lower register:*
> Giving praise to Ptah,
> lord of Maat, king of the Two Lands,
> perfect of face on his Great Throne,[5]
> sole god among the Ennead,
> beloved as king of the Two Lands,
>
> that he may give life, prosperity, health,

Fig. 14. Stela of Neferabu, front and rear surfaces (no. 46a; copyright the Trustees of the British Museum).

alertness, favor, and love,
my eyes seeing Amun in the course of every day,
as is done for a truthful one
who places Amun in his heart;
by the servant in the Place of Truth
Neferabu, true of voice.

Rear surface:
Beginning of the account of the power
of Ptah, South-of-his-Wall,
by the servant in the Place of Truth on the west of Thebes,
Neferabu, true of voice.

He says: I am a man who swore falsely
by Ptah, lord of Maat,
and he caused that I see darkness by day.[6]
I will proclaim his power to those who do not know him and those
        who do,[7]
to the small and the great.

Guard yourselves against Ptah, lord of Maat!
Look, he does not disregard the misdeed of anyone.
Stop yourselves from pronouncing the name
of Ptah in falsehood.
Look, (as for) the one who pronounces it in falsehood, so he is cast
        down.

He made me like dogs of the street,
while I was in his hand (power).
He caused that people and gods look upon me
as a man who had committed an abomination against his lord.
Ptah, lord of Maat, was vindicated against me,
and so he gave me an instruction.

Be merciful to me, look upon me that you may be merciful!—
by the servant in the Place of Truth on the west of Thebes,
Neferabu, true of voice before the great god.

46B. SLAB DEDICATED TO MERETSEGER

Unlike stelae of the traditional shape, this piece is low and rectangular, measuring 0.2 meters in height and 0.54 meters in width (6.5" by 1′8"). Its unusual shape and the position of Meretseger on the right side facing left, rather than the usual position of deities on the left facing right, may indicate that it was designed for a particular location in a chapel. The elongated shape accentuates the form in which the goddess is represented, as a serpent with three heads, of a vulture, a woman, and a serpent. The human and serpent heads both wear plumed crowns. A small offering table in front of her figure bears a vase and a lotus bouquet. Sloping lines incised around her figure may represent the rock shrine with which Meretseger was associated as "Scarp of the West" (Adrom 2004). This epithet is included in the caption that frames her image: Meretseger, lady of the sky, mistress of the Two Lands, whose good name is Scarp of the West. *The rest of the surface is filled with seventeen columns of a hymn. In contrast to Neferabu's hymn to Ptah, this text does not specify the nature of his misconduct, although the consequent affliction is vividly described through the metaphor of the pain of childbirth.*

> Giving praise to the Scarp of the West,
> kissing the ground for her *ka.*
> Let me give praise, hear my appeal,
> (for) I am one truthful upon earth;
> made by the servant in the Place of Truth,
> Neferabu, true of voice.
>
> (I was) an ignorant man, without sense,[8]
> who did not know good from falsehood.
> I performed an act of transgression against the Scarp
> and she gave me an instruction,
> while I was in her hand (power) night and day.
>
> I sat on bricks like a pregnant woman[9]
> and I called out for breath,[10] but it did not come to me.
> I was humble to the Scarp of the West, great of strength,
> to every god and goddess.
>
> Now look, I will speak to those great and small
> who are in the crew:[11] Beware of the Scarp
> because a lion is within her!
> The Scarp strikes

with the blow of a savage lion.
She pursues the one who transgresses against her.

I called to my mistress
and I found her coming to me as a sweet breeze,
and she was merciful to me,
for she had caused me to see her hand (power).

She returned to me in peace
and she caused that I forget the sickness
which had been in my heart.
For she, the Scarp of the West,
is appeased when one calls to her.

Spoken by Neferabu, true of voice,
he says: Look and let every ear listen
that lives upon earth:
Beware of the Scarp of the West!

47. THE STELA OF THE SCULPTOR, QEN

Qen was active as a sculptor during the early part of the reign of Ramesses II; a scene in his tomb (Theban Tomb 4) depicts that king with the vizier Paser (for whom see no. 25), whose latest attestation in this office is in year 21 (see B. G. Davies 1999, 176–78). Alongside his tomb, Qen also dedicated a large number of votive objects, including eleven stelae dedicated to various deities, among whom are the sun-god Re and the deified Eighteenth Dynasty king Amenhotep I, the patron deity of the village who received two stelae (compare McDowell 1999, 92–94). The stela translated here, of which only a lower corner remains (0.2 meters high by 0.14 meters wide, 6.5″ by 4.5″), was found in one of the chapels north of the enclosure wall of the Ptolemaic temple of Hathor at Deir el-Medina (Bruyère 1952, II, 129–31; Bomann 1991, 48). The fragment bears traces of a hand perhaps from a figure of Qen, who was probably represented adoring and offering the prayer to a deity represented in the upper register. The deity's identity is uncertain; his designation as "the Light" could refer to Re, the reigning king, or to Amenhotep I (Borghouts 1982, 25 with n. 116). At Deir el-Medina, Amenhotep I is perhaps most likely. The rest of the fragment bears the first five columns of a text reporting a false oath said to or about a woman known from other objects to have been Qen's wife.

> Giving praise to the Light,
> kissing the ground for the gods,
> the lords of sky and earth.
> May I give praise to (your?) perfect [faces],
> may I propitiate your *kas* every day;
> by the sculptor in the Place of Truth,
> Qen, true of voice.
>
> He says: I am a man who said "As endures" in falsehood[12]
> to the lady of the house, Nefertari, true of voice.
> The power of the god overtook me
> so that (I) would say to the Light,
> to [... ...], to the Moon,
> to Ptah, Thoth, and Amun:
> Be merciful (to) me (?).
> [Let (?) ...]
> [*rest lost apart from traces in the following broken column*]

48. THE STELA OF THE WORKMAN, HUY

Huy's small stela (0.28 meters high and 0.2 meters wide, 9" by 7") probably dates to the Nineteenth Dynasty, perhaps to the reign of Ramesses II, although a number of individuals from the village bore this name. Its findspot is unknown but, as with some other objects presented in this chapter, it was probably dedicated in one of the village chapels. The upper register depicts a barque bearing a lunar disc. The moon was a form of the god Thoth, and this identification is stated in the accompanying caption: Moon Thoth, great god, the merciful. Huy is depicted in the left corner of the lower register, kneeling with his right hand raised in adoration. Over his left shoulder he holds an architectural element, perhaps the upper section of a shrine. The inclusion of such an element is very unusual, and the narrative, inscribed in ten columns in front and around his figure, concerns the false oath Huy swore about this object. This striking feature may constitute a further offering and expression of contrition to the god.

It is the servant of the Moon, Huy,

who says: I am that man who said "As endures" in falsehood[13]
to the Moon concerning the architrave,[14]
and he caused that I witness the greatness of his strength
in the presence of the entire land.

I will relate your power to fish in the river
and birds in the sky,
and they will tell it to the children of their children:
Guard yourselves against the Moon,
the merciful one who was able to avert this![15]

49. The Stela of the Workman, Qenherkhopshef

*Qenherkhopshef is attested in documents from the village from the reign
of Ramesses III to that of Ramesses V. He was the son of a woman called Naunakhte, the owner of a much-discussed legal document that sets out different
inheritances for her children, including Qenherkhopshef (Černý 1945; McDowell
1999, 38–39, no. 14). His stela (0.34 meters by 0.24 meters, 1′1″ by 8″), now in
the British Museum in London, has no archaeological findspot but may have
been set up in the cave sanctuary of Meretseger on the path from Deir el-Medina
to the Valley of the Queens. The upper register of the stela shows Hathor seated
before an offering table. She holds a* wadj-*scepter and wears a solar disc with
plumes. Behind her stands a personified* ankh-*sign, signifying "life," holding a
fan. In front of her are six columns of offering formulas; a further column gives
the name of Qenherkhopshef's mother, Naunakhte.*

*The upper and lower registers of the stela are separated by a horizontal band
that is partially inscribed with the names of two of Qenherkhopshef's sons; these
names may have been added separately, perhaps after the early death of these
sons. In the lower register, Qenherkhopshef is depicted wearing an elaborate
kilt, kneeling with his arms raised in adoration. In contrast to the image of the
goddess in the upper register, Qenherkhopshef's figure is carved in raised relief,
strongly separating him from the twelve columns of text that wrap around him.
These columns present a hymn to Hathor that maps out Qenherkhopshef's own
personal sacred geography by moving him through the Theban West Bank from
sacred areas around Deir el-Bahri (Djesret) to the Valley of the Queens. Allusions to his birth in Hathor's domain at the beginning of the text and to sleeping
in Ptah's presence at the end are probably metaphoric expressions of divine intimacy and protection, although the night spent in Ptah's precinct may have been*

an act of incubation, a practice that is attested in later periods (McDowell 1999, 100; cf. Szpakowska 2003, 144–47).

> *Upper register, before figure of Hathor:*
>> An offering which the king gives to Hathor, mistress of the West,
>> lady of the sky, mistress of the Two Banks,
>> in this her name of Hathor who resides in Djesret.
>> An offering which the king gives to Amun-Re, lord of the perfect
>>> meeting,[16]
>> <and to Hathor> in her name as Mut the great, lady of Asheru.[17]
>> His mother, the songstress of Amun, Naunakhte.

> *Horizontal band between the upper and lower registers:*
>> His son Nebseti, true of voice,
>> and his son Amenemhab, true of voice.
>> [*the rest of the line was never inscribed*]

> *Lower register:*
>> Giving praise to your *ka*, Hathor, mistress of the West,
>> lady of the sky, mistress of all the gods,
>> kissing the ground for your name:

>> I am a *ba* before his lord.[18]
>> I was born in your (Hathor's) precinct,
>> the cave beside Djesret, close to Menset;[19]
>> I ate from the offering loaves of the lector priests beside the great
>>> *akh*-spirits.[20]

>> I walked about in the Place of Perfection,[21]
>> I spent the night in your precinct,
>> drinking water which flowed from the mountain (?)
>> in the precinct of Menet;[22]
>> it waters the rushes and the lotuses for you,[23]
>> in the precinct of Ptah.
>> My body spent the night in the shadow of your (Ptah's) [face],
>> I slept (in) your precinct,
>> I made stelae in the temple beside the lords of Djesret;

>> for the *ka* of one excellent and precise,
>> who fashions the images of all the gods,
>> servant in the Place of Truth,

Qenherkhopshef, true of voice for eternity,
and his father, servant in the Place of Truth, Khaemnun,
his sister, <lady of the house>, Tanefret,
his son Amennakht, true of voice,
and his son ⌜Heqamaatre-⌝Kaemperptah, true of voice.

Caption beneath the arms of Qenherkhopshef:
Her son, (that is) Naunakhte('s).

50. The Stela of the Workman, Ipuy

Now in Vienna, the provenance of this small, badly damaged stela (0.34 meters by 0.26 meters, 1'1" by 9") is unknown, although the owner's title places him at Deir el-Medina. Ipuy is a common name in the village and so cannot help to narrow down the date of the stela. It is inscribed on both front and rear surfaces with a hymn to Hathor which includes the narration of the individual's encounter with the goddess in a dream. The narrative motif of a divinely inspired dream, which is first attested in Eighteenth Dynasty royal inscriptions (Szpakowska 2003, 47–52), is known from a Ramessid biography translated in chapter I (no. 12). The dream episode is inscribed in the lower register on the front, beneath a fragmentary raised relief scene of Ipuy kneeling before Hathor. Only the feet of the goddess, the pillar of her shrine, the offering table, and the corner of Ipuy's kilt are visible. He is depicted again in the lower register in sunk relief, kneeling and adoring to the right of the inscription. The continuation of the hymn fills the back of the stela.

Front surface, lower register:
Giving praise to Hathor who resides in Thebes,
kissing the ground to [... ...] in all her manifestations.
May I give her praise
for the greatness of her name, for the force of her strength.

Love of her is in the hearts of people,
her perfection is before the gods;
the Ennead come to her
bowing before the greatness of her majesty.

And it happened that I saw (her) perfection,

while my heart spent the day in her festival,[24]
when I saw the lady of the Two Lands in a dream,
and she placed joy in my heart.

Then I was refreshed with her sustenance.
There was none who could say of it "would that I had, would that
        we had."
[For he is (?)] ...
[*the final column on this surface is lost*]

Rear surface:
    [*the first two columns are lost, some traces are visible in the third*]
    [...] festival-speech (?) which is given, being taught to[25] (?) ...
    [*over half a column lost*]
    ... and provisions;
    by the servant in the Place of Truth,
    Ipuy, true of voice.

    ⌜He says⌝: ...
    [*ca. half a column lost*]
    who reveals speech.[26]

    The wonders that Hathor performed should be related ...
    [to] those ignorant of it (them?) and those who know.
    And generation should say to generation:
    " ⌜How⌝ perfect [... ... ...]"
    ... her face to the sky;
    one is delighted (?) while drunk through seeing her.[27]

    Her father Amun listens to her,
    (to) all her appeals, propitiated (?) ...
    when he ⌜shines⌝ bearing her perfection.
    He makes lapis lazuli for her hair,
    gold for her limbs.[28]

    The Two Banks of Horus were created for her,
    the god['s mother (?)] is satisfied [through her (?)],
    ... the entire land for the greatness of her love,
    while her perfect countenance joins with his (Amun's) face,[29]
    beloved of (?) [... ... ...]

NOTES

NOTES TO INTRODUCTION

1. A theoretically oriented and partly cross-cultural survey of genres of life-writing, including biography and autobiography, is *Encyclopedia of Life-Writing* (Jolly ed., 2001). The only ancient material included there is Greek and Roman.

2. The most detailed recent typology of Egyptian biography is by Andrea Gnirs (1996, 203–6: English summary 2001); my division draws partly on her analysis. See also Kloth 2002, 227–29 for an assessment of this typology in relation to Old Kingdom material. Van de Walle 1975, 816–17 and Lichtheim 1988, 5–7 represent older approaches to categorizing biography on which these later typologies are based.

3. For examples, see Lichtheim 1980, 58–65; 1989; Jansen-Winkeln 1985, I, 156–67; II, 520–26 (A13); Jansen-Winkeln 2004. For texts belonging to women from earlier periods, see Strudwick 2005, 379–99 (Old Kingdom); Lichtheim 1988, 37–38 (Middle Kingdom).

4. For discussion of the meanings of particular scene types in Eighteenth Dynasty tombs, which are relevant for comparison with Ramessid tombs, see Hartwig 2004.

5. Where the translations in this section are my own, I provide references to hieroglyphic copy-texts as well as to published translations.

6. Major synthesizing studies of Old Kingdom biography include Kloth 2002; Baines 1997; Baud 2005. Anthologies are: Roccati 1982; Strudwick 2005. Much productive and innovative work on Old Kingdom biography, and the biographical genre in general, has emerged from analysis of the relationship of these texts with the emergence of literary genres in the Middle Kingdom: Helck 1972; Assmann 1991 [1983]; Baines 1999b; 1999c.

7. For an anthology and study of Middle Kingdom biography, see Lichtheim 1988. For epithets, which are highly developed in this period, see J. M. A. Janssen 1946; Doxey 1998. Another important study is Gnirs 2000.

8. A synthesizing treatment of Eighteenth Dynasty biography is Guksch 1994. For a discussion of religious concerns in some texts, see Lichtheim 1992, 48–65. A comprehensive study of biographical epithets for the entire New Kingdom, including the Ramessid period, is Rickal 2005. No full study of biography during the Second Intermediate period has been published, but see Kubisch 2003 with references.

9. For translations of biographies from tombs at Amarna, see Murnane 1995, chapter 4; for a study of Amarna texts in relation to later developments, see Assmann 1980. For the visual and textual narrative program in Amarna tombs, see Meyers 1985.

10. For an overview of Ramessid political history, with bibliography, see van Dijk 2000. Useful resources for the Nineteenth Dynasty include Kitchen 1982; Freed 1987; Morris 2005, 343–690. An anthology of sources in translation, mainly royal inscriptions, is B. G. Davies 1997.

11. For the conflict between Sety II and Amenmesse, see Krauss 1997; Dodson 1997. For the end of the Nineteenth Dynasty, see Schneider 2003.

12. For a survey of events in the Twentieth Dynasty, with bibliography, see Grandet 2001. For foreign policy, see Morris 2005, 691–801. For an anthology of a diverse range of sources in translation, see Peden 1994.

13. Accessible surveys of Late Egyptian and linguistic change include Junge 2001, 263–65; 2005; Wente 2001, 56–60.

14. The "god (*ntr*)" in such texts may be a particular deity who is named or referred to, or he or she may be a generic expression of the divine. What the term does not seem to refer to is the one God of later monotheistic religions.

15. An important study of artistic development and innovation is Hofmann 2004.

16. Published: e.g., Martin 2001, 19, pl. 17. Unpublished: Zivie 2002; Leclant and Clerc 1998, 349, pl. 20 (12).

17. A detailed treatment of the phraseology of the Deir el-Medina texts is Vernus 2003.

Notes to Chapter I

1. Sethe (1907, 30 n. 1) considered that the sun determinative inscribed here was to be read as "day 1." It seems more likely that space was left for the day, which was never carved (so KRI III, 283 n. 2a). The date is a significant feature of this text, which parallels Ramesses II's dedicatory inscription in the temple of Sety I at Abydos in both the narrative structure and setting of its opening. That text describes the king's visit to Abydos on day 23 of the third month of *akhet*, in year 1, as he returned north after participating in the Opet festival in Thebes. It records Ramesses' dismay at finding his father's temple at Abydos unfinished and his consequential plans for its completion. Thus, Nebwenenef's installation is closely connected both to the king's assumption of power, which was confirmed by his enacting the Opet festival, and his actions in renewing projects at Abydos.

2. Probably near the temple of Sety I on the Theban West Bank at Qurna.

3. This stanza describes the process of divine selection, which the king mediated; the names of high officials are said to have been read out before the portable cult statue of Amun, an act perhaps to be understood as taking place during the Opet festival. The god then selected Nebwenenef, probably through forward movement of his cult image carried on the priests' shoulders when Nebwenenef's name was said.

4. "Mooring" is a common euphemism for death and transition to the next world. Here it may signify that he will die in office "at home," as well as being provided with a tomb "upon the soil" of Thebes.

5. The "bow-line" and "stern-line" allude to the powers and responsibilities of temple governance with which Nebwenenef is being entrusted. Nautical metaphors are common in Egyptian texts. Here the phrase connects with and develops the preceding verse.

6. The seals and staff are insignia of high priestly office.

7. The solar form of Amun to whom the Eastern temple was dedicated.

8. This enumeration of years in office is striking. Bakenkhons's text has often been used as evidence for the typical trajectory of priestly careers, especially the age at which education and training began, and for discussion of the length of the reign of Sety I (Jansen-Winkeln 1993).

9. This formulation emphasizes that, although the king commissions building works in the temple, Bakenkhons is responsible for their progress and completion.

10. This verse describes the location of the Eastern temple.

11. Bakenkhons's text provides the only evidence for plantations and gardens in the eastern area of Karnak (Cabrol 2001, 425); this passage may also allude to the canal or waterway that passed near this side of the temple complex.

12. One hundred ten years was considered the ideal age.

13. The phrase "made under the charge" may allude to the manufacture of the statue itself. This is also the only occurrence of "overseer of works" in a title string on Bakenkhons's statues,

although it does occur in narrative passages. This text may record the dedication of the statue by Bakenkhons's son or successor, and this could explain the unusual presence of a secondary plinth.

14. "Lady of the sky" is an epithet of the goddess Mut. This passage suggests that Bakenkhons was educated in the temple of Mut in the Karnak complex.

15. The office of "god's father" seems to have permitted the holder access to the cult statue of the god, which may explain why Bakenkhons places particular emphasis on his initiation to this office, rather than his appointment to high priest. This emphasis may also introduce a play between the reference to his human father earlier in the stanza and the title "god's father," perhaps contrasting the humanity of one role with the divine associations of the other. Fatherhood is a central motif in this text, in which the role of father seems to be taken by Amun at the moment of initiation.

16. "Chief of seers of Re" and "*sem*-priest and chief controller of crafts of Ptah" are titles held by the high priests of Re in Heliopolis and Ptah in Memphis respectively. Bakenkhons holds these titles honorifically within the context of the presence of these gods at Thebes.

17. Probably the crew of the sun-god in his passage through the sky and underworld.

18. Note the parallel with the narration of Bakenkhons's initiation on both his Cairo and Munich statues (no. 2).

19. The restoration here is uncertain, but reference to a document issued or approved by Amun seems appropriate in the oracular context that the narrative evokes.

20. This phrase seems to have two levels of meaning: that the work was done on the king's behalf; and that the king's titulary was inscribed on the monument itself (cf. Lefebvre 1929, 21a).

21. If the reading is correct, this may refer to a statue of the king placed within this building.

22. A reference to the cult statue of the god which was carried on the shoulders of priests during procession, usually inside a portable barque shrine.

23. The phrase "as the gift of Amun" may allude to an oracular mandate for Roma's appointment as high priest.

24. This monument may be the preparation chamber (*wʿbt*), the restoration of which is described in Roma's inscription on the eighth pylon (no. 3d), or one of the buildings described on the left side of 3b.

25. The "remainder of the offering service" refers to offerings made to deities, which could then revert to the cults of individuals. Such offerings were highly potent and desirable.

26. These verses refer to the action of cult statues during processions, acknowledging the presence and participation of Roma's statues (compare no. 35a). The word translated here as "assent (*hn*)" is also used in oracular texts to describe the god's positive response to a query (see for example nos. 15, 37).

27. See note 22 to no. 3c above.

28. See note 12 to no. 2a above.

29. A temple in Heliopolis that housed the *benben* stone, an object associated with the solar cult.

30. "Smoothness" may describe the fading away of images or erasures.

31. Alternatively "the place of the south" (as KRI VI, 542, 14c) or "the great place, south of the [lake?]." This may refer to the preparation chamber (*wʿbt*) of the high priests, which was probably in the southern area of the complex, and whose restoration is also described in another of Amenhotep's building narratives (no. 5).

32. Carrying poles were used to bear the portable shrines of deities in processions. This passage, although broken, seems to refer to the refurbishment of this shrine with additional

carrying poles. The narration of the construction of carrying poles for portable shrines is also found in the Twentieth Dynasty text of the high steward Amenmose, where he claims to increase the number of poles used for various shrines (no. 35a). An earlier parallel occurs in the Restoration Stela of Tutankhamun, which states that the king increased the number of poles for the statues of Amun and Ptah (Murnane 1995, 213). This parallel indicates a possible restoration of Amenhotep's text, which may state that Amenhotep "found the image supported by only (for example) 4 poles."

33. Senwosret I (ca. 1918–1875) was a great king of the Middle Kingdom who had at least one structure on the southern axis where Amenhotep's inscriptions were set up (Charles Van Siclen, personal communication; also Björkmann 1971, 91–93). Here Amenhotep seems to be aligning himself with the semi-mythical beginnings of the temple and Amun priesthood, perhaps as a way of asserting his legitimacy.

34. The sacred lake at Karnak. This phrase confirms the location of the preparation chamber near the lake and perhaps in the service area of the temple.

35. The word I translate here as "ochre" also has the meaning "cartouche," and this connection may be significant. A yellow ochre is probably meant, especially as the context here involves the inscription of the royal cartouche, the backgrounds of which were often yellow.

36. This building may have been located in the service and administrative area of the temple, to the south of the sacred lake.

37. For "shouldering" the god, see note 22 to no. 3c.

38. This verse is paralleled by that on the base of the Munich statue of Bakenkhons (no. 2a). In Bakenkhons's case, it concludes with "at dawn he will increase my happiness." Only one group is lost from Amenhotep's text, so his wording must depart from Bakenkhons's at this point.

39. It is likely that this court was in a central part of the temple; Wolfgang Helck (1956, 164) suggested the area in front of the second pylon in Karnak.

40. The "true of voice" after this official's name, which is the same as that of the high priest and could signify that he was dead, is probably inadvertant. The other individuals listed in this text do not bear this epithet.

41. Nesamen and Neferkareemperamen are both attested in the tomb robbery papyri (Helck 1956, 164–65).

42. The "office tax (tpw-$\underline{d}rt$)" is an obscure form of taxation known from Ramessid texts. It was charged against officials and usually consisted of quite valuable commodities (Warburton 1997, 287–91 for a summary).

43. An unidentified style of gold-working.

44. In the images that accompany the scenes, Amenhotep is shown wearing *shebyu*-necklaces and a broad collar. *Shebyu*-necklaces, made from bulbous rings, were particularly associated with royal favor and reward. Broad, flat *wesekh*-collars, made from rows of tubular beads, were associated with significant rituals and with regeneration. Items of adornment are also included on the tables in front of Amenhotep in both scenes.

45. The amounts of gold and silver enumerated are generous. A *deben* was a standard measurement of weight, equivalent to 91 grams, 3 1/8 ounces. Ten *deben*, therefore, amounts to 9.1 kilograms (20 lbs). One *deben* of gold was enough to buy an ox. In the reign of Ramesses III, it was also equivalent to 4560 liters of grain (8024 pints). A workman at Deir el-Medina received 115.32 liters of barley and 307.52 liters of emmer as a monthly ration, so Amenhotep's reward of gold is equivalent to almost ten years of a well-paid artisan's grain rations.

46. Various forms of vessels are shown on the tables in front of Amenhotep, but relating these depictions to the vessels listed in the text is problematic.

47. For much of Egyptian history, silver was more valued than gold (the ratio of gold to silver was usually 2:1). However, in the Nineteenth Dynasty, silver declined sharply in value (J. J.

Janssen 1975, 158), which may explain why Amenhotep receives more silver than gold.

48. A *qeb* was a standard vessel type for the storage and transport of beer. It probably did not correspond to any fixed measure.

49. A *hin* is ca. 5.03 liters (8.85 pints).

50. An aroura is equivalent to 2756.5 square meters, so the gift here was of 55,130 square meters of land, or fourteen acres.

51. This stanza seems to express that Amenhotep has been granted the harvest of this grain-land as a yearly allocation, probably without having to pay taxes on it.

52. This may be a reference to the preparation chamber whose restoration is described in other inscriptions of Amenhotep (nos. 4–5). The chamber is described in these texts as being reserved for the high priesthood. Here the king's generosity may be due to the building's function as a place where offerings were prepared, as well as its association with the high priests.

53. Literally "to wash your heart."

54. These amounts of food and beer could be allocated as a reward for one period of work or could endow future work.

55. This title is an elaboration of the ancient and prestigious title "controller of the lord's kilt."

56. This refers to the administrative institution of the king's mortuary temple. The temple itself was never built, while the institution was probably located in the temple of Ramesses IV on the Theban West Bank (Polz 1998, 280).

57. The mortuary temple of Ramesses III, often named Medinet Habu.

58. These lines narrate the death and burial of Amenhotep's father, the high priest of Amun Ramessesnakht. The inclusion of this event in a biographical text, with a date, is unusual.

59. Alternatively "to cause it (the House of Gold) to be planned for" or "to cause it (gold) to be trebled" (with Wente 1966, 80, n. 14b). The "House of Gold" can refer, in texts relating to the royal domain, to the palace or part of the treasury (E. Schott 1977, 739), although in these contexts it can also be associated with ritual performance and transformation (e.g., Frood 2003, 79). In the biography of Amenmose (no. 35a) the emphasis on cult equipment suggests that it designates sanctified space for the storage of such materials or perhaps the sanctuary itself (with Gardiner 1948, 21 n. 1). It is possible therefore that this stanza in Amenhotep's text concerns a cult statue.

60. This refers to Amenhotep's imprisonment during the period of civil war in Thebes. "He" here probably refers to the viceroy of Nubia, Panehsy, who temporarily seized power (see Morales 2001). Amenhotep may have been held in the mortuary temple of Ramesses III (Medinet Habu) on the West Bank. A later testimony in one of the tomb robbery papyri refers to "nine whole months of the suppression of Amenhotep, who used to be high priest of Amun" (Wente 1966, 73).

61. Merybastet was both the name of Amenhotep's grandfather and his brother, although it seems most likely that it is the grandfather who is referred to here (compare with the genealogy given with the central scene of the reward tableau: no. 7).

62. This temple was probably part of the Ptah temple complex in Memphis.

63. This is the final verse in a blessing, probably directed to those who honor Amenhotep's memory, in contrast to the threat that follows. The verse refers to the good burial of the high priest and is the counterpart of the final verse of the threat. The use of "we" to refer to Amenhotep himself and the members of his priesthood, who are perhaps family members, is distinctive and gives the sense of direct speech.

64. This is the second reference to Amenhotep's restoration of a building set up by this Twelfth Dynasty king some eight hundred years earlier (see no. 5, with n. 33). It is possible that

both references refer to the same building. Senwosret I also had a number of buildings in this central area of the temple and Amenhotep may be referring to these in this text.

65. The opening line of the text, "there was a man," signals a literary, fictive context, since it begins two known Middle Kingdom tales, the Tale of Nefer[...] (Parkinson 2002, 302) and the Tale of the Eloquent Peasant (Parkinson 1997, 58; see also Morenz 1998). A broad equivalent in the English-language literary tradition would be "once upon a time."

66. Or "she protected me in a painful moment" (with Vernus 1978, 121–22). My translation is based on thematic parallels in the penitential hymns from Deir el-Medina (nos. 45–48). In these texts, the individual suffers in isolation before experiencing divine intervention. Such a contrast of isolation and ordeal with divine protection may be alluded to both in the present verse and in the following stanza. Samut, however, does not concede any wrongdoing. In this, his text may be closer to motifs of ordeal and aid in the biography of the high priest of Amun, Amenhotep (no. 8), and the Qadesh poem of Ramesses II (Lichtheim 1976, 65–66).

67. Although especially frequent in biographical texts from the Amarna period, the often fictional motif of humble beginnings is a common means of emphasizing the protagonist's singular advancement either through his own ability, through the intervention of the king (as in the Amarna texts) or a god, as in this text.

68. These verses concern the removal of Samut and his possessions from human responsibility, both on an informal level, through reference to robbery, and on the formal and official level of legal action. The protection of Samut's property and punishments resulting from any attempt to overturn his decision lie with the goddess, surpassing any potential human intervention.

69. Or "there is no son of mine who will arrange burial for me" (with Assmann 1999, 403). It seems more likely that Mut's responsibility for burial is referred to here (with Gnirs 2003, 182).

70. Since the determinative to the word is lost, it is possible that it refers to "birthplace," a euphemism for the necropolis (Gnirs 2003, 182). However, Meskhenet is the personification of birthplace and is an appropriate reading considering the numerous goddesses that are alluded to throughout the text as aspects of Mut.

71. The "ways of life" could be veins or nostrils.

72. The text moves onto the north wall of the tomb at this point and is less badly damaged.

73. The few known depictions of Egyptian women giving birth show them crouched on bricks; these bricks are also referred to in literary texts and are attested archaeologically (compare no. 46b). For discussion of the evidence for birthing bricks in connection with a category of magical object, see Roth and Roehrig 2002.

74. The word for "contract" here seems to refer to a supplementary maintenance income or annuity (Menu 1980, 143–44). Thus, Samut's donation to the temple not only ensures his burial and cult, but also a pension for his old age.

75. The meaning of this passage is disputed and has juridical implications for the whole text. Vernus (1978, 135–37) proposes that the passage represents an "exclusion clause": Samut denies the existence of heirs to his property in order to exclude them from inheritance. Bernadette Menu (1980, 142) argues instead that the form of the clause indicates that Samut left his property to Mut because he had no heirs. Vernus (1980, 145–46) responds in support of his original position citing a passage in 11a, where Samut states: "Not one of my family shall divide it." This question is difficult to resolve, and these clauses may be more concerned with binding Samut closely to Mut at the general expense of the human sphere rather than with specific family matters.

76. This is the beginning of a threat directed against those who would seek to overturn

Samut's endowment. For the use of blessing and threat formulas in a similar context see the inscription on the stela from Bilgai (no. 33).

77. "Gold" and "eye of Re" are epithets of Hathor.

78. *"Hely"* also occurs as a personal name, which suggests that it is here a term of endearment for the goddess, emphasizing the intimacy of Djehutyemheb's relationship with her (Assmann 1978, 32, n. t). The traces of the word "Mut" visible here can be read both as the name of the goddess and as "(my) mother." Thus, the aspect of Hathor evoked is also maternal, as well as establishing a connection with the goddess Mut (Szpakowska 2003, 229–31). Karl Joachim Seyfried (1995, 73) considers the possibility that the lost image of a goddess beneath 12b showed Mut rather than Hathor.

79. "Your place" refers to Djehutyemheb's tomb.

80. It is also possible to translate this verse as "that I may carve your form in my tomb," as an allusion to the images of the goddess on the walls of the hall and the shrine (Assmann 1978, 28, with n. y). Both meanings are possible and this may be a deliberate word play.

81. An epithet of Ptah. The references to the Memphite deities Ptah, Sokar, and Nefertem may indicate that this text was composed in Memphis or based on Memphite stock materials. This can be compared with the inclusion of northern deities in the biography of Samut (no. 11a).

82. The god Penpen occurs in Ramessid nonroyal tombs in association with offerings and in one case with writing (Leitz et. al. 2002, III, 37).

83. An epithet of Osiris.

84. In funerary literature, this object signals the wearer's justified and rejuvenated state in the next world (Derchain 1955; M. Bell 1987, 57). Spell 19 of the Book of the Dead, which is attested from the Late period onward, is specifically centered on its transformative potential (Riggs 2005, 81–82).

85. Or "I am the priest of the great one who is in Abydos."

86. "*Weba*-servant" is a priestly title first attested in the New Kingdom. Here "Wenennefer" is a name of Osiris.

87. Referring to the violent defense of Osiris from his enemies, particularly Seth.

88. The *ames-* and the *iaat*-weapons occur in the Pyramid Texts (Old Kingdom) and Coffin Texts (Middle Kingdom: van der Molen 2000, 4–5, 12) as part of the regalia of Osiris and the transfigured dead, but are rare in nonroyal contexts. The mention of them, as well as the earlier reference to the "wreath of triumph," signal Wenennefer's privileged access to portentous ritual objects.

89. The lack of movement indicates a negative answer.

90. The *wab*-priests probably represent four of those depicted with the barque in the lunette scene. These may have been more senior priests, paired with juniors who are unnamed.

91. This may be a reference to the god's tomb or more generally to "the West."

92. If this reading is correct, it may refer to cult equipment, perhaps to a type of portable shrine or barque.

93. Wenennefer's title and filiation are incorporated into the narrative rather than marking its beginning, as in the standard formulation: "X, true of voice, son of Y, true of voice, he says . . . " This marks the point at which the biography shifts into the third person.

94. The "exceptional youth" probably refers to Wenennefer in his youthful role as a processional priest who was one of the bearers of a cult image. The phrase could also designate the cult statue of the divine child Horus-Ihy that was carried in procession. The potential dual readings here may identify the priest with the god, an assimilation that is developed more explicitly in the following verses.

95. Wenennefer is compared with the child-god Ihy, whose name means literally "the sistrum player." This reference to Ihy seems to be part of a play on words associated with music and sistrum players, but the reading of these later words is not certain. "Ihy" is written here with plant determinatives, which indicate that the simile also operates through imagery of plant life, literally "like swamp plants in the marsh." The idea of fertile growth is mobilized by the verbs "to grow strong (*swrḏ*)" and "to flourish (*ȝḥ3ḥ*)."

96. This detailed description of the celebratory, ritual activity surrounding Wenennefer's promotion, which he terms his "day of favor," is very rare. By contrast, the biographies of the high priests of Amun, Bakenkhons (no. 2) and Roma (no. 3b), present initiation as a moment of divine intervention between god and priest alone. The language in Wenennefer's text is elliptical and some readings are uncertain. The presence of young people, as well as that of "others" who seem to play a witnessing role, is emphasized. This "god's eye" perspective on the event may be enabled by the third person voice.

97. It is likely that this self-created goddess is Isis. Goddesses such as Mut and Neith are described as self-creating beings in later religious texts (Stadler 2004, 12) and this aspect of Isis would be appropriate to the birth-house context (see the introductory paragraph to this text).

98. This stanza presents the moment of Wenennefer's initiation, which is enacted by a goddess, probably Isis. The key phrase refers to the revealing of Wenennefer's "form" through her action. *jrw*, "form," is normally used only of gods; since the divine child is alluded to throughout the text, *jrw* may refer to Wenennefer as assimilated with Horus-Ihy. The identification of priests with Horus is a central element of biographies that describe the performance of the Osiris mysteries (no. 14a; Frood 2003, 73–75). This process transforms Wenennefer's prestige and status in a way that is not specified. The allusions to royal presence and the palace suggest that the king ratified the appointment.

99. The final stanza presents Wenennefer's beneficent actions for the gods of Abydos—"those who are within it"—and their reciprocal assurance that he will attain an afterlife, "perfection."

100. The ancient name of el-Mashayikh was "Eastern Behdet."

101. This title relates to Anhurmose's earlier military career prior to his promotion to the position of high priest. The successful performance of his military duties is described in later stanzas of the biography after the description of his childhood and education.

102. Or, more freely, "who only had to look for a thing in order to find it" (with Gardiner 1938, 125), as an evocation of quick intelligence and understanding.

103. As well as evoking delight, the religious, ritual, and festival associations of dancing are appropriate to the theme of priestly activity and role developed in the verses that follow. Joy and dance are contrasted with the powerful image of a "protector" in the next verse.

104. The statement that Anhurmose was one whom Shu "chose" may refer to an oracular event or initiation to priestly office comparable to those narrated by the high priests of Amun, Nebwenenef (no. 1), Bakenkhons (no. 2), and Roma (no. 3b–c). The transition from a military role to a priestly one seems to begin in the preceding stanza describing royal favor.

105. A general term for a group of the highest officials in Upper Egypt.

106. A distinctive epithet that may be an elaboration of the traditional epithet "pure of hands" characteristic of priestly biographies, particularly those associated with the Osiris mysteries (for which see no. 14a).

107. At this point the text moves onto the east wall of the transverse hall.

108. This stanza, with its different formulation, marks a shift in topic, from Anhurmose's proper performance of temple ritual to his moral character and right action toward dependants.

109. The word for "shepherd (*mnjw*)" has a house determinative, evoking meanings related to shelter and physical protection.

110. A possible reference to Anhurmose's tomb.

111. An epithet of Osiris.

112. This verse expresses Anhurmose's desire to be like Thoth, "the Filler," in terms of wisdom and accurate judgment. The epithet "Filler" refers to Thoth's mythical role healing ("filling") the eye of Horus.

113. Unless there was a local manifestation of Atum, his inclusion here may be a reference to Heliopolis. The cattle could relate to the Mnevis bull, an earthly aspect of the sun-god.

114. The word I translate as "support," *rk*, usually refers to time or close vicinity. The context seems to require a meaning connected with physical proximity. A more literal translation might be: "I was the one who was (always) close by them."

115. This stanza is the final, culminating passage of the biography and closes with a quintessential statement of relationship with a single deity. A summation and series of afterlife wishes follows.

116. This epithet describes the king as one who advanced and promoted Anhurmose.

117. The shrine is probably the royal burial, which here is understood to be symbolically within the domain of Amun-Re.

118. The "children of Nut" are stars, but the passage also alludes to Shu, the partner of Nut, as the local deity. This passage is a striking description of the birth of Anhurmose's name, therefore his self, at sunrise.

119. This seems to allude to a mythical episode involving the *neshmet*-barque, which was perhaps enacted during the Osiris mysteries (see no. 14a).

120. The "following" probably refers to the entourage of priests and officials who accompany the cult statue in procession. This stanza expresses Anhurmose's desire to partake of offerings made before this entourage as well as alluding to the possibility that his tomb was a point in the procession.

121. The god's cast-offs were valuable to a mortal in this world and in the next. This is a poetic extension of the desire, commonly expressed in funerary wishes, that offerings revert from the gods to favored individuals and their cults (see also note 25 to no. 3c in this chapter).

Notes to Chapter II

1. The word "bouquet" has the same root as the word for "life" (*ꜥnḫ*) so the verse refers both to garlands that were components of divine offerings and more broadly to the perpetual life bestowed on Userhat through his receipt of these offerings. The "remainder" from offerings that had been placed before deities were highly desirable for an individual's mortuary cult.

2. Literally "the earth-hacker," a deity otherwise known from royal religious texts, including a spell in the Old Kingdom Pyramid Texts and in underworld books inscribed on the walls of New Kingdom royal tombs. In Userhat's text, he seems to be a manifestation of Osiris.

3. The "attack" refers to the defense of Osiris against his enemies, in which Wepwawet and Horus play a central role.

4. An epithet of Osiris. "Weariness" or "inertness" was often ascribed to the dead in Egyptian texts.

5. The "testament" or transfer deed is a legal document concerned with the disposition of offices or possessions. Here it refers to the legal judgment, which resolves, in some versions of the myth, the dispute between Horus and Seth for the throne of Osiris. Thoth, as the god of writing and knowledge, played a central role in this mediation.

6. A mythical locality, here functioning as a court in which the legal dispute between Horus and Seth for the throne of Osiris was settled before the "Sole Lord," Re. A full narrative of this

myth, in which the dispute over the inheritance is argued out before the sun god in a range of mythical locations, is the Tale of Horus and Seth, known from a Twentieth Dynasty papyrus (Lichtheim 1976, 214–23; Wente in Simpson [ed.] 2003, 91–103).

7. This epithet is attested in spells in the Pyramid Texts (Old Kingdom). However, a city determinative is visible beneath the damaged section, perhaps as a metaphor for the sky as a dwelling place, a city, of the gods. Alternative renderings include "who are within the city of Nut" or "who are in Khen-nut," an otherwise unattested place name.

8. An ideal location in the next world where the dead lived and worked.

9. The efflux of Osiris, which includes all the liquids that issue from his body such as sweat and putrefaction, was associated with the Nile and therefore believed to have purifying and healing powers.

10. In the next world.

11. A ritual gesture of welcome, here performed for Re by the sky goddess as he sets in the underworld.

12. Hesret was a name of the necropolis of Hermopolis, the city of Thoth. Hutyebet is the name of a shrine to Thoth in Hermopolis.

13. Horus and Seth. For Thoth's role in their dispute see note 5 to no. 19a above.

14. Kheritjehenu is the place name of an area perhaps near Memphis. This stanza introduces the list of gods, which fills the next five and a half lines.

15. Shepses, "the noble one," was a manifestation of Thoth (Gardiner 1947, II, 47*, no. 358). The goddess Wenut personifies Wenu, an ancient name for Hermopolis.

16. The goddess Nehmetawy is one of Thoth's consorts, a role that Sekhmet can also take. For Hutyebet, see note 12 to this text.

17. Herwer is a locality, slightly to the north of Hermopolis, where Khnum and Hathor were the local deities. Although I read "ruler goddess" as a rare epithet of Hathor here, the verse could refer to two separate goddesses attested in this region, Heqet (of Herwer) and Hathor (Kessler 1981, 145–46, doc. 23). Cusae is a city ca. 40 kilometers south of Hermopolis. The epithet of Hathor "daughter of Pre-who-protects-the-effective-One" is not otherwise known; the "effective One" is a characteristic epithet of Thoth and this designation of Hathor may evoke him (Leitz et. al. 2002, I, 564).

18. Agenu, Hutsnefru (both perhaps to be equated with modern Asfun el-Mataina), and Hefat (modern el-Mo'alla) are all names for towns located in the third Upper Egyptian nome, near Esna. Haroeris, "Horus the elder," is a form of Horus. The god Hemen is usually depicted as a falcon. Tod is also in southern Upper Egypt, ca. 15 kilometers south of Thebes. A cult of Anubis of Tahedj is attested near Tod (Gardiner 1947, II, 20*, nos. 327–29).

19. Hebenu, north of Hermopolis, was capital of the sixteenth Upper Egyptian nome and the location of the tomb of the high steward Nefersekheru (no. 24). The lioness-headed goddess Pakhet of Set was worshipped at Speos Artemidos, a few kilometers north of Hermopolis. Roinet was used to name various localities, including a place north of Hermopolis.

20. The falcon god Nemty may evoke the eighteenth Upper Egyptian nome, with which he was associated (Gardiner 1947, II, 97*, no. 384B). Saka is in the seventeenth Upper Egyptian nome. These nomes are immediately north of Hermopolis. Gesy, modern Qus, is in Upper Egypt, ca. 10 kilometers south of Coptos. The list ends with the two *herty* goddesses equated with Isis and Nephthys in their role as mourners of Osiris (Gardiner 1947, I, 53, n. 6). This may be a culminating reference to Abydos, where Userhat's chapel was dedicated.

21. Possibly a reference to the action of a divine oracle. In a Twenty-first Dynasty account of oracular decisions, the protagonist approaches Amun's cult statue on the "ground of silver of the domain of Amun . . . in order to consult on matters of this land" (Kruchten 1986, 60–

63, 66, 325–26). Jean-Marie Kruchten suggests that the "ground of silver" may be a stand on which the barque was set. If this allusion is correct, the stanza seems to fuse both the rivergoing, ceremonial, royal boat with a portable barque shrine of a god.

22. A euphemism for death (see note 4 to no. 1, chapter I).

23. Behbet el-Hagar in the twelfth nome of Lower Egypt, the site of the most important cult of Isis in Lower Egypt.

24. Thoth in his role as guardian of the scales of judgment in the next world.

25. The epithet "⸢sharp of⸣ eyes" precedes "open of ears" in the parallel text from the Saqqara tomb of Pay (Raven 2005, 44–45, pl. 75).

26. Pay's version of the text continues at this point with: "⸢precise of⸣ words when he opens his mouth to (speak) truth, who is silent concerning the secrets in ⸢the palace⸣… [*half a line lost*] … I performed Maat while I was on earth, without an evil act. I have done … ." After this, the text closes with hymns to Thoth and Maat (Raven 2005, 44–45, pl. 75).

27. These festivals are probably those from which Amenemone wished to receive offerings and in which he wished to participate perpetually. The list is partially restored on the basis of a parallel on a statue dedicated in Karnak for Amenhotep son of Hapu, one of the highest officials under the Eighteenth Dynasty king Amenhotep III (Ockinga 2004, 85, n. c). Jansen-Winkeln (in Ockinga 2004, 92–94) has observed other parallels between these texts and suggests that Amenhotep's may have provided the direct model for Amenemone's.

28. Probably designating a temple, although "Great Mansion" can also refer to palaces and tombs (Ockinga 2004, 86, n. o).

29. The parallels on the tomb statue (no. 20a) and on the statue of Amenhotep son of Hapu (see note 27 to this text) suggest that this stanza was part of an address to Amenemone; the statements in the preceding stanza therefore also probably relate to him.

30. The text would have continued into a ninth column in the lost upper block.

31. Cults of these Eighteenth Dynasty kings were active in the Theban area in the Ramessid period. Nefertari, or more fully Ahmose Nefertari, was the queen of the founder of the Eighteenth Dynasty, Ahmose, and also became an important cult figure in the late New Kingdom. She was most closely linked in deification to her son, Amenhotep I.

32. Montuhotep II (ca. 2010–1960) was the king of the Eleventh Dynasty who was seen as the founder of the epoch now known as the Middle Kingdom. His mortuary temple called Akhset, which is alluded to here and included in the list of temples later in this text, lies beside the temple of the later Eighteenth Dynasty female king Hatshepsut, in the area now called Deir el-Bahri. Didia also dedicated a granodiorite stela bearing religious texts and appeals in Montuhotep's temple (Lowle 1976, 94–95).

33. The directions of sailing are not appropriate to the statue's Theban context as Abydos is downstream from Karnak. Therefore this formula is probably Memphite in origin.

34. The name of a festival associated with the beginning of the Sokar festival. All known references to it are on Theban monuments (Gaballa and Kitchen 1969, 43–45).

35. The "staff for the coffin" seems to refer to the responsibility for funeral preparations, including the coffin, which is handed over at the end of a person's life.

36. Akhmenu is the festival temple of Thutmose III in Karnak. Menset is a lost temple at Dra Abu el-Naga, in the northern part of the Theban West Bank, probably dedicated to Amun with the deified Ahmose Nefertari (see note 31 to this text). For Akhset see note 32 to this text. Djeserakhet is the Amun temple of Thutmose III beside Deir el-Bahri. Djeserdjeseru is the temple of Hatshepsut at Deir el-Bahri. Henketankh is the lost mortuary temple of Thutmose III on the Theban West Bank.

37. A phyle is a group of people who served as part-time priests on rotation.

38. An island in the first cataract, approximately three kilometers south of Aswan.

39. An island in the first cataract ca. 3 kilometers upstream from Sehel (see previous note), which seems to have formed the frontier of Egypt.

40. El-Rizeiqat, north of Gebelein.

41. A reference to future visitors to the necropolis who could be called upon to give offerings for the mortuary cult of Nakhtdjehuty.

42. Although I render "barque," the word *sšm-ḥw* also encompasses the stand on which the barque rested. This more inclusive meaning is confirmed both by the determinative, which depicts this stand, and by the images of barques and stands on the tomb facade.

43. A goddess. Khnum and Nebetuu were the principal deities of the temple of Esna, some 50 kilometers south of Thebes (Gardiner 1947, II, 10*; Leitz et. al. 2002, IV, 34–35).

44. No local cults of the god Geb are currently known.

45. A cult place also associated with Sokar.

NOTES TO CHAPTER III

1. The numerous graffiti of visitors in tombs that express delight at the images and texts within point to the potentially pleasurable and recreational aspect of visits to cemeteries by the living, alongside the pious honoring of the dead and the maintenance of their cults. Here Maya addresses these chance visitors, encouraging them to read and enjoy his inscription. This sentiment is also strongly expressed on the stela of Bakaa (no. 39).

2. Comparable phraseology is found in a scene from the south side of the columned hall of the tomb: "I was the mouth of the king in order to make splendid the temples, to fashion the images of the gods. I was one who entered and saw the Mansion of Gold, in order to propitiate their statues" (Graefe 1975, 210, fig. 3a; van Dijk 1995, 33). These verses are inscribed in a column behind standing figures of Maya and his wife. Maya's brother, Nehuher, stands before them, censing. Title strings of Maya on the jambs of the pylon also include the title "keeper of secrets in the Mansion of Gold in the temples of all the gods" (van Dijk in Martin et al. 1988, 13).

3. It seems that Maya had only daughters and no son, and the identity of the "eldest son" mentioned here is uncertain. Van Dijk (in Martin et al. 1988, 12, n. 20) notes a parallel in an Eighteenth Dynasty biographical stela where the "eldest son" seems to refer to a god, although the context is obscure: "I entered before the august image of Atum; it was his [eldest (?)] son (Shu) who ..." (Fischer 1986, 126, fig. 49). In a later discussion, van Dijk (1993, 19) suggests that the title may refer to Horemheb in his capacity as heir to Tutankhamun, attributing to him the commissioning of Maya's tomb; Horemheb bears the title "eldest son of Horus" in the description of his role as heir and crown prince in the text that narrates his succession to the throne (Murnane 1995, 231).

4. The metaphor of the individual as balance, which is attested from the Middle Kingdom onward, expresses an ideal of honest, impartial social action and alignment with the deities Thoth and Maat.

5. The province in which Nefersekheru's tomb was located.

6. Nefersekheru's name translates as "perfect of plans," and this verse and its parallel in the truth claim later in the text probably make play with this. A verse in the harper's song in the shrine of the tomb is even more explicit in its reference to his name: "When you have had a life of perfect plans, you will be rejuvenated in your time ..." (Osing 1992, 66–72, pl. 42). Such plays signal that these texts were composed for Nefersekheru, rather than being entirely drawn from stock materials.

7. The Mansion of Life seems to be a bureau concerned, in part, with the administration

of palace resources, particularly food provisions. Titles associated with the Mansion of Life, including those of doctors, indicate that roles in this bureau were also intimately connected with the physical person of the king, and the ritual and ceremonial surrounding him.

8. The term for "protected chamber," $k\cancel{3}p$, often involves the presence of children, hence the common alternative translation "nursery." The $k\cancel{3}p$ is usually considered part of the king's inner apartments. Here it is stated to be in the outer palace ($ḥnty$) and may be an intermediary zone between the interior and the outside world, as suggested by the reference to messengers in the next line.

9. A similar phrase in the Middle Kingdom Tale of Sinuhe, "my name was not heard in the herald's mouth" (Parkinson 1997, 29), points to the meaning of this verse. Presumably an individual's name would be reported by the herald if he was sought by the authorities for wrongful behavior or criminal activity.

10. If the restoration of "preparation chamber (w^cbt)" and "horizon ($\cancel{3}ht$)" is correct (with Osing 1992, 46, 50, pl. 35) this may designate an area of the palace connected with butchery and the preparation of meat for the king's meal. "Horizon" was used for the butcheries at Akhenaten's capital, Amarna. This intepretation is supported by the office "royal scribe of the meal for the king" to which Nefersekheru is appointed.

11. "My Horus" is the king, although it may also allude to the local god of Hebenu, Horus, who is often mentioned elsewhere in Nefersekheru's tomb. A statue of Horus of Hebenu sits in the shrine.

12. This description corresponds with the iconography of the accompanying image of Nefersekheru, who is shown adorned with gold collars and an incense cone on his head.

13. This statement has a proverbial quality that can be compared with the final line of the text.

14. Epithets of Osiris.

15. Nefersekheru enjoins visitors to his tomb to offer prayers for him. "Son-who-loves" is a reference to Horus as protector and ritual actor for his father Osiris, expressing the ideal that sons should maintain and ensure the continuity of their fathers' funerary cults.

16. The Egyptian name for the town at Zawyet Sultan where Nefersekheru's tomb is located.

17. The final verses of these funerary wishes describe the cycle of the sun and may also be a metaphor for Nefersekheru's own life, which attains its zenith at his reward.

18. In the next world.

19. The word which I read here (with Osing 1992, 48, 53) as "fate ($š\cancel{3}y$)" is written with only $\mathcal{W}$. A reading as "snake" may also be possible: "there will be no snake ($ḥf\cancel{3}w$) for (that is, against) him." A comparable concept is found in Old Kingdom threat formulas: "May the crocodile be against him in water, the snake ($ḥf\cancel{3}w$) against him on land—(that is) the one who will do anything against this tomb" (see Strudwick 2005, 253, 260). Nefersekheru may be evoking the language of these ancient curses.

20. "Keeper of the balance" is an epithet of Thoth. These verses refer to judgment in the next world.

21. This text closes with a proverbial statement well known from wisdom literature and from the Middle Kingdom tale, The Story of the Shipwrecked Sailor, where comparable phrases come at both the beginning and the end.

22. This sequence of titles was a traditional component of the vizierial titulary in the Ramessid period (Raedler 2004, 289–90). The ancient title "mouth of Nekhen (Hierakonpolis)," in sequence with the honorary title "dignitary ($s\cancel{3}b$)," signals, in part, the bearer's juridical role as well as his access to restricted domains within the palace and in relation to the king (Franke

1984). "He of the curtain (*t3jtj*)" also refers to restricted access, alluding to screened off areas behind the throne.

23. An epithet of Thoth.

24. Here Maat is assimilated with the cobra goddess, Great-of-Magic, as the uraeus on the king's brow, a further sign of his legitimate kingship.

25. The crook and the flail are held by the king and Osiris in depictions (see fig. 8) and, as symbols of care (crook) and authority (flail), are central accoutrements of kingship.

26. These verses describe Sety's accession to the throne using a sequence of events and phraseology comparable to the accession inscription of Horemheb (Murnane 1995, 232; Gnirs 1996, 234, n. 231). Thus Paser aligns his own promotions to high offices with the king's assumption of power, a narrative strategy that can be compared with that of the high priest of Amun, Nebwenenef, who links his appointment to office with the first Opet festival of Ramesses II (no. 1, note 1, chapter I).

27. The designation of Paser as "the Osiris of" may indicate that he had died by the time this inscription was carved. He does not bear this designation in the text dedicated to Sety I (no. 25a).

28. These restorations are suggested by Assmann (1980, 6–7, n. 22), who bases them on parallels in a hymn to Khonsu on a Nineteenth Dynasty statue of a royal scribe, Roy. The motif of the individual as the king's creation, which is central to biographies of the Amarna period (Assmann 1980; Gnirs 1996, 232–34), is alluded to in the following stanzas of this text. This theme is also strongly expressed, using comparable phraseology, in a speech to Sety I accompanying the reward scene of the overseer of the royal harem, Hormin (not translated in this book): "O ruler who made me among people, the one whom he raised through his *ka*, joy and perfection are for your retinue, who listen to your teaching. I was one humble whom you raised, a noble whom you created" (KRI I, 309, 8–10).

29. Kitchen (1993, 239) restores these very damaged verses more fully; reading "There is nothing (that) [one can conceal] in the presence of the Sovereign, so that His Majesty sees (even) from (within) the innermost sanctum, [past?] the keepers of the secret doors." I suggest that the verses may concern Paser's access to the king, which culminates with his reward in the following verses.

30. Comparable motifs of privileged and exclusive entry through the palace gates occur in Eighteenth Dynasty biographies such as that of Rekhmire (see the introductory paragraph to this text): "I reached the door of the palace gate; the courtiers bowed, the elders of the forecourt clearing the way for me . . ." (N. de G. Davies 1943, I, 80; II, pls. 11–12).

31. The illegible signs here are probably a priestly title, perhaps related to Tawer.

32. A similar statement is also made by the vizier Paser (see no. 25) on a statue of his set up in the mortuary temple of the Eleventh Dynasty king Montuhotep II on the Theban West Bank: "I was the son of an established man and I was born on your (Amun-Re's) ground" (KRI III, 18, 3–4: not translated here). In this case the verse is set within an offering formula and afterlife wishes.

33. The restoration of "portal (*sbḫt*)" is likely, although the determinative of a seated man, which is certain, is unusual for this word. The motif of Prehotep as both a curtain (*t3jtj*) and portal occurs throughout this text, making play with the formulaic use of the title "he of the curtain" in the traditional vizieral title string (see n. 22 to no. 25a in this chapter). Here the terms express that Prehotep both protects the king and can facilitate access to him. In a later verse, Prehotep is said to be the "curtain of the sky, portal of the earth," perhaps alluding to divine and earthly aspects of the king. The pairing of metaphors is a feature of this text, seen also in Prehotep's identification as the king's eyes and ears and as one who speaks on his behalf and reports to him as a herald.

34. An ancient and prestigious title that expressed a particularly close relationship to the king. It is probably an archaism in this context.

35. In these epithets Prehotep relates himself to the king's dual nature. While Upper and Lower Egypt can refer to geographical divisions in certain contexts, here these designations characterize different aspects of kingship. *njsw* is the premier title for the king, referring to political and historical manifestations of power, while *bjty* alludes to religious and ancestral conceptions of kingship and its obligations.

36. An epithet of the Apis bull. The bull was a special manifestation of the god Ptah.

37. "Mansion of Eternity" refers to the cult chapel Prehotep probably dedicated at Saqqara in which this stela was set up.

38. "Filler" is an epithet of Thoth, referring to his mythical role healing, that is completing or "filling," the eye of Horus. See also next note.

39. The word which I read as "grain-measure" is written with the *wedjat*-eye, which represented concepts relating to completeness. Component parts of this hieroglyph were used to indicate fractions in the measurement of amounts of grain, for which the full eye represented a complete totality. See also previous note.

40. This obscure verse seems to refer to reciprocity of action: people did not bow or give thanks to Prehotep without his performing a service for them.

41. This is a metaphor for Prehotep as a vessel for Maat and the truth and justice she embodies, on which the following verse elaborates.

42. Prehotep's name was not inscribed at the end of this column due to lack of space.

43. A temple in Heliopolis.

44. The "balance post" is the central vertical on which the crossbar rests. For the metaphor of the balance, of which the "plumbline" in the preceding verse is an elaboration, see note 4 to the biography of Nefersekheru (no. 24) in this chapter.

45. From the New Kingdom, "Great Throne" could refer to the sanctuary or whole temple area, as well as an actual seat or barque stand.

46. This striking phrase seems to refer to potentially evil, polluting elements within the necropolis, a domain that is usually presented positively in funerary texts as desirable and divine (for example, see face 4). For discussion of the meanings of "abomination (*bwt*)" in temple contexts and in relation to the physical body, spheres that are comparable with or relevant to the necropolis, see Frandsen 1999; 2001.

47. Damage to the text makes the reading of this verse uncertain. It may continue the ideas relating to corruption and partiality in the previous verse. A passage in a New Kingdom papyrus recording variant maxims from the Middle Kingdom instruction text, The Teaching of Ptahhotep, may point toward a possible meaning: "Do not be partial [... ...] two men, leaning to one side is the *bwt* (abomination) of god" (Frandsen 2001, 173). The verse may allude alternately to taboo elements in the necropolis, which are referred to on face 2 (see previous note).

48. In contrast to the statements of adoration that open the other texts on this object, this text begins and ends with phrases concerning Tia's integration with the community of Osiris (Smith 1987, 75–79; 2006) who is depicted in the scene.

49. A reference to the process of mummification with which Anubis was particularly associated.

50. The "*tjenenet*-shrine" has Memphite associations and is especially connected with Sokar. It is also a component of epithets of Ptah and Osiris (Leitz et. al. 2002, V, 876). From the First Intermediate period onward, it can designate the tomb of Osiris (Schlögl 1980, 105–06; see also spell 1B in the Book of the Dead: Faulkner 1985, 36).

51. A euphemism for the next world.

52. This clause seems to express Tia's desire to be as far-sighted as the falcon-god Horus, whose epithet here emphasizes this particular quality.

53. The texts on the right and left front of the naos fan out from a central *ankh*-sign that is not itself to be read. The sharing of centrally placed signs and columns of inscription between the right and left halves is a feature of the organization of inscriptions on this statue (compare no. 30).

54. See note 50 to no. 27 in this chapter.

55. References to Memphis and Abydos throughout the inscriptions could indicate a provenance in either place. As few statues from Memphite temples survive, Abydos is perhaps more likely especially as it had areas with Memphite associations.

56. I follow Ahmed Badawi's (1944, 203) suggested restoration. A title string would be expected here; the exact sequence is uncertain.

57. This unusual designation, "monumental hall (*wsḫt mnw*)," may describe a broad hall with monuments surrounding and extending before it.

58. The Libyan war inscription of Merenptah at Karnak provides a possible parallel to Huy's text, in which people are made to seem foolish by an external manifestation of royal and divine power: "I am the god who shepherds you ... like a father who sustains his children. Are you silly (*swg³*) like birds? Do you not know the perfection of what he does?" (KRI IV, 4,5–7; Manassa 2003, 28 renders differently).

59. Or "I am the favored one of the great one who is in Abydos (Osiris)."

60. For the "*tjenenet*-shrine" see note 50 to no. 27 in this chapter. Its occurrence here may allude to the areas of Abydos with Memphite associations.

61. An epithet of Osiris. The *djam*-scepter (*ḏˁm*) occurs in a similar context of divine adornment in the Litany of Re, a text included in some New Kingdom royal tombs: "I establish the *djam*-scepter of Orion, I give the *nemes* to the Hidden-of-Name" (Hornung 1975–1976, I, 233–34; II, 91).

62. The *nemes* (*nms*) is a cloth headdress, commonly depicted on the king that was also a component of ritual performance, especially in connection with Osiris, and in personal transfiguration in the next world (Goebs 1995; see also previous note).

63. The Abydos fetish is a pole topped with a rounded, mound-like object and adorned with elements usually found on headdresses, such as fillets and double feathers. Kha's role in attaching the plumes perhaps rendered it complete and potent for use in ritual.

64. A reference to the ritual defence of Osiris from his enemies during the Osiris mysteries (see no. 14a).

65. The translation of this passage (with Anthes 1974, 45, fig. 5) is uncertain, and I know of no parallel for "the-place-which-protects-its-lord." If correctly read, it may refer to the tomb of Osiris in Umm el-Qaab where rituals associated with his resurrection were performed.

66. This tentatively read clause may refer to maintaining eternal life by pronouncing the protagonist's name in the mouths of the living.

67. An epithet of Osiris more usually found in mortuary texts.

68. One hundred and ten years was the ideal age.

69. The reading of this verse is uncertain, but it seems to refer to Bay's privileged, sole access to the king.

70. The erased cartouche may be that of Siptah.

71. These titles and name are restored from the reverse of the stela (with Gardiner 1912, 50). The temple of Sety II in this title may be identified with the chapel of Sety II in the first court of Karnak temple (Drenkhahn 1980, 8–9).

72. The size of the erased section fits the word "benefactress (*rpˁyt*)," which is to be restored here and elsewhere on the stela. This title refers to Tawosret in her capacity as regent and is

attested on other monuments of hers. The Eighteenth Dynasty female king Hatshepsut also bore this title during her regency for Thutmose III, prior to her assumption of full royal titles.

73. Similar statements are found in the biographical and legal texts of Samut (no. 11), where he asserts that no member of his family is to have access to the property that he bequeathed to the goddess Mut. This suggests that the protagonist of the Bilgai stela too may have made a personal endowment of property to the temple.

74. This seems to refer to potential suppression of cult activity relating to Amun. Through negligence of the temple, the overseers to which this threat is directed may prevent it from being visited by the cult statue during its rituals and processions.

75. The sense seems to be that, although colleagues and relatives of the disgraced overseer will remain, they will not continue his cult or maintain the memory of his name.

76. This motif of the successful completion of a specific task powerfully contrasts with the corresponding statement in the preceding curse that "nothing that he does will succeed."

77. David Warburton (1997, 185) observes that this volume of wine is nearly half the volume (62,000) that Ramesses III claimed he had donated to the temple of Amun throughout his entire reign.

78. Possibly meaning that Nedjem, during his tenure as high steward, did not achieve anything comparable to the yields managed by the protagonist.

79. The relative value of the amount of honey laid claim to here may be obtained through comparison with the 1370 amphorae Ramesses III recorded that he gave to the temple of Amun during the course of his reign (Warburton 1997, 185).

80. If "sack ($ḥ^3r$)" is the correct restoration, this represents a significant amount of grain. One sack is equivalent to 48 liters (12½ gallons), so 140,000 sacks is 6,720,000 liters (1,764,000 gallons). The monthly rations of an ordinary workmen at Deir el-Medina included 5½ sacks of grain (barley and emmer) each month. In this context, Warburton (1997, 184) notes two administrative texts that record that one field worker could be expected to produce 200 sacks annually. He calculates on this basis that 700 workers on an area of land between 7,000 and 14,000 arouras (ca. 4767 to 9534 acres) would be needed to produce 140,000 sacks of grain.

81. This is perhaps a hyperbolic statement that the protagonist was more vigilant than anyone in fulfilling his duties.

82. That the opening offering formula is on behalf of the king, rather than the owner of the stela, as traditionally, is a striking feature of this text.

83. A variation on the standard writing of this title as "fanbearer on the right of the king," possibly an elaboration or a scribal error.

84. Gardiner (1948, 20) suggested, on the basis of the waterlogged character of the area Amenmose says he reclaimed in this text and the designation "Western River," that Na-Amun-Re was somewhere in the west of the Delta. He also noted that Na-Amun-Re is named as the location of vineyards on wine-jars from the Ramesseum.

85. The "House of Gold" may refer here to an area for storing cult equipment (further see note 59 to no. 8, chapter I).

86. See note 45 to no. 27 in this chapter.

87. Statues of baboons adoring the rising sun were sometimes incorporated as architectural features in the outer areas of temples and around the bases of obelisks.

88. The scribe statue of the high priest of Amun, Amenhotep, provides a parallel for increasing the number of carrying poles for shrines (no. 4, with note 32, in chapter I).

89. This may refer to the action of the cult statue in acknowledging other divine images and statues during a procession (compare the text on the back pillar of no. 3c, chapter I).

90. This seems to evoke the texts relating to divine favor and Amenmose's property endowments that are inscribed upon the statue. It is also possible that it refers to images and works within the temple itself.

91. That the god's staff is given a portable shrine transforms it into a separate cult image.

92. Here Amenmose describes his reclamation of flooded land in the area of Na-Amun-Re in order to build a temple complex that is designated as part of the estate of the Amun.

93. The mortuary temple of Ramesses III at Medinet Habu on the Theban West Bank.

94. This word, which I translate as "barques (*sšm-ḥw*)," has a broader meaning, including, for example, the stands on which the barques were placed (see also no. 22a, with note 42, in chapter II).

95. A parallel for Amenmose's endowment of personal property to the god's estate is the Nineteenth Dynasty biography and legal text of Samut (no. 11).

96. If this reading as "brightness (*ꜣsb*)" is correct, it may refer to the inlaid eyes of a cult statue.

97. This reading is very tentative. Amenmose may be referring to the expulsion of delinquent servants (*bꜣkw*) but the context and meaning is not clear. The reading as "servants" is supported by the human determinatives. By either ignoring the determinatives, thus reading *bꜣkw* as "quotas," or reading as "labor quotas (*bꜣkw-rmṯ*)," the passage could be translated as: "because of the quotas which I did away with." This could mean that he managed to fulfil his quotas so quickly and effortlessly that they went out almost immediately. Similar statements are made in the stela from Bilgai (no. 33). Charles Van Siclen (1980, 189–90) offers a very different rendering of this passage, considering the reference to servants to be an epithet of Ahmose Nefertari: "the Primeval One on the West of Thebes, the advocate (?) for the lesser name of servants. They come (?) to me in my position of power, my office to which they. . . ."

98. The parallel for the continuation of this passage on the left half of the base of Amenmose's Delta statue (no. 35a) suggests that these verses may be part of a list of possessions that Amenmose had endowed to the temple of Amun. The probable inclusion of singers could refer to the singing that was part of temple cult and from which Amenmose's mortuary cult may have also benefited.

99. This section of the line, which is inscribed at the back of the base, could not be collated by Kitchen so the readings are all uncertain. It seems to close with the name of an individual who perhaps acted as a witness and guarantor for the endowment.

100. I suggest that this section of the text refers to the statue itself, which is seated before this line of inscription. The word "heir" (*jmy-ḥt*, "one who comes after"), which I propose to restore here, signifies that the statue will act as a representative of Amenmose, a component of his personhood, within the temple. Parallels for such a concept are found on Ramessid statues such as the statue of Panehsy (no. 28) and Amenemone (no. 36), as well as one belonging to the viceroy of Nubia, Setau (no. 41), which gives the statue itself a voice: "I am your (Setau's) watchman who is in this temple" (KRI III, 82,7).

Notes to Chapter IV

1. This may refer to a time when a cult statue was accessible to supplicants, perhaps during procession. An alternative interpretation is: "I will repeat them to my mistress in exchange for offerings" (Pinch 1993, 334). Both readings are appropriate to the context; they may constitute a deliberate word play.

2. "Gold" is an epithet of Hathor. This stanza is a vivid description of the bald-headed statue with its palm cupped to its mouth.

3. A euphemistic allusion to the next world that may also refer to the statue's position within the temple.

4. This epithet may refer to Isis in relation to a male deity, possibly Re (Goyon 1990, 59, n. 32).

5. The Seth animal, which determines the word for uproar here, has been erased.

6. This verse may introduce Penre's next promotion. Jean-Claude Goyon (1990, 59) restores the passage more fully and with a different emphasis: "I returned to Egypt in a position of [command ... the decision to promote me among the] companions as chief of Medjay was communicated to me" (my rendering).

7. "Stopping" and "assenting" are part of the standard terminology for oracular communication: the cult statue halts before (*smn ḥr*) the supplicant in order to grant a decision and then indicates agreement by assent (*ḥn*). In some cases, lack of movement, stopping, can indicate a negative response to a query (no. 15). Here the oracle may ratify Penre's promotion to office by indicating that he would succeed the current chief of Medjay. This decision may also relate to others among Penre's offices.

8. The identity of Bunakhtef (alternatively rendered Nebnakhtef) is unclear, although it is likely that he was the chief of Medjay whom Penre would succeed. Charles F. Nims (1956, 148) suggested that Bunakhtef was Penre's father.

9. The verses before the lost section record Isis's speech to Penre, apparently bestowing favors upon him comparable to those received by Bunakhtef. The goddess's speech probably ends in the lacuna. The strong statement of agreement, "saying 'yes' emphatically," may express the enthusiastic response of those who witness the event as, for example, in the biographies of Userhat (no. 19b) and Nefersekheru (no. 24). Alternatively it may record Penre's commitment to honor the goddess in return for her favor (with Römer 1994, 481). One action he promises is to create this stela to record the event, as stated in the next verse (compare no. 45).

10. This verse is a general statement of divine power: the one who follows the goddess, placing her in his heart, will be promoted, just as Penre was promoted.

11. Or: "to [consult on] every plan with me."

12. A comparable blend of military action with ceremonial can be found in the biography of the overseer of soldiers, Nehesy (no. 40) and in earlier texts such as the Eighteenth Dynasty biography of the soldier Amenemhab (*Urk.* IV, 895,9–12; Freier in Blumenthal et. al. 1984, 313; Baines in preparation).

13. For mooring as a metaphor for dying see note 4 to no. 1, chapter I.

14. This verse alludes to a passage in Coffin Text spell 335 (Middle Kingdom) and spell 17 of the Book of the Dead (New Kingdom), which expresses a complementary relationship between Re and Osiris: "As for yesterday, it is Osiris. As for tomorrow, it is Re ..." (Faulkner 1985, 44 for the Book of the Dead). In New Kingdom underworld books, Osiris and Re are merged.

15. This stanza evokes the process of judgment in the next world, set out in spell 125 of the Book of the Dead and depicted in its vignettes (Faulkner 1985, 29–34).

16. Literally "released of heart."

17. This is the first of two speeches addressed to Nehesy as a component of the performance surrounding his integration into the council of thirty. In this first verse, the title "count (*ḥȝty-ꜥ*)" is distinctive: with "member of the *pat*" it was one of the ancient ranking titles identifying members of the inner elite and presenting the closeness of their connection to the king. This statement mobilizes the associations of the title to emphasize the transformation of Nehesy's status. "Step (*nmtt*)" may make play with the statement on the left jamb where Nehesy guides the journeys (*nmtt*) of his own subordinates.

18. Or "he gives, he is brought" (Anthes 1965, 87), perhaps in reference to the reciprocity that bound the king and the elites: the protagonist acts for, and pays honor to, the king, and in return, is favored with promotion and elevation among his peers. My rendering (with Rickal 2005, I, 285) gives the verse a proverbial quality, perhaps relating to the ceremonial associated with the promotion.

19. I read this verse as a speech made by Nehesy to the king, which may refer to some sort of ceremonial role that Nehesy performed in relation to him, perhaps bearing a *ka*-standard. This statement can be compared with those of priests who narrate roles bearing cult statues in procession (e.g., nos. 3c, 16, 17) and is comparable to the ceremonial role alluded to in the biography of Khetef (no. 38, with note 12).

Notes to Chapter V

1. Roinet was a name given to various places, typically wadi mouths with sacred associations. Here it probably refers to a locality near Elkab.

2. "She of the upper district" is depicted as a snake-headed goddess on the left interior wall of the temple, in a row of three scenes showing Ramesses II offering before goddesses, one of whom is Nekhbet and the other of uncertain identification. Philippe Derchain (1971, 69) suggests, on the basis of the scene arrangement on this wall, that the three goddesses were also named in Setau's text, Nekhbet and "she of the upper district" framing the now-lost third name.

3. Derchain (1971, 70) suggests that Horus of Nekhen is the last of the three gods named here. These may correspond to those depicted on the right interior wall of the temple: Thoth, a falcon god, and Horus-who-protects-his-father identified with Horus of Nekhen.

4. The text begins with the full titulary of Ramesses II, constructed of five separate components: the Horus name, relating the king to Horus; the Two Ladies name, relating him to the goddesses of Upper and Lower Egypt, Nekhbet and Wadjet; the Golden Horus name (which is poorly understood); and the prenomen and nomen (for which see the glossary).

5. Or: "[When] the herald was speechless, I clarified words" (Helck 1975, 87–89: my rendering).

6. With Wente (1985, 351). Or: "I was provided with complete rations as scribe of the horned cattle, [without] neglecting books in school" (Helck 1975, 89: my rendering).

7. This vivid metaphor is developed further in a damaged text of a high-ranking official from Serabit el-Khadim, inscribed on the edge of a stela of Ramesses IV. In that text (not translated here), the individual claims that he was one who "filled the magazines with the child of the granaries," as a reference to grain (KRI VI, 27,3).

8. The reading of these lines is based on Helck (1975, 89) with Rickal (2005, II/1, 1182) and narrates the honoring of the king by his subjects. Wente's (1985, 351) alternative reading is also compatible with the traces: "I [cleared] all the (irrigation) canals. I did not deal with this land so that the growth of any child was stunted. I caused those who were young to pay honor to his Majesty."

9. With Wente (1985, 351), in whose rendering the passage describes Setau in the role of priestly actor, performing rituals for Amun on the king's behalf. Helck's (1975, 89–91) reading of these very indistinct lines requires a different interpretation, perhaps linking the recognition of Setau with the honoring of Amun: "he distinguished me, as he [honored (?)] my god in order to create his forms, and he will grant him eternity as lord of the Two Lands" (my rendering).

10. Akerty, more normally Akuyata, is probably the area of Wadi Allaqi, a gold mining zone in Lower Nubia, stretching further south in the Eastern Desert. Irem designated a region in central Sudan, upstream of the fifth cataract, in the area of the Shendi reach (O'Connor 1987).

11. The temple of Wadi el-Sebua.

12. This perhaps refers to the fact that the rear section of the temple, including the hypostyle hall and sanctuary, was rock-cut (Wente 1985, 357, with n. rr).

13. This may refer to a statue of the deified Ramesses II set up in the sanctuary in the

presence of other gods including Horus of Quban who is mentioned next in the text. The epithet "lord of the ways" is attributed to Amun on some of the smaller client stelae dedicated with Setau's (e.g., no. 42) and may be local.

14. Quban was one of the most important New Kingdom settlements in Lower Nubia, controlling access to the gold mines of Wadi Allaqi.

15. The group after Maat is clear, but its reading is problematic. Neither Wente's (1985, 358, n. hhh) reading "his great mother," nor Helck's (1975, 93) "Maat, whom he greatly loves," seem satisfactory. I leave the group untranslated.

16. The temple of Wadi el-Sebua (see no. 41b).

17. This may refer to Ramose's role in assembling a smaller specialist force from the larger troop.

18. The determinative to the signs suggests this was the end of a personal name.

19. The temple of Ramesses II at el-Derr, which was ca. 20 kilometers north of Aniba on the Korosko bend of the Nile. This statement specifies the district belonging to the town associated with the temple.

20. The long deceased first queen of Ramesses II, who had a statue with a cult in the temple at Aniba.

21. As a measure of length, a *khet* is equivalent to 100 cubits (ca. 46 meters). It seems to have been used as a measure of area in texts in Nubia in particular (Helck 1986, 27), where it is equivalent to 100 cubits squared (ca. 2116 square meters, ca. 1900 square yards).

22. Miu is an area on the east bank of the Nile near Toshka, ca. 25 kilometers downstream from Aniba. It is also the name of another locality some 600 kilometers upstream at Kurgus.

23. Helck (1986, 28) identified this goddess as a form of Hathor whose cult center was at Faras, a site ca. 30 kilometers north of the second cataract.

24. Probably land that had no owner, either for lack of an heir or because there was no claimant.

25. Mery may have been Penniut's predecessor in office.

26. Probably Serra, south of Faras (see note 23 to this text) and a little north of the second cataract.

27. Meaning uncertain. Helck (1986, 29) suggested that the term may associate the land with foreign settlers, perhaps from Alasiya.

28. Rendering uncertain. It seems to give a calculation for the value of the endowed, somewhat poor quality land, in relation to *arouras* of normal, arable land. Thus Penniut's endowment equates to a little under 4 *arouras* (ca. 3 acres).

29. These notations indicate that the donation had been formally and officially ratified, recorded, and "fixed (*smn*)" to ensure that it would not be subject to requisition from any future royal administration or other claimants.

30. Although associated with water and perhaps located near the river, the character of this type of land is uncertain (see Helck 1986, 30–31).

31. Helck (1986, 31) suggested that *khelel* (*ḫll*) could be the cutting for a canal.

32. Armant (*jwny*), located a little over 6 kilometers south of Thebes (modern Luxor), was a major cult center of Montu.

33. See note 10 to no. 41b in this chapter.

NOTES TO CHAPTER VI

1. Probably referring to the building in which the stela was dedicated.

2. Or "He (Nebre) made adorations before his name … he made humble supplications before his face."

3. If the reading as "cow" is correct, this could refer to an offering for the god that Nakhtamun may have misappropriated (Borghouts 1982, 28 with n. 137). A possible parallel is provided by a Second Intermediate period inscription from Coptos that relates measures undertaken against an individual who may have stolen sacrificial animals from the temple (Goebs 2003). The Nauri Decree of Sety I also details penalties imposed on those who sold or stole temple cattle (Goebs 2003, 33 with n. 33 and refs). An alternative reading is "his evil (action)" (*jsft*: with KRI III, 654, 11; Lichtheim 1976, 106–7).

4. This statement probably refers to the punishment inflicted on Nakhtamun by Amun, which was subsequently withdrawn and forgiven.

5. For the associations of "Great Throne," see note 45 to no. 27, chapter III.

6. The motif of "seeing darkness by day" occurs in a number of hymns and prayers from Deir el-Medina (Borghouts 1982, 7 with n. 31; Galán 1999). It is possible that these relate actual cases of temporary blindness; Borghouts notes examples of individuals seeking medical treatment for blindness where the cause is connected with divine anger. However, it is likely that the majority of such references in hymns are metaphors, expressing the power of the god both to punish and show mercy.

7. Or "I will proclaim his power to those who do not know it and those who do."

8. Literally "without my heart." For the Egyptians, heart was the center of thought and emotion.

9. For birthing bricks, see note 73 to no. 11a, chapter I.

10. Or "to the wind," evoking one possible manifestation of the goddess. In the next stanza, Meretseger comes to Neferabu as a "sweet breeze."

11. The term used for the workforce at Deir el-Medina.

12. This formulation is based on the standard Ramessid structure of oaths, for example, "As Amun endures and as the ruler endures, I will do . . ." It therefore expresses Qen's false oath without repeating the dangerous words themselves.

13. For the meaning of this phrase, see the previous note.

14. The translation "architrave" for *šdyt* is uncertain. Borghouts (1982, 6 n. 26, followed by McDowell 1999, 102) renders "scoop," based on the word *šdj*, which in medical texts designates a type of container. However, identification of the word with the object on Huy's shoulders seems more likely here (with Tosi and Roccati 1972, 78).

15. "This" may refer to the punishment inflicted on Huy by the Moon, which only the god then has the power to reverse. Alternatively it could refer to Huy's misdeed, the effects of which the god can remedy and forgive.

16. A form of Amun associated with the cliff path to the Valley of the Kings (Vernus 2002, 240).

17. The identification of Hathor with Mut may be a way of indirectly identifying her with Amun, her consort at Karnak.

18. This may be a play on the more traditional statement "I am a servant," which is also an alternative reading.

19. This may refer to a small cave or unfinished tomb in the cliffs above the temples of Deir el-Bahri in Djesret, which might have been considered sacred space. Its walls were inscribed with numerous graffiti, some of which have been understood to associate the cave with places of healing (Marciniak 1981; but see Philips 1986). Menset is the name of the temple of Amun and the deified Eighteenth Dynasty queen Ahmose Nefertari on the Theban West Bank (see note 36 to no. 21, chapter II, and no. 35b).

20. Or "I ate loaves during/from the festival" (Vernus 2000, 334). The "great *akh*-spirits" may refer to stelae dedicated to ancestors, termed "effective *akh*-spirits," which were set up in the local chapels (for which see Demarée 1983).

21. The Valley of the Queens.

22. The rendering "mountain" is appropriate to the context, but very uncertain. Vernus (2000, 335) offers a range of readings, including "I drank the water flooding down as a sheet of water in the precinct of Menet" (my rendering) in reference to torrents of water which flowed through the sanctuary. He suggests that "Menet" could be the cave-sanctuary associated with Hathor and Taweret at the western end of the Valley of the Queens, which was occasionally flooded due to desert storms. For this sanctuary, see Desroches Noblecourt 1990, esp. 10–18.

23. Or "I have watered the rushes and the lotuses for you" (Vernus 2000, 334).

24. Satzinger (1985, 252; see also Szpakowska 2003, 136–37, 142) suggests that this phrase indicates that Ipuy was not physically present at a festival when the dream was received. For discussion of this text as evidence for blurred boundaries between public and private spheres of religious practice and devotion, see Depauw and Smith 2004, 90.

25. This reference to teaching evokes the instruction which Djehutyemheb received through his dream (no. 12a).

26. A common epithet, probably ending a self-characterization of Ipuy.

27. Drunkenness, with which Hathor was particularly associated, was a key component of some festival participation (see Depauw and Smith 2004, 86–89).

28. This evokes the conceptualization of the bodies of deities as composed of precious materials, as a way of describing and manifesting textually what could not be apprehended.

29. Hathor was Amun's daughter and consort, and this line seems to refer both to embrace and physical union.

Sources

Included here are the main editions used in preparing the translations, as well as some other translations, sources for photographs, object descriptions where available, and key additional discussions for some texts. Full lists, especially of older publications, can be found in the volumes of PM, KRI, and Schulz 1992 for statues.

1. Theban Tomb 157. PM I^2, 1, 267 (8). Editions: Sethe 1907, with translation; KRI III, 282,13 – 285,3. Further translation: Kitchen 2000, 201–3. Photographs: Borchardt 1931, pls. 1–2; L. Bell 1969, 32 upper; Hofmann 2004, 33, fig. 35. Line drawing: Kitchen 1982, 47, fig. 16.

2a. Munich, Staatliche Sammlung Ägyptischer Kunst Gl. WAF. 38. Editions: KRI III, 297,4–299,6; Plantikow-Münster 1969, with translation and discussion. Further translation: Kitchen 2000, 212–13. Photograph and description: Schulz 1992, I, 428–29, cat. 253; II, pl. 112. Important discussions include: Yoyotte 1957; Schoske 1987 (for this statue and the Cairo statue, with photographs); Jansen-Winkeln 1993; Hofmann 2004, 141–43.

2b. Cairo, Egyptian Museum CG 42155. Editions: Legrain 1909, 21–23, pl. 18; KRI III, 295,7–297,3. Translations: Lichtheim 1997, 47–49; Kitchen 2000, 212–13. Photographs and description: Schulz 1992, I, 255–56, cat. 140; II, pl. 58b–c.

3a. Cairo, Egyptian Museum JE 37874. Editions: Lefebvre 1929, 16–18, with translation; KRI IV, 131,8–15. Further translation: Kitchen 2003, 99. Photographs and description: Schulz 1992, I, 291–92, cat. 161; II, pl. 71a–d.

3b. Cairo, Egyptian Museum CG 42186. Editions: Lefebvre 1929, 18–26, with translation; KRI IV, 208,4–209,15. Further translation: Kitchen 2003, 150–51. Photographs and description: Schulz 1992, I, 280–81, cat. 154; II, pl. 67c–d.

3c. Cairo, Egyptian Museum CG 42185. Editions: Lefebvre 1929, 4–16, with translation; KRI IV, 129,1–131,7. Further translation: Kitchen 2003, 98–99. Photographs and description: Schulz 1992, I, 278–79, cat. 153; II, pl. 67a–b.

3d. Karnak, temple of Amun. PM II^2, 177 (527b–d). Editions: Lefebvre 1929, 26–39, with translations and a photograph; KRI IV, 210,1–16; 287,10 – 289,11. Further translations: Kitchen 2003, 151–52; 206–8. Photograph: Schwaller de Lubicz 1999, pl. 378.

4. Cairo, Egyptian Museum JE 36348. Editions: Legrain 1904, 21 (mistakenly referred to as a stela), with discussion p. 17; KRI VI, 542,11–543,3.

5. Karnak, temple of Amun. PM II^2, 172 (506c). Edition: KRI VI, 534,10–536,10. Translation: Breasted 1906, 238–40, §§488–89.

6. Karnak, temple of Amun. PM II², 172 (506d–f). Editions: Lefebvre 1929, 47–54, with translation; KRI VI, 540,3–542,2. Photograph of door thickness: Schwaller de Lubicz 1999, pl. 374.

7. Karnak, temple of Amun. PM II², 172 (505). Editions: Lefebvre 1929, 55–69 with translation and a photograph of the north reward scene (pl. 2); Helck 1956, with translation and discussion; KRI VI, 455,6–458,16; 539,1–540,2. Further translation: Breasted 1906, 241–45, §§ 492–98 (north scene only). Further photographs: Hermann 1963, pl. 10, with discussion; Schwaller de Lubicz 1999, pls. 376–77.

8. Karnak, temple of Amun. PM II², 174 (516). Editions: Wente 1966, with translation and discussion; KRI VI, 536,11–538,13. Further translation: Breasted 1906, 240–41, §§ 490–91.

9. Karnak, temple of Amun. Editions: Sauneron 1966, with translation and photograph; KRI VI, 532,8–533,16.

10. Brussels, Musées royaux d'Art et d'Histoire E 4661. PM II², 395. Editions: Speleers 1923, 64, no. 268; KRI III, 845,13–846,3. Translation: Kitchen 2000, 565.

11a–b. Theban Tomb 409. PM I², 1, 462 (4)–(6). Editions: KRI III, 336,1–341,12; Negm 1997, pls. XLIV–LXIII, with translation pp. 37–46. Further translations: Wilson 1970; Vernus 1978, with discussion; Assmann 1999, 401–6, no. 173 (11a only); Kitchen 2000, 243–47. Further photographs: Muhammed 1966, pls. 39–41, 47–51. Important discussions include: Assmann 2002 [1996], 229–46 (with partial translation); Morenz 1998; 2000; Gnirs 2003.

12a–b. Theban Tomb 194. PM I², 1, 301 (14). Editions: Assmann 1978, with translation and discussion; KRI VII, 153,5–155,4; Seyfried 1995, pls. 35–36, with translation pp. 69–73 (texts 119–120). Further translations: Assmann 1999, 399–401, no. 172 (12a only); Szpakowska 2003, 138–41 (with discussion), 195–96 (12a only).

13. Theban Tomb 158. PM I², 1, 270 (19). Editions: Seele 1959, pl. 29A; KRI V, 410,10–411,1.

14a. Paris, Louvre A. 66. Edition: Anthes 1974, 41–43 (partial edition and translation); KRI III, 452,4–453,5. Further translation: Kitchen 2000, 322–23.

14b. Cairo, Egyptian Museum CG 34505. Editions: Mariette 1880, 36–37, pl. 41 (reversed); KRI III, 453,6–454,6. Translation: Kitchen 2000, 323. Photograph and discussion: Loukianoff 1956 [1937], 768, 772, fig. 3.

15. Cairo, Egyptian Museum JE 43649. Editions: Legrain 1916, 161–70, with translation and photograph; KRI III, 464,2–465,4. Translations: John A. Wilson, in Pritchard (ed.) 1969, 448; Kitchen 2000, 330.

16. Manchester, The Manchester Museum 2699. Edition: Petrie 1903, 36, pl. 37 [upper], with translation by Francis Llewellyn Griffith p. 45. Translation with photographs and discussion: Frood 2006.

17. Paris, Louvre C 219. Edition: KRI IV, 296,13–297,13. Translations: Kruchten 1989, 180–81 (partial; mistakenly referring to the object as a statue); Kitchen 2003, 214–16.

18. el-Mashayikh, tomb of Anhurmose. Editions: Kees 1937 (first sections); KRI IV, 143,6–144,15 (first sections, based on Kees and a copy-text of Mariette); KRI VII,

226,1–232,2 (based on materials provided by Boyo Ockinga); Ockinga and al-Masri 1988, pls. 18–31, with translation pp. 31–47. Further translation: Kitchen 2003, 108–9 (based on the earlier copy-text in KRI IV).

19a. Leiden, Rijksmuseum van Oudheden K.9. Edition: KRI I, 357,5–362,10. Translations: Lichtheim 1992, 68–71 (extracts); Kitchen 1993, 292–98. Photographs: Boeser 1913, 9, pls. 33–36.

19b. Leiden, Rijksmuseum van Oudheden V.1. Edition: KRI VII, 26,14–29,13. Translations with discussions: Gardiner 1947, I, 51–53; Kruchten 1992; Willems 1998. Photograph: Boeser 1911, 1–2, pl. 1. Other important discussions include: Guksch 1983; van Dijk 1995.

20a–b. Cairo, Egyptian Museum TN 8/6/24/10 (statue); TN 17/6/25/1 (block). Edition and translation: Ockinga 2004, 83–92, pls. 27–29 and pp. 72–73, with an excursus by Karl Jansen-Winkeln pp. 92–94.

21. Cairo, Egyptian Museum CG 42122. Edition: KRI VII, 24,7–26,3. Translation: Lowle 1976, 96–98. Photographs and description: Schulz 1992, I, 249–50, cat. 136; II, pl. 56a–c.

22a–b. Theban Tomb 189. PM I², 1, 295 (2), (5)–(6). Editions: Kitchen 1974, with translation and discussion; KRI III, 350,2–352,12. Further translation: Kitchen 2000, 252–54.

23. The tomb of Maya at Saqqara is not yet published. My translation is based on materials kindly supplied to me by Jacobus van Dijk who is preparing the inscriptions for publication, and is presented here with his permission, as well as that of the excavator Geoffrey T. Martin, and of the Egypt Exploration Society. A discussion and preliminary translation by van Dijk is given in Martin et al. 1988, 11–12.

24. Zawyet Sultan, tomb of Nefersekheru. Edition and translation: Osing 1992, 43–53, pl. 35. Further translation: Assmann 2005, 187–88.

25a–b. Theban Tomb 106. PM I², 1, 222, Ba; 224, Ga. Editions: KRI I, 298,7–299,16; KRI III, 8,14–9,8. Translations: Kitchen 1993, 243–44; Kitchen 2000, 7–8.

25c. Theban Tomb 106. PM I², 1, 221 (5). Editions: Wilkinson 1878, III, pl. 64; KRI I, 291,11–293,6. Translations: Redford 1970, 220–22 (partial); Kitchen 1993, 238–39.

26a. Boston, Museum of Fine Arts 03.891. Editions: Petrie 1903, 36, pl. 35, no. 2 (photograph); pl. 37 lower, with translation by Francis Llewellyn Griffith p. 45; KRI III, 63,13–64,7; Further translation: Kitchen 2000, 44. Photograph and description: Schulz 1992, 90–91, cat. 026; II, pl. 10.

26b. Cairo, Egyptian Museum JE 48845. Editions: KRI III, 53,7–55,16; Moursi 1981, with photographs, translation, and discussion. Further translation: Kitchen 2000, 36–38.

27. Cairo, Egyptian Museum JE 89624. Editions: Zayed 1964, with photographs, translation, and discussion; KRI III, 366,1–367,15; Martin 1997, pls. 95–97, no. 331, with translation by Jacobus van Dijk pp. 46–47. Further translation: Kitchen 2000, 264–66. Photograph: Grimm and Wildung (eds.) 1978, no. 54.

28. London, British Museum EA 1377. Editions: KRI III, 136,1–137,13; Bierbrier 1982, pls. 49–51 (line-drawings and photographs), with description p. 42. Trans-

lations: Kitchen 2000, 92–93; Assmann 2003a, 14 (texts around the base only).

29. Small Ptah temple, Memphis; current location unknown. Editions: Badawi 1944, 202–4, pl. 22 with translation; KRI III, 169,1–13. Translation: Kitchen 2000, 114.

30. Paris, Louvre A. 65. Editions: Anthes 1974, 45–46 (partial edition and translation); KRI III, 224,1–14. Translation: Kitchen 2000, 157–58. Description: Schulz 1992, I, 469–70, cat. 281. Photograph: Delange 2001, 126–27, cat. 41.

31. New York, Metropolitan Museum of Art 17.2.5. Editions: Anthes 1974, 45–47 (partial edition and translation); KRI III, 151,10–152,10. Translation: Kitchen 2000, 102–3. Description and photograph: Hayes 1959, 348–49, fig. 218.

32. Theban West Bank, temple of Montuhotep II. PM II², 386. Editions: Naville 1910, pl. 10K; KRI IV, 370,4–15. Translation: Kitchen 2003, 268–69.

33. Cairo, Egyptian Museum JE 43341. Editions: Gardiner 1912, with translation and discussion; KRI IV, 341,5–343,16. Further translations: B. G. Davies 1997, 335–42; Warburton 1997, 182–83 (partial); Kitchen 2003, 246–48. Other discussions include: Haring 1997, 152–53; Morschauser 1991, 189–92 (threat formula).

34. Berlin, Staatliche Museen 2081. Edition: KRI VI, 439,4–440,10; Translation: Breasted 1906, IV, 236, §§ 484–85 (partial).

35a. Cairo, Egyptian Museum JE 87194. Editions: Hamada 1947, with photographs and translation; KRI V, 415,6–416,11. Translation and discussion: Gardiner 1948.

35b. Cairo, Egyptian Museum CG 1221. Editions: Borchardt 1934, 116–17, with photograph pl. 170; KRI V, 416,12–417,9. Translation: Van Siclen 1980, 189–90.

36. Luxor, Luxor Museum J 141. Editions include: Lipińska 1969, with translation (right side); KRI III, 274,7–275,7 (right side); KRI VII, 128,2–13 (left side); Lipińska 1984, 21–24, no. 18, with translation, and figs. 66–68 (photographs); Clère 1995, figs. 31a–c, and pls. VI–VII, doc. B, with description and translation pp. 87–92. Further translations include: Kitchen 2000, 195 (right side); Pinch 1993, 334 (left side). Further descriptions and photographs include: Romano 1979, 149, cat. 227; Schulz 1992, I, 360–61, cat. 207; II, pl. 93a.

37. Oxford, Ashmolean Museum 1894.106d. Editions: Petrie 1896, pl. 19 upper, with translation by Francis Llewellyn Griffith pp. 15–16; KRI III, 270,10–271,14. Further translations: Nims 1956, 147–48 (checked by John Barns); Goyon 1990, 59–60; Kitchen 2000, 192–93.

38. Paris, Louvre C. 95. Editions: Pierret 1878, 1–2; KRI III, 265,3–10. Translation: Kitchen 2000, 188–89.

39. London, British Museum EA 164. Editions: James 1970, pls. 21–21a (photograph and line-drawing), with description pp. 25–26; KRI II, 386,8–388,3. Translation: Kitchen 1993, 215–17.

40. Mit Rahina, excavation nos. Mit. 1737, 1738. Editions: Anthes 1965, fig. 9, nos. 12–13, pl. 29b–c, with translation collated by William Kelly Simpson pp. 85–87. Further translations: Budka 2001, 238–39, no. 249; Rickal 2005, I, 283–86.

41a. Elkab, Thoth chapel, PM V, 187–88. Editions: Derchain 1971, pls. 28–30, with translation pp. 69–70; KRI III, 84,1–85,4. Further translation: Kitchen 2000, 58–59.

41b. Cairo, Egyptian Museum JE 41395 (stela); JE 41398 (jambs). PM VII, 55 (mistakenly located in the outer court of Wadi el-Sebua). Editions: Barsanti and Gauthier 1911, 77–81, pl. 5; Helck 1975 with translation and discussion; Kitchen 1975–1976, with translation; KRI III, 91,6–94,11; Wente 1985 with translation. Further translation: Kitchen 2000, 63–65. Photograph: Gauthier 1912, II, pl. 66A. Discussion: Raedler 2003, esp. 157–59.

42. Cairo, Egyptian Museum JE 41403. Editions: Barsanti and Gauthier 1911, 83–85, pl. 4; KRI III, 95,4–15. Translations: Yoyotte 1951, 13–14, with pl. 1; Kitchen 2000, 65–66.

43. Sai Island, excavation no. S.103. Editions: Vercoutter 1958, 156–57, pl. 45a, with partial translation; KRI III, 110,6–14. Further translation: Kitchen 2000, 75.

44a–b. Aniba, tomb of Penniut, PM VII, 76–77 (5)–(6). Edition: KRI VI, 350,11–353,10. Translations: Breasted 1906, 231–35, §§ 474–83; Helck 1961, II, 231–32 (1013–14), 295–97 (1077–79) (sections of 44a); Menu 1970, 118–21 (section of 44a); Helck 1986 (44a only); Fitzenreiter 2004, 178–79 (44b only), with discussion. Photographs: Steindorff 1935–1937, II, pls. 101–2. Line-drawing of 44b: Hermann 1963, 62–63, with discussion. Further discussion of the tomb: Fitzenreiter 1998; 2001; 2003.

45. Berlin, Staatliche Museen 20377. PM I², 2, 683. Editions: Erman 1911, 1087–95, pl. 16; Roeder 1924, 158–62; KRI III 653,1–655,7. Further translations: Gunn 1916, 83–85; Lichtheim 1976, 105–7; Assmann 1999, 371–75, no. 148; Kitchen 2000, 444–46; Edward F. Wente in Simpson (ed.) 2003, 284–86.

46a. London, British Museum EA 589. Editions: James 1970, pls. 31–31a (photograph and line-drawing), with description p. 36; KRI III, 771,7–772,8. Translations: Gunn 1916, 88–89; Assmann 1999, 377–78, no. 150; Lichtheim 1976, 109–110; Kitchen 2000, 517–18; Edward F. Wente in Simpson (ed.) 2003, 287–88.

46b. Turin, Museo Egizio 50058. Editions: Tosi and Roccati 1972, pl. 286, pp. 94–96 with translation; KRI III, 772,9–773,9. Further translations: Gunn 1916, 86–87; Lichtheim 1976, 107–9; Assmann 1999, 375–76, no. 149; McDowell 1999, 98–100, no. 71; Kitchen 2000, 518–19; Edward F. Wente in Simpson (ed.) 2003, 286–87; Adrom 2005, with discussion. Further photograph: Andreu (ed.) 2002, 279, no. 225.

47. Deir el-Medina, excavation no. 320. PM I², 2, 694. Editions: Bruyère 1952, 130–31, fig. 215; KRI III, 687,1–8. Translations: Borghouts 1982, 6, with discussion; Kitchen 2000, 462.

48. Turin, Museo Egizio 50044. Editions: Tosi and Roccati 1972, pl. 279, pp. 78 with translation; KRI III 795,1–8. Further translations: Gunn 1916, 89; Borghouts 1982, 6, with discussion; Assmann 1999, 379, no. 151; McDowell 1999, 101–2, no. 73B; Kitchen 2000, 532.

49. London, British Museum EA 278. Editions: Bierbrier 1982, pl. 86, with description pp. 37–38; KRI VI, 275,5–276,4. Translations: Assmann 1999, 382–83, no. 155; McDowell 1999, 100–101, no. 72; Vernus 2000; 2002, with photograph and discussion.

50. Vienna, Kunsthistorisches Museum Inv. Nr. 8390. Edition: Satzinger 1985, 249–54, with translation. Further translation: Szpakowska 2003, 135–37 (with discussion), 194–95.

Glossary

The glossary contains definitions of terms and proper names used in this book, as well as some principal titles and places. It also includes a small number of divine epithets, whose meaning may not be immediately clear from the translation. Standard consonantal translations are given for all Egyptian words.

A

Abydos (*3bḏw*). A town in Upper Egypt, ca. 100 kilometers north of Thebes (modern Luxor), which was the primary cult center of Osiris

Abydos standard or fetish. A staff, sometimes resting on a mountain hieroglyph (*ḏw*), topped with a rounded object that is adorned with headdress elements

aegis. An amuletic fitting, usually representing the head and neck of a god or goddess with a broad collar necklace, that could be held in the hand or attached to the prow and stern of a portable barque

akh (*3ḫ*). The transfigured spirit of a deceased individual, often translated as "spirits"

akhet (*3ḫt*). The inundation season

Amun (*jmn*). Principal god of the Theban triad and dominant deity throughout much of the New Kingdom; often merged with Re as Amun-Re

Amunet (*jmnt*). The female aspect of Amun and one of his consorts

Anat (*ʿnt*). Syrian goddess of war important in Egypt, especially in the Delta, from the Second Intermediate period onwards

ankh (*ʿnḫ*). The hieroglyph that writes the word "life" and also symbolizes the gift of life

Anubis (*jnpw*). Jackal god of the dead and guardian of the underworld

Anukis (*ʿnqt*). Goddess of the cataracts of Lower Nubia

Apis (*ḥpj*). Bull god, manifestation of and intermediary for Ptah

aroura (*st3t*). A measure of area, equivalent to 2,756 square meters or roughly two-thirds of an acre, 0.275 of a hectare

Asheru (*jšrw*). The name of the precinct of Mut in the Karnak temple complex

atef-**crown** (*3tf*). A crown particularly associated with Osiris, consisting of double plumes, ram horns, and a disc

Atum (*jtm*). Primeval creator god of complete and perfect totality, closely associated with Re

B

ba (*b3*). A component of the human self and of gods, probably activated at death. Although connected to the body, the *ba* was free to leave the tomb and seek earthly pleasures; often depicted as a bird with a human head.

bah-land (*bʿḥ*). Lands used for the cultivation of vines, fruit-, and oil-bearing trees

barque (*wj3*). A portable sacred boat used to carry an image of the god during cult performance, often borne on the shoulders of priests via carrying poles (see fig. 11). It also refers to the sacred rivergoing boat used to carry the king in festivals, and which was the vehicle for the sun-god across the sky and through the underworld.

Behdetite (*bḥdt*). An epithet of Horus describing him as the "one of Behdet," a cult place of this god; often applied to the protective winged disc associated with representations of the king and of deities

block statue. A type of nonroyal stone statue, first attested in the Middle Kingdom, which shows its owner seated with his knees drawn tightly to his chest and his arms folded across the knees; the statue's block-like form provides a convenient surface for inscription (see fig. 3)

brother (*sn*). Can refer to close, intragenerational kinship or to a collegial relationship

Busiris (*ḏdw*). Town in the central Delta and the cult center of Osiris in Lower Egypt

Buto. Town in the northern Delta (modern Tell el-Faraʿin), termed Pe (*p*) and Dep (*dp*) in Egyptian sources; a cult center of the goddess Wadjet

C

cartouche (*mnš*). An oval ring, symbolically a protective, knotted cord, in which the name of the king was written; separate cartouches enclosed the prenomen and nomen (compare "*shen*-ring")

chief controller of crafts(men) (*wr-ḫrpw-ḥmwt*). Title of the high priest of Ptah in Memphis, often in conjunction with the title *sem*-priest

chief of seers (*wr-m3w*). Title of the high priest of Re in Heliopolis, also used in relation to deities connected with Re such as Shu

companion (*smr*). Ranking title expressing an individual's position among the inner elite around the king

council of thirty (*mʿb3yt*). A select group of the highest officials; can also refer to a mythical court of judges in the next world

count (*h3ty-ʿ*). Ranking title expressing an individual's position among the inner elite, often following "member of the *pat* (*jry-pʿt*)"; when used with the name of a town, it has the meaning "mayor" (no. 29)

D

day-barque (*mʿnḏt*). The solar barque that carried the sun-god through the daytime sky

Dendara (*jwnt*). Town approximately 60 kilometers north of Thebes (modern Luxor) and cult center of the goddess Hathor

dignitary (*sꜣb*). The lowest possible title for men, often used as a title for the father of the deceased who may or may not have had other titles

djed-**pillar** (*ḏd*). A symbolic pillar, perhaps originally of a plant material, which came to be considered the backbone of Osiris; as a hieroglyph it writes "stability" or "permanence" and is an important amuletic object

Djesret (*ḏsrt*). The ancient name of the bay in the cliffs of Western Thebes, now known as Deir el-Bahri, where the temples of Montuhotep II, Hatshepsut, and Thutmose III are located

E

Edfu (*msn*). Town located midway between Thebes (modern Luxor) and Aswan that was a major cult center of Horus

effigy-form. Undifferentiated bodily form in which some gods can be depicted, especially Ptah and Osiris, symbolizing processes of death and regeneration; kings can also be represented in this way

electrum (*ḏꜥm*). A naturally occurring alloy of silver and gold

embalming place (*wt*). The word *wt* probably did not originally have this meaning, but by the New Kingdom it seems, in some contexts, to be connected with embalming and the preparation of the body; often associated with Anubis, whose ancient epithet *imiut* was reinterpreted as "the one who is in *wt*"

Ennead (*psḏt*). Term for a large group of related deities, notionally nine, who were associated with a place or connected by a creation myth

eye of Re (*jrt-rꜥ*). A powerful destructive and creative force, often personified as a goddess, Re's daughter and protector; also termed the solar eye

F

first time (*sp-tpy*). Primeval, mythical time before history when creator gods ruled Egypt

G

Geb (*gb*). Earth god, partnered with the sky goddess Nut

god's father (*jt-nṯr*). High-ranking priestly office that may have granted the holder access to the cult image of a deity

Great-of-Magic (*wrt-ḥkꜣw*). Epithet of a lioness- and snake-formed goddess who protected the king, manifest as the uraeus; could be identified with various goddesses

H

Hapy (*ḥꜥpy*). Personification of the Nile-flood as a deity

Heliopolis (*jwnw*). Town in Lower Egypt, now an eastern sector of modern Cairo, which was the cult center of Re

henu-barque (*ḥnw*). The barque of the god Sokar

Heqet (*ḥqt*). A goddess of birth, often depicted as a frog

Hermopolis (*ḫnmw*). Town in Middle Egypt (modern el-Ashmunein) that was the cult center of Thoth; its name means "Eight-town" and it was associated with the Ogdoad

Hidden-of-Name (*jmn-rn.f*). An epithet that describes the potent, hidden, and secret aspect of a deity, particularly of Amun and Osiris

His Person (*ḥm.f*). See "Person"

Horakhty (*ḥr-ȝḫty*). Literally "Horus of the horizon" or "Horus of the two horizons"; a manifestation of the falcon god Horus that was closely identified with the sun (see also Re-Horakhty)

horizon of eternity (*ȝḫt-nḥḥ*). A general term for a space with heightened sanctity, such as a temple or palace area

Horus (*ḥr*). Falcon god and embodiment of living kingship, identified with the reigning king

Horus-who-protects-his-father (*ḥr-nḏ-ḥr-jt.f*). The manifestation of Horus in his role as avenger of the murder of Osiris

I

Ihy (*jḥy*). A child-god, son of Hathor, whose name means "the sistrum player"

Isis (*ȝst*). Consort to Osiris and mother of Horus, who embodies the healing potential of maternal love

imperishable stars (*jḫmw-sk*). Stars in the northern sky that are identified with the transfigured dead (compare "unwearying stars")

J

justified (also "justification"). See "true of voice"

K

ka (*kȝ*). A component of the self of humans and gods associated with their life-force and power, as well as with the passage of identity down the generations in the male line

Kamutef (*kȝ-mwt.f*). Literally "Bull of his Mother"; an epithet describing the potent regenerative power of a god, often Amun or Min

Khentimentu (*ḫnty-jmntw*). Literally "foremost of the Westerners"; a form of Osiris

Khepri (*ḫprj*). The manifestation of the sun-god at dawn, often depicted as a scarab beetle

Khnum (*ḫnmw*). Ram-headed creator god, sometimes represented in the role of a potter who fashions humankind on his wheel

Khonsu (*ẖnsw*). A moon and child god, the third in the Theban triad with Amun and Mut

L

l.p.h. Standard modern abbreviation of the epithet "life, prosperity, health (ʿnḫ wḏꜣ snb)," which very often follows the king's name; a feature of writing and probably not pronounced in antiquity
lector priest (*ẖry-ḥbt*). Priestly title associated with the recitation of ritual texts
Lower Egypt (*mḥw*). Northern Egypt, encompassing the Nile Valley north of the Fayyum and the area of the Delta to the Mediterranean coast

M

Maat (*mꜣʿt*). All-encompassing principle of harmony, justice, and truth, often personified as a goddess
Mansion of Gold (*ḥwt-nbw*). A place where temple equipment was crafted and consecrated prior to presentation to the gods; both craftsmen and priests were active there
Mansion of the Official (*ḥwt-sr*). Name given to sections of temples of, for example, Re in Heliopolis and Amun in Karnak
Mehit (*mḥt*). Lioness-headed goddess worshipped at Thinis
member of the *pat* (*jry-pʿt*). Most senior of the ranking titles, designating its bearer as belonging to the inner elite social group, often followed by "count (hꜣty-ʿ)"
Memphis (*mn-nfr*). Primary capital city throughout much of Egyptian history, ca. 20 kilometers upstream of Cairo; its main necropolis was Saqqara
Meretseger (*mrt-sgr*). Goddess of the West Bank at Thebes, often shown as a snake or snake-headed woman
Meskhenet (*msḫnt*). Goddess of birth
Min (*mn*). Ithyphallic god, associated with fertility
Montu (*mnṯw*). War god of the Theban area
Mut (*mwt*). Goddess whose name means "mother," consort to Amun at Karnak

N

naophorous statue. A type of nonroyal stone statue, first attested in the New Kingdom, which shows its owner sitting or kneeling and holding a naos (see below) in front of his body; the naos usually contains one or more figures of statues or emblems of deities (see fig. 9)
naos. A shrine in which divine statues were kept
Nefertem (*nfr-tm*). God of the lotus blossom and third in the Memphite triad with Ptah and Sekhmet
Neith (*nt*). Creator goddess, also associated with war and motherhood

Nekhbet (*nḫbt*). Vulture goddess whose cult center was at Nekheb, tutelary goddess of Upper Egypt

Nekheb (*nḫb*). Upper Egyptian town (modern Elkab), some 70 kilometers south of Thebes (modern Luxor), opposite Nekhen

Nekhen (*nḫn*). Upper Egyptian town, also known by the Greek name Hierakonpolis, opposite Nekheb

Nephthys (*nbt-ḥwt*). Protective goddess often partnered with Isis in mourning Osiris; consort to Seth

Nepri (*npr*). Divine personification of grain

neshmet-**barque** (*nšmt*). Name of the barque of Osiris at Abydos

night-barque (*msktt*). The solar barque that carried the sun-god through his night journey

nine bows (*psḏt-9*). Collective designation for the foreign enemies of Egypt

nomen. The king's birth name, in cartouche, with optional epithets

Nubia. Designates the land up the Nile between Aswan and the River Atbara

Nut (*nwt*). Primeval creator goddess who embodies the arching firmament of the sky

O

offering which the king gives (*ḥtp-dj-njsw*). Formula (exact rendering disputed) relating to offerings given to deities for the benefit of deceased individuals

Ogdoad (*ḫmnw*). Term for a group of eight deities, associated especially with Hermopolis

Onuris (*jn-ḥrt*). A god associated with hunting and an alternate form of the god Shu; local deity of the Thinite area, near Abydos

Opet (*jpt*). An annual festival at Thebes, consisting of a procession of Amun, Mut, Khonsu, and the king from Karnak to Luxor temple where rituals were performed that reinforced the king's relationship with his father Amun, who endowed him with the powers of kingship

Orion. The Greek name of the southern constellation, for whom the Egyptian name was Sah (*s³ḥ*), also a manifestation of Osiris

Osiris (*wsjr*). God of the dead and king of the underworld

the Osiris of. An epithet assigned to the deceased that describes his or her integration with the community of the transfigured dead in the next world; conventionally rendered "Osiris NN"; my translations follow the interpretation of Mark Smith (1987, 75–79; 2006).

ostracon (pl. ostraca). Flakes of limestone or sherds of pottery used as a writing surface

P

pat (*pˁt*). See "member of the *pat*"

pectoral. A flat, generally rectangular, pendant attached to necklaces and worn on the chest; often bearing a scene of the king and deities

Perception (*sj3*). Divine personification of creative thought

peret (*prt*). The season of growing, when crops begin to appear

Perfect God (*ntr-nfr*). Designation of the king, which assigns him junior divine status in relation to major gods

Person (*ḥm*). The physical presence of the king as "His Person" or "My Person"; often translated as "His Majesty" and "My Majesty" in Egyptological literature. Also used in reference to deities

Place of Truth (*st-mȝˤt*). Ancient name of the Valley of the Kings and associated areas

Poqer (*pqr*). Ancient name of the Early Dynastic royal necropolis of Umm el-Qaab, in the desert at Abydos (also Ropoqer), believed to be the tomb of Osiris in the New Kingdom

Pre (*pȝ-rˤ*). A variant form of the name of the sun-god Re with a prefixed article, also Pre-Horakhty

prenomen. One of the names of the king, written within a cartouche, assumed at accession, relating him to the sun-god Re

Ptah (*ptḥ*). Creator deity and chief god of Memphis, associated with craftsmanship

Ptah-Tatenen (*ptḥ tȝ-tnn*). A form of Ptah that personified the primeval mound

Q

qemy-**unguent** (*qmj*). A fine quality, scented gum or resinous oil

R

ranking title. Title that expresses an individual's rank or status rather than designating an administrative role or function; often also termed an honorific title

Re (*rˤ*). God of the sun, embodying life-force and the cyclical patterning of the cosmos

Re-Horakhty (*rˤ-ḥr-ȝḫty*). Falcon form of Re who embodied the height of his power (see Horakhty)

Renenet (*rnnt*). Goddess personifying the notion of "fortune"

Rettawy (*rˤt-tȝwy*). Female counterpart of Re, whose name means literally "(female) Re-of-the-Two-Lands"

Ropoqer (*rȝ-pqr*). See "Poqer"

Rosetjau (*rȝ-stȝw*). Name used for necropolis sites, especially at Giza and Saqqara, and an underworld locality

S

Saqqara. Old Kingdom pyramid field and the main nonroyal necropolis for Memphis; the principal elite cemetery of the Ramessid period

Satet (*stt*). Goddess associated with areas of rough sailing in Nubia, including the first cataract

sed-festival (*ḥb-sd*). Festival of renewal of the king, held in principle after 30 years of rule

Sekhmet (*sḫmt*). Lioness-headed Memphite goddess often associated with disease and violence, but also with healing

sem-priest (*sm*) (**also setem-priest**). High ranking priestly title linked with Horus and particularly associated with mortuary rituals and those related to the enlivening of gods (especially Osiris) or deceased individuals

Seshat (*sšȝt*). Goddess of writing and measurement, a counterpart of the god Thoth

Seth (*swtḫ*). God associated with chaos and wrongful aggression, often represented as the enemy of Osiris; also associated positively with aspects of royal power, especially in the Ramessid period

shabti (**also ushabti**). Servant statuette placed in tombs that performed labor for the deceased in the next world

Shay (*šȝy*). God personifying the notion of "fate"

shebyu-necklace (*šbyw*). A necklace of bulbous gold rings given as a mark of royal favor and reward

shen-ring (*šn*). A circular ring shown as a gift of the gods to the king that symbolized eternity and protection (compare "cartouche")

shetayt (*štȝyt*). An area of the Memphite necropolis; also a shrine associated with Ptah-Sokar-Osiris in Memphis and other cult areas

shomu (*šmw*). The summer, harvest and "hot" season

Shu (*šw*). Primeval god of light and air, also associated with Onuris

sister (*snt*). Close female kin; "his sister" often designates a man's wife

sistrophorous statue. A type of nonroyal stone statue, first attested in the New Kingdom, which shows its owner sitting or kneeling and holding the emblem of a sistrum (see below) in front of his body

sistrum (**pl. sistra**). A musical instrument similar to a rattle, often associated with ritual and festival performance, particularly in the cults of Isis and Hathor

Sobek (*sbk*). Crocodile god of water and marshes

Sokar (*skr*). Hawk-headed god of the Memphite necropolis, also worshipped in other parts of Egypt, closely associated with Ptah and Osiris

souls of Pe and Nekhen (*bȝw p nḫn*). Two groups of deities representing, in part, the royal ancestors; those of Pe (Buto) are falcon-headed and those of Nekhen (Hierakonpolis) are jackal-headed

South-of-his-Wall (*rsy-jnbw.f*). Epithet of Ptah, describing his relationship to his city of Memphis (also known as "White Walls (*jnbw-ḥḏ*)") where he was chief god

sun-folk (*ḥnmmt*). A type of high status being, alongside people and gods, also with a divine or mythic aspect; particularly associated with Heliopolis

T

Tawer (*tȝ-wr*). Ancient name for the Abydos area

Tefnut (*tfnt*). Primeval goddess of moisture; consort to Shu

temple of millions of years (*ḥwt nt ḥḥw m rnpwt*). Name for royal mortuary temples

Thebes (*w3st*). Principal city of Upper Egypt and sometimes capital of Egypt (modern Luxor), which was the cult center of Amun and associated deities; the Valley of the Kings, royal mortuary temples, and a major nonroyal necropolis are located on the Theban West Bank

Thinis (*tny*). Capital of the eighth Upper Egyptian nome, a province that included Abydos; "Thinite nome" refers to the whole province

Thoth (*dhwty*). God of wisdom and writing, associated with fair judgment, and the local god of Hermopolis; often depicted as a baboon or ibis, or in human form with an ibis head

Thoth festival (*dhwtt*). An annual festival held on day 19 of the first month of the New Year (1 *akhet*) in celebration of the New Year; the whole of this month was associated with Thoth

true of voice (*m3ʿ-hrw*). Epithet following personal names that describes the transfigured state of a deceased individual who has successfully undergone judgment in the next world; also translated in Egyptological literature as "justified" and "justification"

Two Lands (*t3wy*) **or Two Banks** (*jdbwy*). Designation of Egypt, expressing the dual unity of Upper and Lower Egypt

U

unwearying stars (*jhmw-wrd*). Stars of the southern sky, which rise and set in the night sky, hence their association with the sun-god and their role pulling the solar barque (compare "imperishable stars")

Upper Egypt (*šmʿw*). Southern Egypt, roughly the Nile Valley from the Fayyum to the border with Nubia

uraeus (pl. uraei). Cobra goddess Wadjet, depicted attached to the king's brow, often as a component of crowns or headdresses; a protective and aggressive force also identified as the sun-god's eye and daughter

V

venerated or veneration (*jm3hy*). The state of a deceased individual as one who receives a mortuary cult

vizier (*t3ty*). Title of the head of the administration; the full title is "vizier, dignitary, he of the curtain (*t3ty s3b t3jtj*)," often with the additional title "mouth of Nekhen (*r3-nhn*)"

voice-offering (*prt-hrw*). A spoken recitation of lists of offerings centering on food and drink, reflecting the Egyptian belief in the efficacious power of the spoken word

W

wab-priest (*wʿb*). A lower-order priest, literally "pure-one"

wadj-scepter (*wȝḏ*). A papyrus scepter, symbolizing regenerative power; usually held by goddesses

Wadjet (*wȝḏt*). Cobra goddess whose cult center was at Buto; tutelary deity of Lower Egypt

wag-festival (*wȝg*). An annual festival held on day 18 of the first month of the New Year (1 *akhet*) and associated with funerary rituals, as well as wine and celebration

was-scepter (*wȝs*). A scepter with a rounded top, symbolizing divine or royal power and dominion

wedjat-eye (*wḏȝt*). A part hawk, part human eye that can represent all celestial eyes, symbolizing wholeness, healing, and protection; symbolically the eye of Horus, shattered by Seth and rendered whole by Thoth

Wenennefer (*wnn-nfr*). An epithet of Osiris that can stand alone as one of his names, meaning "he who exists in a state of perfection"

Wepwawet (*wp-wȝwt*). Jackal god of the desert and guardian of the necropolis, whose name means "one who opens the ways"

West (*jmntt*). Signifies the necropolis and the next world

BIBLIOGRAPHY

Adrom, Faried. 2004. "Der Gipfel der Frömmigkeit? Überlegungen zur Semantik und religiösen Symbolik von * t3-dhn.t*." *Lingua Aegyptia* 12: 1–20.

———. 2005. "'Der Gipfel der Frömmigkeit' (Soziale und funktionale Überlegungen zu Kultstelen am Beispiel der Stele Turin CG 50058 des *Nfr-ʿbw*)." *SAK* 33: 1–28.

Andreu, Guillemette, ed. 2002. *Les artistes de Pharaon: Deir el-Médineh et la Vallée des Rois*. Exhibition catalogue. Turnhout: Brepols.

Anthes, Rudolf. 1928. *Die Felseninschriften von Hatnub, nach den Aufnahmen Georg Möllers*. Untersuchungen zur Geschichte und Altertumskunde Aegyptens 9. Leipzig: Hinrichs.

———. 1965. *Mit Rahineh 1956*. Museum Monographs. Philadelphia: The University Museum, University of Pennsylvania.

———. 1974. "Die Berichte des Neferhotep und des Ichernofret über das Osirisfest in Abydos." Pages 15–49 in *Festschrift zum 150jährigen Bestehen des Berliner Ägyptischen Museums*. Staatliche Museen zu Berlin, Mitteilungen aus der Ägyptischen Sammlung 8. Berlin: Akademie-Verlag.

Arnold, Dieter. 2003. *The Encyclopedia of Ancient Egyptian Architecture*. Translated by Sabine H. Gardiner and Helen Strudwick. London: I. B. Taurus.

Assmann, Jan. 1978. "Eine Traumoffenbarung der Göttin Hathor: Zeugnisse 'Persönlicher Frömmigkeit' in thebanische Privatgräbern der Ramessidenzeit." *RdE* 30: 22–50.

———. 1980. "Die 'Loyalistische Lehre' Echnatons." *SAK* 8: 1–32.

———. 1983. *Sonnenhymnen in thebanischen Gräbern*. Theben 1. Mainz am Rhein: von Zabern.

———. 1991 [1983]. "Schrift, Tod und Identität. Das Grab als Vorschule der Literatur im alten Ägypten." Pages 169–99 in Jan Assmann, *Stein und Zeit: Mensch und Gesellschaft im alten Ägypten*. Munich: Wilhelm Fink.

———. 1987. "Priorität und Interesse: Das Problem der ramessidischen Beamtengräber." Pages 31–41 in *Problems and Priorities in Egyptian Archaeology*. Edited by Jan Assmann, Günter Burkard, and Vivian Davies. Studies in Egyptology. New York: Kegan Paul International.

———. 1995 [1983]. *Egyptian Solar Religion in the New Kingdom: Re, Amun and the Crisis of Polytheism*. Translated by Anthony Alcock. Studies in Egyptology. New York: Kegan Paul International.

———. 1999. *Ägyptische Hymnen und Gebete*. 2nd edition, 1st edition 1975. OBO. Fri-

274 BIOGRAPHICAL TEXTS FROM RAMESSID EGYPT

bourg and Göttingen: Universitätsverlag; Vandenhoeck & Ruprecht.

———. 2001. *Tod und Jenseits im alten Ägypten*. Munich: Beck.

———. 2002 [1996]. *The Mind of Egypt: History and Meaning in the Time of the Pharaohs*. Translated by Andrew Jenkins. New York: Metropolitan Books.

———. 2003a. "Einwohnung." Pages 1–14 in *Menschenbilder – Bildermenschen: Kunst und Kultur im alten Ägypten*. Edited by Tobias Hofmann and Alexandra Sturm. Norderstedt: n.p.

———. 2003b. "The Ramesside Tomb and the Construction of Sacred Space." Pages 46–52 in *The Theban Necropolis: Past, Present and Future*. Edited by Nigel Strudwick and John H. Taylor. London: British Museum Press.

———. 2005. "Zeitkonstruktion, Vergangenheitsbezug und Geschichtsbewusstsein im alten Ägypten." Pages 112–214 in *Der Ursprung der Geschichte: Archaische Kulturen, das alte Ägypten und das frühe Griechenland*. Edited by Jan Assmann and Klaus E. Müller. Stuttgart: Klett-Cotta.

Badawi, Ahmad. 1944. "Zwei Denkmäler des grossen Gaugrafen von Memphis Amenophis Ḥwjj." *ASAE* 44: 181–206.

Baines, John. 1989. "Ancient Egyptian Concepts and Uses of the Past: 3rd to 2nd Millennium BC Evidence." Pages 131–49 in *Who Needs the Past? Indigenous Values and Archaeology*. Edited by Robert Layton. One World Archaeology. London: Unwin Hyman.

———. 1991. "Society, Morality, and Religious Practice." Pages 123–200 in *Religion in Ancient Egypt: Gods, Myths, and Personal Practice*. Edited by Byron E. Shafer. Ithaca and London: Cornell University Press.

———. 1996. "Classicism and Modernism in the Literature of the New Kingdom." Pages 157–74 in *Ancient Egyptian Literature: History and Forms*. Edited by Antonio Loprieno. PdÄ 10. Leiden: Brill.

———. 1997. "Kingship before Literature: The World of the King in the Old Kingdom." Pages 125–74 in *Selbstverständnis und Realität: Akten des Symposiums zur ägyptischen Königsideologie Mainz 15–17.6.1995*. Edited by Rolf Gundlach and Christine Raedler. ÄAT 36, Beiträge zur Ägyptischen Königsideologie 1. Wiesbaden: Harrassowitz.

———. 1998a. "Ancient Egyptian Kingship: Official Forms, Rhetoric, Context." Pages 16–53 in *King and Messiah in Israel and the Ancient Near East: Proceedings of the Oxford Old Testament Seminar*. Edited by John Day. Journal for the Study of the Old Testament, Supplement Series 270. Sheffield: Sheffield Academic Press.

———. 1998b. "The Dawn of the Amarna Age." Pages 271–312 in *Amenhotep III: Perspectives on His Reign*. Edited by Eric H. Cline and David O'Connor. Ann Arbor: University of Michigan Press.

———. 1999a. "Feuds or Vengeance? Rhetoric and Social Forms." Pages 11–20 in *Gold of Praise: Studies in Ancient Egypt in Honor of Edward F. Wente*. Edited by Emily Teeter and John A. Larson. SAOC 58. Chicago: The Oriental Institute of the University of Chicago.

———. 1999b. "Forerunners of Narrative Biographies." Pages 23–37 in *Studies on Ancient Egypt in Honour of H. S. Smith*. Edited by Anthony Leahy and John Tait. Occasional Publications 13. London: Egypt Exploration Society.

———. 1999c. "Prehistories of Literature: Performance, Fiction, Myth." Pages 17–41 in *Definitely: Egyptian Literature. Proceedings of the Symposium "Ancient Egyptian Literature: History and Forms"*, Los Angeles, March 24–26, 1995. Edited by Gerald Moers. Lingua Aegyptia, Studia Monographica 2. Göttingen: Seminar für Ägyptologie und Koptologie.

———. 2001. "Egyptian Letters of the New Kingdom as Evidence for Religious Practice." *JANER* 1: 1–31.

———. in preparation. *Les biographies égyptiennes en monuments, images et textes*. Paris: Cybèle.

Baines, John, and Jaromir Malek. 2000. *Cultural Atlas of Ancient Egypt*. Revised edition. New York: Checkmark Books.

Barbotin, Christophe. 1994. "Une statue du grand prêtre d'Amon Bakenkhonsou II." *RdE* 45: 11–15.

———. 2005. *La voix des hiéroglyphes: Promenade au département des antiquités égyptiennes du Musée du Louvre*. Paris: Musée du Louvre, Institut Khéops.

Barsanti, Alexandre and Henri Gauthier. 1911. "Stèles trouvées à Ouadi es-Sabouâ (Nubie)." *ASAE* 11: 64–86.

Barthelmess, Petra. 1992. *Der Übergang ins Jenseits in den thebanischen Beamtengräbern der Ramessidenzeit*. SAGA 2. Heidelberg: Heidelberger Orientverlag.

Baud, Michel. 2005. "The Birth of Biography in Ancient Egypt: Text Format and Content in the IVth Dynasty." Pages 91–124 in *Texte und Denkmäler des ägyptischen Alten Reiches*. Edited by Stephan Seidlmayer. Berlin-Brandenburgische Akademie der Wissenschaften, Thesaurus Linguae Aegyptiae 3. Berlin: Achet.

Bell, Lanny. 1969. "Return to Dra Abu el-Naga." *Expedition* 11, no. 3: 26–37.

Bell, Martha. 1987. "Regional Variation in Polychrome Pottery of the 19th Dynasty." *Cahiers de la Ceramique Egyptienne* 1: 49–76.

Bickel, Susanne. 2003. "'Ich spreche ständig zu Aton . . .': Zur Mensch-Gott-Beziehung in der Amarna Religion." *JANER* 3: 23–45.

Bickel, Susanne, and Bernard Mathieu. 1993. "L'écrivain Amennakht et son Enseignement." *BIFAO* 93: 31–51.

Bierbrier, Morris L. 1982. *Hieroglyphic Texts from Egyptian Stelae etc.* 10. London: British Museum Publications.

Björkman, Gun. 1971. *Kings at Karnak: A Study of the Treatment of the Monuments of Royal Predecessors in the Early New Kingdom*. Acta Universitatis Upsaliensis Boreas 2: Uppsala Studies in Ancient Mediterranean and Near Eastern Civilizations. Uppsala and Stockholm: Almqvist and Wiksell.

Blumenthal, Elke, Ingeborg Müller, and Walter F. Reineke. 1984. *Urkunden der 18. Dynastie: Übersetzung zu Heften 5–16*. Berlin: Akademie-Verlag.

Boeser, Pieter Adriaan Aart. 1911. *Beschreibung der aegyptischen Sammlung des Niederländischen Reichsmuseums der Altertümer in Leiden IV: Die Denkmäler des Neuen Reiches I: Gräber*. Hague: Martinus Nijhoff.

———. 1913. *Beschreibung der aegyptischen Sammlung des Niederländischen Reichsmuseums der Altertümer in Leiden VI: Die Denkmäler des Neuen Reiches III: Stelen*. Hague: Martinus Nijhoff.

Bomann, Ann H. 1991. *The Private Chapel in Ancient Egypt: A Study of the Chapels in the Workmen's Village at El Amarna with Special Reference to Deir el Medina and Other Sites*. Studies in Egyptology. New York: Kegan Paul International.

Borchardt, Ludwig. 1931. "Die Königin bei einer feierlichen Staatshandlung Ramses' II." *ZÄS* 67: 29–31.

———. 1934. *Statuen und Statuetten von Königen und Privatleuten in Museum von Kairo, IV: Nos 1–1294*. Catalogue Général des Antiquités Egyptiennes du Musée du Caire. Berlin: Reichsdruckerei.

Borghouts, Joris. F. 1982. "Divine Intervention in Ancient Egypt and Its Manifestation (*b3w*)." Pages 1–70 in *Gleanings from Deir el-Medîna*. Edited by Robert J. Demarée and Jac J. Janssen. Egyptologische Uitgaven 1. Leiden: Nederlands Instituut voor het Nabije Oosten.

Breasted, James Henry. 1906. *Ancient Records of Egypt, IV: The Twentieth to the Twenty Sixth Dynasties*. Chicago: University of Chicago Press.

Bruyère, Bernard. 1952. *Rapport sur les fouilles de Deir el Médineh (1935–40)* II. FIFAO 20/2. Cairo: IFAO.

Budka, Julia. 2001. *Der König an der Haustür: Die Rolle des ägyptischen Herrschers an dekorierten Türgewänden von Beamten im Neuen Reich*. Beiträge zur Ägyptologie 19. Wien: Institute für Afrikanistik und Ägyptologie der Universität Wien.

Burkard, Günter. 1996. "Metrik, Prosodie und formaler Aufbau ägyptischer literarischer Texte." Pages 447–63 in *Ancient Egyptian Literature: History and Forms*. Edited by Antonio Loprieno. PdÄ 10. Leiden: Brill.

Cabrol, Agnès. 2001. *Les voies processionnelles de Thèbes*. OLA 97. Leuven: Peeters.

Černý, Jaroslav. 1945. "The Will of Naunakhte and the Related Documents." *JEA* 31: 29–53.

Clère, Jacques J. 1959. "Un hymne à Abydos sur un stèle inédite d'époque ramesside." *ZÄS* 84: 86–104.

———. 1968a. "Deux statues 'gardiennes de porte' d'époque ramesside." *JEA* 54: 135–48.

———. 1968b. "La légende d'une scène d'oracle." Pages 45–49 in *Festschrift für Siegfried Schott zu seinem 70. Geburtstag am 20. August 1967*. Edited by Wolfgang Helck. Wiesbaden: Harrassowitz.

———. 1995. *Les chauves d'Hathor*. OLA 63. Leuven: Peeters.

Coulon, Laurent. 1997. "Véracité et rhétorique dans les autobiographies égyptiennes de la Première Période Intermédiaire." *BIFAO* 97: 108–38.

Davies, Benedict G. 1997. *Egyptian Historical Inscriptions of the Nineteenth Dynasty*. Documenta Mundi: Aegyptiaca 2. Jonsered: Åströms.

———. 1999. *Who's Who at Deir el-Medina: A Prosopographic Study of the Royal Workmen's Community*. Egyptologische Uitgaven 13. Leiden: Nederlands Instituut voor het Nabije Oosten.

Davies, Norman de Garis. 1922–1923. *The Tomb of Puyemrê at Thebes*. 2 vols. Metropolitan Museum of Art Egyptian Expedition, Robb de Peyster Tytus Memorial Series 2–3. New York: Metropolitan Museum of Art.

———. 1943. *The Tomb of Rekh-mi-Rēʿ at Thebes*. 2 vols. Metropolitan Museum of Art Egyptian Expedition 11. New York: Metropolitan Museum of Art.

Delange, Elisabeth. 2001. *Egito faraônico, terra dos deuses, 27 de setembro de 2001 a 7 de abril de 2002*. Exhibition catalogue. São Paulo: Museu de Arte de São Paulo.

Delvaux, Luc. 1988. "La statue Louvre A 134 du premier prophète d'Amon Hapouseneb." *SAK* 15: 53–67.

Demarée, Robert J. 1983. *The ꜣḫ iḳr n Rꜥ-stelae: On Ancestor Worship in Ancient Egypt*. Egyptologische Uitgaven 3. Leiden: Nederlands Instituut voor het Nabije Oosten.

Depauw, Mark, and Mark Smith. 2004. "Visions of Ecstasy: Cultic Revelry before the Goddess Ai/Nehemanit. Ostraca Faculteit Letteren (K.U.Leuven) dem. 1–2." Pages 67–93 in *Res Severa Verum Gaudium: Festschrift für Karl-Theodor Zauzich zum 65. Geburtstag am 8. Juni 2004*. Edited by Friedhelm Hoffmann and Heinz Josef Thissen. Leuven: Peeters.

Derchain, Philippe. 1955. "La couronne de la justification: Essai d'analyse d'un rite ptolémaïque." *CdE* 30: 225–87.

———. 1971. *Elkab I: Les monuments religieux à l'entrée de l'Ouady Hellal*. Publications du Comité des Fouilles Belges en Egypte. Brussels: Fondation Egyptologique Reine Elisabeth.

Desroches Noblecourt, Christiane. 1990. "Le message de la grotte sacrée." *Les Dossiers d'Archéologie* 149–150: 4–21.

Dodson, Aidan. 1997. "Messuy, Amada, and Amenmesse." *JARCE* 34: 41–48.

Doxey, Denise M. 1998. *Egyptian Non-Royal Epithets in the Middle Kingdom: A Social and Historical Analysis*. PdÄ 12. Leiden: Brill.

Drenkhahn, Rosemarie. 1980. *Die Elephantine-Stele des Sethnacht und ihr historischer Hintergrund*. Ägyptologische Abhandlungen 36. Wiesbaden: Harrassowitz.

Dziobek, Eberhard. 1994. *Die Gräber des Vezirs User-Amun, Theben Nr. 61 und 131*. AVDAIK 84. Mainz am Rhein: von Zabern.

Eakin, Paul John. 1992. *Touching the World: Reference in Autobiography*. Princeton: Princeton University Press.

Edwards, I. E. S. 1986. "The Shetayet of Rosetau." Pages 27–36 in *Egyptological Studies in Honor of Richard A. Parker*. Edited by Leonard H. Lesko. Hanover, N.H.: University Press of New England.

Eigner, Diethelm. 1983. "Das thebanische Grab des Amenhotep, Wesir von Unterägypten: Die Architektur." *MDAIK* 39: 39–50.

Espinel, Andrés D. 2005. "A Newly Identified Stela from Wadi el-Hudi (Cairo JE 86119)." *JEA* 91: 55–70.

Erman, Adolf. 1911. "Denksteine aus der thebanischen Gräberstadt." *Sitzungsberichte der Preussischen Akademie der Wissenschaften zu Berlin* 1911: 1086–1110.

Faulkner, Raymond. 1985. *The Ancient Egyptian Book of the Dead*. Edited by Carol Andrews. London: British Museum Press.

Fecht, Gerhard. 1965. *Literarische Zeugnisse zur "Persönlichen Frömmigkeit" in Ägypten: Analyse der Beispiele aus den ramessidischen Schulpapyri*. AHAW 1965: 1. Heidelberg: Carl Winter, Universitätsverlag.

———. 1993. "The Structural Principle of Ancient Egyptian Elevated Language." Pages 69–94 in *Verse in Ancient Near Eastern Prose*. Edited by Johannes C. de Moor and Wilfred G. E. Watson. AOAT 42. Kevelaer: Butzon & Bercker, Neukirch-ener Verlag.

Fischer, Henry G. 1986. *L'écriture et l'art de l'Egypte ancienne: Quatre leçons sur la paléographie et l'épigraphie pharaoniques.* Paris: Presses Universitaires de France.

Fischer-Elfert, Hans-Werner. 2002. "Quelques textes et une vignette du Papyrus magique no. 1826 de la Bibliothèque nationale d'Athènes." Pages 167–84 in *La magie en Egypte: À la recherche d'une définition.* Edited by Yvan Koenig. Louvre Conférences et Colloques. Paris: Musée du Louvre, La documentation Française.

——. 2003. "Representations of the Past in New Kingdom Literature." Pages 119–37 in *"Never had the like occurred": Egypt's View of Its Past.* Edited by John Tait. Encounters with Ancient Egypt. London: UCL Press.

Fischer-Elfert, Hans-Werner and Alfred Grimm. 2003. "Autobiographie und Apotheose: Die Statue des *Zš(š)n Z3-Ḥw.t-Ḥrw* im Staatlichen Museum Ägyptischer Kunst München." *ZÄS* 130: 60–80.

Fisher, Marjorie M. 2001. *The Sons of Ramesses II.* 2 vols. ÄAT 53. Wiesbaden: Harrassowitz.

Fitzenreiter, Martin. 1998. "Konzepte vom Tod und dem Toten im späten Neuen Reich – Notizen zum Grab des Pennut (Teil II)." Pages 27–71 in *Die ägyptische Mumie: Ein Phänomen der Kulturgeschichte.* Edited by Martin Fitzenreiter and Christian Loeben. Internet-Beiträge zur Ägyptologie und Sudanarchäologie 1. http://www2.hu-berlin.de/nilus/net-publications/ibaes1/Publikation/ibaes1.pdf

——. 2001. "Innere Bezüge und äussere Funktion eines ramessidischen Felsgrabes in Nubien – Notizen zum Grab des Pennut (Teil I)." Pages 131–59 in *Begegnungen: Antike Kulturen im Niltal. Festgabe für Erika Endesfelder, Karl-Heinz Priese, Walter Friedrich Reineke, Steffen Wenig.* Edited by Caris-Beatrice Arnst, Ingelore Hafemann and Angelika Lohwasser. Leipzig: Helmar Wodtke and Katharina Stegbauer.

——. 2003. "Ahnen an der Ostwand: Notizen zum Grab des Pennut Teil III." Pages 294–317 in *Umwege und Weggefährten: Festschrift für Heinrich Balz zum 65. Geburtstag.* Edited by Jürgen Thiesbonenkamp and Helgard Cochois. Neuendettelsau: Erlanger Verlag für Mission und Ökumene.

——. 2004. "Identität als Bekenntnis und Anspruch – Notizen zum Grab des Pennut (Teil IV)." *Der Antike Sudan: Mitteilungen der Sudanarchäologischen Gesellschaft zu Berlin e.V.* 15: 169–93.

Frandsen, Paul John. 1999. "On Fear of Death and the Three *bwt*s Connected with Hathor." Pages 131–48 in *Gold of Praise: Studies on Ancient Egypt in Honor of E. F. Wente.* Edited by Emily Teeter and John A. Larson. SAOC 58. Chicago: The Oriental Institute of the University of Chicago.

——. 2001. "*Bwt* in the Body." Pages 141–74 in *Social Aspects of Funerary Culture in the Egyptian Old and Middle Kingdoms: Proceedings of the International Symposium Held at Leiden University 6–7 June, 1996.* Edited by Harco Willems. OLA 103. Leuven: Peeters.

Franke, Detlef. 1984. "Ursprung und Bedeutung der Titelsequenz *Z3b R3-Nḫn.*" *SAK* 11: 209–17.

Freed, Rita E., ed. 1987. *Ramses II: The Great Pharaoh and His Time*. Exhibition catalogue. Denver: Denver Museum of Natural History.

Frood, Elizabeth. 2003. "Ritual Function and Priestly Narrative: The Stelae of the High
Priest of Osiris, Nebwawy." *JEA* 89: 59–81.

———. 2006. "A Ramessid Statue from Abydos Bearing a Sacred Emblem." *JEA* 92:
250–55.

Gaballa, Gaballa A. 1977. *The Memphite Tomb-Chapel of Mose*. Warminster: Aris and
Phillips.

Gaballa, Gaballa A., and Kenneth A. Kitchen. 1969. "The Festival of Sokar." *Orientalia*
38: 1–76.

———. 1981. "Ramesside Varia IV: The Prophet Amenemope, His Tomb and Family."
MDAIK 37: 161–80.

Galán, José M. 1999. "Seeing Darkness." *CdE* 74: 18–30.

Gardiner, Alan H. 1910. "The Goddess Nekhbet at the Jubilee Festival of Rameses III."
ZÄS 48: 47–51.

———. 1912. "The Stele of Bilgai." *ZÄS* 50: 49–57.

———. 1938. "The Idiom *it in*." *JEA* 24: 124–25.

———. 1947. *Ancient Egyptian Onomastica*. 3 vols. Oxford: Oxford University Press.

———. 1948. "The Founding of a New Delta Town in the Twentieth Dynasty." *JEA* 34:
19–22.

Gardiner, Alan H., and T. Eric Peet. 1952–1955. *The Inscriptions of Sinai*. 2 vols. 2nd
edition. Egypt Exploration Society, Memoir 45. London: Egypt Exploration
Society.

Gauthier, Henri. 1912. *Le temple de Ouadi es-Sebouâ*. 2 vols. Les Temples Immergés
de la Nubie. Cairo: IFAO.

Gnirs, Andrea. 1996. "Die ägyptische Autobiographie." Pages 191–241 in *Ancient
Egyptian Literature: History and Forms*. Edited by Antonio Loprieno. PdÄ 10.
Leiden: Brill.

———. 2000. "The Language of Corruption: On Rich and Poor in The Eloquent
Peasant." Pages 125–55 in *Reading the Eloquent Peasant: Proceedings of the
International Conference on The Tale of the Eloquent Peasant at the University
of California, Los Angeles, March 27–30, 1997*. Edited by Andrea Gnirs. Lingua
Aegyptia 8. Göttingen: Seminar für Ägyptologie und Koptologie.

———. 2001. "Biographies." Pages 184–89 in *The Oxford Encyclopedia of Ancient Egypt* I.
Edited by Donald B. Redford. Oxford: Oxford University Press.

———. 2003. "Der Tod des Selbst: Die Wandlung der Jenseitsvorstellungen in der
Ramessidenzeit." Pages 175–99 in *Grab und Totenkult im alten Ägypten*. Edited
by Heike Guksch, Eva Hofmann, and Martin Bommas. Munich: Beck.

Goebs, Katja. 1995. "Untersuchungen zu Funktion und Symbolgehalt des *nms*." *ZÄS*
122: 154–81.

———. 2003. "*hftj ntr* as Euphemism – The Case of the Antef Decree." *JEA* 89: 27–37.

Goyon, Jean-Claude. 1990. "Penrê, conducteur des travaux au Ramesseum, et son
étrange histoire." *Memnonia* 1: 53–65.

Graefe, Erhart. 1975. "Das Grab des Schatzhausvorstehers und Bauleiters Maya in
Saqqara." *MDAIK* 31: 187–220.

Grandet, Pierre. 2000. "L'exécution du chancelier Bay: O. IFAO 1864." *BIFAO* 100: 339–45.

———. 2001. "New Kingdom: Twentieth Dynasty." Pages 538–43 in *The Oxford Encyclopedia of Ancient Egypt* II. Edited by Donald B. Redford. Oxford: Oxford University Press.

Griffith, Francis Llewellyn. 1889. *The Inscriptions of Siût and Dêr Rîfeh*. London: Trübner.

Grimm, Günther, and Dietrich Wildung, eds. 1978. *Götter, Pharaonen*. Exhibition catalogue. Haus der Kunst, Munich. Mainz am Rhein: von Zabern.

Guksch, Heike. 1983. "*Wsr-ḥȝt* und *Hȝtjȝjj* zur Zeit Sethos I." *GM* 64: 23–24.

———. 1994. *Königsdienst: Zur Selbsdarstellung der Beamten in der 18. Dynastie*. SAGA 11. Heidelberg: Heidelberger Orientverlag.

Gunn, Battiscombe. 1916. "The Religion of the Poor in Ancient Egypt." *JEA* 3: 81–94.

Habachi, Labib. 1938. "Découvertes de Karnak (1936–1937)." *ASAE* 38: 69–84.

———. 1969. *Features of the Deification of Ramses II*. ADAIK, Ägyptologische Reihe 5. Glückstadt: Augustin.

Hamada, A. 1947. "Statue of the Fanbearer [*jmn-ms*]." *ASAE* 47: 15–21.

Haring, Ben. 1997. *Divine Households: Administrative and Economic Aspects of the New Kingdom Royal Memorial Temples in Western Thebes*. Egyptologische Uitgaven 12. Leiden: Nederlands Instituut voor het Nabije Oosten.

Hartwig, Melinda. 2004. *Tomb Painting and Identity in Ancient Thebes, 1419–1372 BCE*. Monumenta Aegyptiaca 10, Série Imago 2, Fondation Egyptologique Reine Elisabeth. Turnhout: Brepols.

Harvey, Stephen. 1998. "The Cults of King Ahmose at Abydos." Ph.D. diss., University of Pennsylvania.

Hayes, William C. 1959. *The Scepter of Egypt: A Background for the Study of the Egyptian Antiquities in the Metropolitan Museum of Art* II: *The Hyksos Period and the New Kingdom (1675–1080 B.C.)*. New York: Metropolitan Museum of Art.

Helck, Wolfgang. 1956. "Die Inschrift über die Belohnung des Hohenpriesters *Jmn-ḥtp*." *Mitteilungen des Instituts für Orientforschung der Deutschen Akademie der Wissenschaften zu Berlin* 4: 161–78.

———. 1961. *Materialien zur Wirtschaftsgeschichte des Neuen Reiches* II. Akademie der Wissenschaften und der Literatur in Mainz, Abhandlungen der Geistes- und Socialwissenschaftlichen Klasse 11. Wiesbaden: Franz Steiner.

———. 1972. "Zur Frage der Entstehung der ägyptischen Literatur." *WZKM* 63/64: 6–26.

———. 1975. "Die grosse Stele des Vizekönigs *Stȝw* aus Wadi es-Sabua." *SAK* 3: 85–112.

———. 1984. "Zur Datierung der Hohenpriesterinschrift PM II², 174 (516)." *Orientalia* 53: 52–56.

———. 1986. "Die Stiftung des *Pn-nwt* von Aniba." *Beiträge zur Sudanforschung* 1: 24–37.

Hermann, Alfred. 1940. *Die Stelen der thebanischen Felsgräber der 18. Dynastie*. Ägyptologische Forschungen 11. Glückstadt: Augustin.

———. 1963. "Jubel bei der Audienz: Zur Gebärdensprache in der Kunst des Neuen Reiches." *ZÄS* 90: 49–66.

Hofmann, Eva. 1995. *Das Grab des Neferrenpet gen. Kenro (TT 178).* Theben 9. Mainz am Rhein: von Zabern.

———. 2004. *Bilder im Wandel: Die Kunst der ramissidischen Privatgräber.* Theben 17. Mainz am Rhein: von Zabern.

Hornung, Erik. 1975–1976. *Das Buch der Anbetung des Re im Westen (Sonnenlitanei).* 2 vols. Ægyptiaca Helvetica 2–3. Geneva: Editions de Belles Lettres.

Houlbrooke, Ralph. 1998. *Death, Religion, and the Family in England 1480–1750.* Oxford Studies in Social History. Oxford: Clarendon.

Iser, Wolfgang. 1993. *The Fictive and the Imaginary.* Baltimore: Johns Hopkins University Press.

Jacquet-Gordon, Helen. 1999. *Le trésor de Thoutmosis Ier: Statues, stèles et blocs réutilisés.* Karnak-Nord 8, FIFAO 39. Cairo: IFAO.

James, Thomas Garnet Henry. 1970. *Hieroglyphic Texts from Egyptian Stelae etc.* 9. London: British Museum.

Jansen-Winkeln, Karl. 1985. *Ägyptische Biographien der 22. und 23. Dynastie.* 2 vols. ÄAT 8. Wiesbaden: Harrassowitz.

———. 1993. "The Career of the Egyptian High Priest Bakenkhons." *JNES* 52: 221–25.

———. 2004. "Bermerkungen zu den Frauenbiographien der Spätzeit." *AF* 31: 358–73.

Janssen, J. M. A. 1946. *De traditioneele egyptische autobiografie vóór het Nieuwe Rijk.* 2 vols. Leiden: Brill.

Janssen, Jac J. 1975. "Prolegomena to the Study of Egypt's Economic History during the New Kingdom." *SAK* 3: 127–85.

Jolly, Margaretta, ed. 2001. *Encyclopedia of Life-Writing: Autobiographical and Biographical Forms.* 2 vols. London and Chicago: Fitzroy Dearborn.

Junge, Friedrich. 2001. "Language." Pages 258–67 in *The Oxford Encyclopedia of Ancient Egypt* II. Edited by Donald B. Redford. Oxford: Oxford University Press.

———. 2005. *Late Egyptian Grammar: An Introduction.* Translated by David Warburton. 2nd edition. Oxford: Griffith Institute.

Kampp-Seyfried, Friederike. 1996. *Die thebanische Nekropole: Zum Wandel des Grabgedankens von der XVIII. bis zur XX. Dynastie.* 2 vols. Theben 13. Mainz am Rhein: von Zabern.

———. 2003. "The Theban Necropolis: An Overview of Topography and Tomb Development from the Middle Kingdom to the Ramesside Period." Pages 2–10 in *The Theban Necropolis: Past, Present and Future.* Edited by Nigel Strudwick and John H. Taylor. London: British Museum Press.

Kees, Hermann. 1937. "Die Laufbahn des Hohenpriesters Onhurmes von Thinis." *ZÄS* 73: 77–90.

Kessler, Dieter. 1981. *Historische Topographie der Region zwischen Mallawi und Samalut.* Beihefte zum Tübinger Atlas des Vorderen Orients B 30. Wiesbaden: Reichert.

Kitchen, Kenneth. A. 1974. "Nakht-Thuty – Servitor of Sacred Barques and Golden Portals." *JEA* 60: 168–74.

———. 1975–1976. "The Great Biographical Stela of Setau, Viceroy of Nubia." Pages 295–302 in *Miscellanea in honorem Josephi Vergote*. Edited by P. Naster, H. De Meulenaere and J. Quaegebeur. *OLP* 6–7. Leuven: Departement Oriëntlistiek.

———. 1975–1991. *Ramesside Inscriptions, Historical and Biographical*. 8 vols. Oxford: Blackwell.

———. 1982. *Pharaoh Triumphant: The Life and Times of Ramesses II, King of Egypt*. Warminster: Aris & Phillips.

———. 1993. *Ramesses I, Sethos I and Contemporaries*. Vol. I of *Ramesside Inscriptions, Translated and Annotated, Translations*. Oxford: Blackwell.

———. 2000. *Ramesses II, His Contemporaries*. Vol. III of *Ramesside Inscriptions, Translated and Annotated, Translations*. Oxford: Blackwell.

———. 2003. *Merenptah and the Late Nineteenth Dynasty*. Vol. IV of *Ramesside Inscriptions, Translated and Annotated, Translations*. Oxford: Blackwell.

Kloth, Nicole. 2002. *Die (auto-)biographischen Inschriften des ägyptischen Alten Reiches: Untersuchungen zu Phraseologie und Entwicklung*. SAK Beihefte 8. Hamburg: Helmut Buske.

Krauss, Rolf. 1997. "Untersuchungen zu König Amenmesse: Nachträge." *SAK* 24: 161–84.

Kruchten, Jean-Marie. 1986. *Le grand texte oraculaire de Djéhoutymose, intendant du domaine d'Amon sous le pontificat de Pinedjem II*. Monographies Reine Elisabeth 5. Brussels: Fondation Egyptologique Reine Elisabeth.

———. 1989. *Les annales des prêtres de Karnak (XXI–XXIIImes dynasties) et autres textes contemporains relatifs à l'initiation des prêtres d'Amon*. OLA 32. Leuven: Departement Oriëntalistiek.

———. 1992. "Un sculpteur des images divine ramesside." Pages 107–18 in *L'atelier de l'orfèvre: Mélanges offerts à Ph. Derchain*. Edited by Michèle Broze and Philippe Talon. Leuven: Peeters.

———. 2001. "Oracles." Pages 609–12 in *The Oxford Encyclopedia of Ancient Egypt* II. Edited by Donald B. Redford. Oxford: Oxford University Press.

Kubisch, Sabine. 2003. "Kindheit und Erziehung in den Biographien der 13.–17. Dynastie." Pages 179–91 in *Menschenbilder – Bildermenschen: Kunst und Kultur im alten Ägypten*. Edited by Tobias Hofmann and Alexandra Sturm. Norderstedt: n.p.

Kuhlmann, Klaus P., and Wolfgang Schenkel. 1983. *Das Grab des Ibi, Obergutsverwalters der Gottesgemahlin des Amun (thebanisches Grab Nr. 36)*. AVDAIK 15. Mainz am Rhein: von Zabern.

Leclant, Jean, and Gisèle Clerc. 1998. "Fouilles et travaux en Egypte et au Soudan, 1996–1997." *Orientalia* 67: 315–444.

Lefebvre, Gustave. 1929. *Inscriptions concernant les grands prêtres d'Amon, Romê-Roÿ et Amenhotep*. Paris: Geuthner.

Legrain, Georges. 1904. "Rapport sur les travaux exécutés à Karnak du 31 Octobre 1902 au 15 Mai 1903." *ASAE* 5: 1–43.

———. 1916. "Un miracle d'Ahmès Ier à Abydos sous le règne de Ramsès II." *ASAE* 16: 161–70.

———. 1909. *Statues et statuettes de rois et de particuliers* II: *Nos. 42139–42191*. Catalogue Général des Antiquités Egyptiennes du Musée du Caire. Cairo: IFAO.

Leitz, Christian (ed.), Dagmar Budde, Peter Dils, Lothar Goldbrunner, and Daniela Mendel. 2002. *Lexikon der ägyptischen Götter und Götterbezeichnungen*. 8 vols. OLA 110–16, 129. Leuven: Peeters.

Lichtheim, Miriam. 1971–1972. "Have the Principles of Ancient Egyptian Metrics been Discovered?" *JARCE* 9: 103–10.

———. 1973. *The Old and Middle Kingdoms*. Vol. I of *Ancient Egyptian Literature: A Book of Readings*. Berkeley: University of California Press.

———. 1976. *The New Kingdom*. Vol. II of *Ancient Egyptian Literature: A Book of Readings*. Berkeley: University of California Press.

———. 1980. *The Late Period*. Vol. III of *Ancient Egyptian literature: A Book of Readings*. Berkeley: University of California Press.

———. 1988. *Ancient Egyptian Autobiographies Chiefly of the Middle Kingdom: A Study and an Anthology*. OBO 84. Fribourg and Göttingen: Universitätsverlag; Vandenhoeck & Ruprecht.

———. 1989. "The Stela of Taniy, CG 20564: Its Date and Its Character." *SAK* 16: 203–15.

———. 1992. *Maat in Egyptian Autobiographies and Related Studies*. OBO 120. Fribourg and Göttingen: Universitätsverlag; Vandenhoeck & Ruprecht.

———. 1997. *Moral Values in Ancient Egypt*. OBO 155. Fribourg and Göttingen: Universitätsverlag; Vandenhoeck & Ruprecht.

Lipińska, Jadwiga. 1969. "Amenemone, Builder of the Ramesseum." *Études et Travaux* 3: 41–49.

———. 1984. *The Temple of Tuthmosis III: Statuary and Votive Monuments*. Deir el-Bahari 4. Warsaw: PWN–Editions Scientifiques de Pologne.

Loprieno, Antonio. 1996. "Linguistic Variety and Egyptian Literature." Pages 515–29 in *Ancient Egyptian Literature: History and Forms*. Edited by Antonio Loprieno. PdÄ 10. Leiden: Brill.

Loukianoff, Grégoire. 1956 [1937]. "Une statue-caryatide d'Unnefer." *Archaiologike Ephemeris* 140: 767–75.

Lowle, Donald A. 1976. "A Remarkable Family of Draughtsmen-Painters from Early Nineteenth-Dynasty Thebes." *Oriens Antiquus* 15: 91–106.

Malek, Jaromir. 1992. "A Meeting of the Old and New: Saqqâra during the New Kingdom." Pages 57–76 in *Studies in Pharaonic Religion and Society in Honour of J. Gwyn Griffiths*. Edited by Alan B. Lloyd. Occasional Publications 8. London: Egypt Exploration Society.

Manassa, Colleen. 2003. *The Great Karnak Inscription of Merneptah: Grand Strategy in the 13th Century BC*. Yale Egyptological Studies 5. New Haven: Yale Egyptological Seminar.

Marciniak, Marek. 1981. "Un texte inédit de Deir el-Bahari." *Bulletin du Centenaire = BIFAO 81 Supplément*: 283–91.

Mariette, Auguste. 1880. *Abydos: Description des fouilles exécutées sur l'emplacement de cette ville* II. Paris: Franck-Vieweg; Imprimerie Nationale.

Martin, Geoffrey Thorndike. 1991. *The Hidden Tombs of Memphis: New Discoveries from the Time of Tutankhamun and Ramesses the Great*. London: Thames and Hudson.

———. 1997. *The Tomb of Tia and Tia: A Royal Monument of the Ramesside Period in the Memphite Necropolis*. Excavation Memoir 58. London: Egypt Exploration Society.

———. 2001. *The Tombs of Three Memphite Officials: Ramose, Khay and Pabes*. Excavation Memoir 66. London: Egypt Exploration Society.

Martin, Geoffrey Thorndike, Maarten J. Raven, Barbara Greene Aston, and Jacobus van Dijk. 1988. "The Tomb of Maya and Meryt: Preliminary Report on the Saqqâra Excavations, 1987–8." *JEA* 74: 1–14.

McDowell. Andrea G. 1999. *Village Life in Ancient Egypt: Laundry Lists and Love Songs*. Oxford: Oxford University Press.

Menu, Bernadette. 1970. "La gestion du 'patrimoine' foncier d'Hekanakhte." *RdE* 22: 111–29.

———. 1980. "Note sur les inscriptions de S^3-*mwt* surnommé *Kyky*." *RdE* 32: 141–44.

Meyers, Elizabeth L. 1985. "Component Design as a Narrative Device in Amarna Tomb Art." Pages 35–51 in *Pictorial Narrative in Antiquity and the Middle Ages*. Edited by Herbert L. Kessler and Marianna Shreve Simpson. Studies in the History of Art 16. Hanover, N.H.: University Press of New England.

Morales, Antonio J. 2001. "The Suppression of the High Priest Amenhotep: A Suggestion to the Role of Panhesi." *GM* 181: 59–75.

Morenz, Ludwig. 1998. "Sa-mut/*kyky* und Menna, zwei reale Leser/Hörer des *Oasenmannes* aus dem Neuen Reich?" *GM* 165: 73–81.

———. 2000. Review of Negm, Maged, *The Tomb of Simut Called Kyky*. *BiOr* 57: 313–23.

Morris, Ellen. 2005. *The Architecture of Imperialism: Military Bases and the Evolution of Foreign Policy in Egypt's New Kingdom*. PdÄ 22. Leiden: Brill.

Morschauser, Scott. 1991. *Threat-Formulae in Ancient Egypt: A Study of the History, Structure and Use of Threats and Curses in Ancient Egypt*. Baltimore: Halgo.

Moursi, Mohamed. 1981. "Die Stele des Vezirs Re-Hotep (Kairo JdE 48845)." *MDAIK* 37: 321–29.

Murnane, William, J. 1995. *Texts from the Amarna Period in Egypt*. SBL Writings from the Ancient World 5. Atlanta: Scholars Press.

Muhammed, M. Abdul-Qader. 1966. "Two Theban Tombs: Kyky and Bak-en-Amun." *ASAE* 59: 157–84.

Naville, Edouard. 1910. *The XIth Dynasty Temple at Deir el-Bahari* II. Egypt Exploration Fund, Memoir 30. London: Egypt Exploration Fund.

Negm, Maged. 1997. *The Tomb of Simut Called Kyky: Theban Tomb 409 at Qurnah*. Warminster: Aris & Philips.

Nims, Charles F. 1956. "A Stela of Penre, Builder of the Ramesseum." *MDAIK* 14: 146–49.

Ockinga, Boyo G. 2004. *Amenemone the Chief Goldsmith: A New Kingdom Tomb in the Teti Cemetery at Saqqara*. Australian Centre for Egyptology Reports 22. Oxford: Aris & Phillips.

Ockinga, Boyo G., and Yahya al-Masri. 1988. *Two Ramesside Tombs at el-Mashayikh I: The Tomb of Anhurmose – The Outer Room*. Sydney: Ancient History Documentary Research Centre, Macquarie University.

———. 1990. *Two Ramesside Tombs at el-Mashayikh II: The Tomb of Anhurmose – The Inner Room and the Tomb of Imiseba*. Sydney: Ancient History Documentary Research Centre, Macquarie University.

O'Connor, David. 1987. "The Location of Irem." *JEA* 73: 99–136.

Osing, Jürgen. 1992. *Das Grab des Nefersecheru in Zawyet Sultan*. AVDAIK 88. Mainz am Rhein: von Zabern.

Parkinson, Richard. 1991. *Voices from Ancient Egypt: An Anthology of Middle Kingdom Writings*. London: British Museum Press.

———. 1997. *The Tale of Sinuhe and Other Ancient Egyptian Poems, 1940–1640 BC*. Oxford: Clarendon.

———. 2002. *Poetry and Culture in Middle Kingdom Egypt: A Dark Side to Perfection*. Athlone Publications in Egyptology and Ancient Near Eastern Studies. London: Continuum.

———. in preparation. *Among Other Histories: Reading Ancient Egyptian Poetry from 1850 BC to the Present*. Oxford: Blackwell.

Peden, A. J. 1994. *Egyptian Historical Inscriptions of the Twentieth Dynasty*. Documenta Mundi; Aegyptiaca 3. Jonsered: Åströms.

Peet, Thomas Eric. 1930. *The Great Tomb-Robberies of the Twentieth Egyptian Dynasty*. Oxford: Clarendon.

Petrie, W. M. Flinders. 1896. *Koptos*. London: Bernard Quaritch.

———. 1903. *Abydos* II. Egypt Exploration Fund, Memoir 24. London: Egypt Exploration Fund.

Petrucci, Armando. 1998. *Writing the Dead: Death and Writing Strategies in the Western Tradition*. Translated by Michael Sullivan. Figurae: Reading Medieval Culture. Stanford: Stanford University Press.

Philips, Allan K. 1986. "Observation on the Alleged New Kingdom Sanatorium at Deir el-Bahari." *GM* 89: 77–83.

Pierret, Paul. 1878. *Recueil d'inscriptions inédites du Musée égyptien du Louvre* II. Etudes Egyptologiques 8. Paris: A. Franck.

Pinch, Geraldine. 1993. *Votive Offerings to Hathor*. Oxford: Griffith Institute.

Pirelli, Rosanna. 1998. "The Monument of Imeneminet (Naples, INV. 1069) as a Document of Social Changes in the Egyptian New Kingdom." Pages 871–84 in *Proceedings of the Seventh International Congress of Egyptologists, Cambridge, 3–9 September 1995*. OLA 82. Edited by Christopher J. Eyre. Leuven: Peeters.

Plantikow-Münster, Maria. 1969. "Die Inschrift des *B3k-n-ḫnsw* in München." *ZÄS* 95: 117–35.

Polz, Daniel. 1998. "The Ramsesnakht Dynasty and the Fall of the New Kingdom: A New Monument in Thebes." *SAK* 25: 257–93.

Porter, Bertha, and Rosalind L. B. Moss, with Ethel W. Burney and Jaromír Málek (from 1973). 1927–1952. *Topographical Bibliography of Ancient Egyptian Hieroglyphic Texts, Reliefs, and Paintings*. 7 vols. 2nd edition 1960–. Oxford: Griffith Institute.

Pritchard, James B., ed. 1969. *Ancient Near Eastern Texts Relating to the Old Testament*. 3rd edition. Princeton: Princeton University Press.

Raedler, Christine. 2003. "Zur Repräsentation und Verwirklichung pharaonischer Macht in Nubien: Der Vizekönig Setau." Pages 129–73 in *Das Königtum der Ramessidenzeit: Voraussetzungen – Verwirklichung – Vermächtnis, Akten des 3. Symposiums zur ägyptischen Königsideologie in Bonn 7.– 9. 6. 2001*. Edited by Rolf Gundlach and Ursula Rössler-Köhler. ÄAT 36, Beiträge zur Altägyptischen Königsideologie 3. Wiesbaden: Harrassowitz.

———. 2004. "Die Wesire Ramses' II – Netzwerke der Macht." Pages 277–416 in *Das ägyptische Königtum im Spannungsfeld zwischen Innen- und Aussenpolitik im 2. Jahrtausend v. Chr.* Edited by Rolf Gundlach and Andrea Klug. Königtum, Staat und Gesellschaft Früher Hochkulturen 1. Wiesbaden: Harrassowitz.

Raue, Dietrich. 1995. "Zum memphitischen Privatgrab im Neuen Reich." *MDAIK* 51: 255–68.

———. 1998. "Ein Wesir Ramses' II." Pages 341–51 in *Stationen: Beiträge zur Kulturgeschichte Ägyptens, Rainer Stadelmann gewidmet*. Edited by Heike Guksch and Daniel Polz. Mainz am Rhein: von Zabern.

Raven, Maarten J. 2005. *The Tomb of Pay and Raia at Saqqara*. Excavation Memoir 74. London: Egypt Exploration Society. Leiden: National Museum of Antiquities.

Riggs, Christina. 2005. *The Beautiful Burial in Roman Egypt: Art, Identity and Funerary Religion*. Oxford Studies in Ancient Culture and Representation. Oxford: Oxford University Press.

Redford, Donald B. 1970. *A Study of the Biblical Story of Joseph (Genesis 37–50)*. Supplements to Vetus Testamentum 20. Leiden: Brill.

Richards, Janet. 2002. "Text and Context in Late Old Kingdom Egypt: The Archaeology and Historiography of Weni the Elder." *JARCE* 39: 75–102.

Rickal, Elsa. 2005. "Les épithètes dans les autobiographies de particuliers du Nouvel Empire égyptien." 3 vols. Doctoral dissertation: Université de Paris IV–Sorbonne.

Roccati, Alessandro. 1982. *La littérature historique sous l'Ancien Empire égyptien*. Littératures Anciennes du Proche-Orient. Paris: Editions du Cerf.

Roeder, Günther. 1924. *Aegyptische Inschriften aus den Staatlichen Museen zu Berlin* II: *Inschriften des Neuen Reichs*. Leipzig: Hinrichs.

Romano, James F. 1979. *The Luxor Museum of Ancient Egyptian Art: Catalogue*. Cairo: American Research Center in Egypt.

Römer, Malte. 1994. *Gottes- und Priesterherrschaft in Ägypten am Ende des Neuen Reiches: Ein religionsgeschichtliches Phänomen und seine sozialen Grundlagen*. ÄAT 21. Wiesbaden: Harrassowitz.

Roth, Ann Macy, and Catharine H. Roehrig. 2002. "Magical Bricks and the Bricks of Birth." *JEA* 88: 121–39.

Satzinger, Helmut. 1978. "Der Leiter des Speicherwesens Si-êse Sohn des Qeni und seine Wiener Statue." *Jahrbuch der Kunsthistorischen Sammlungen in Wien* 74: 7–28.

———. 1985. "Zwei Wiener Objekte mit bemerkenswerten Inschriften." Pages 249–59 in *Mélanges Gamal Eddin Mokhtar* II. Edited by Paule Posener-Kriéger. Bibliothèque d'Etude 97. Cairo: IFAO.

Sauneron, Serge. 1966. "La restauration d'un portique à Karnak par le grand-prêtre Amenhotpe." *BIFAO* 64: 11–17.

Säve-Söderbergh, Torgny. 1956. "Eine ramessidische Darstellung vom Töten der Schildkröte." *MDAIK* 14: 175–80.

Schlögl, Hermann Alexander. 1980. *Der Gott Tatenen: Nach Texten und Bildern des Neuen Reiches.* OBO 29. Fribourg and Göttingen: Universitätsverlag; Vandenhoeck & Ruprecht.

Schneider, Thomas. 2003. "Siptah and Beja: Neubeurteilung einer historischen Konstellation." *ZÄS* 130: 134–46.

Schoske, Sylvia. 1987. "Historisches Bewusstsein in der ägyptischen Kunst: Beobachtungen an der Münchner Statue des Bekenchons." *Münchner Jahrbuch der Bildenden Kunst* 38: 7–26.

Schott, Erika. 1977. "Goldhaus." Columns 739–40 in *Lexikon der Ägyptologie* II. Edited by Wolfgang Helck and Eberhard Otto. Wiesbaden: Harrassowitz.

Schott, Siegfried. 1957. *Wall Scenes from the Mortuary Chapel of the Mayor Paser at Medinet Habu.* Translated by Elizabeth B. Hauser. SAOC 30. Chicago: University of Chicago Press.

Schulz, Regine. 1992. *Die Entwicklung und Bedeutung des kuboiden Statuentypus: Eine Untersuchung zu den sogenannten "Würfelhockern."* 2 vols. Hildesheimer Ägyptologische Beiträge 33–34. Hildesheim: Gerstenberg.

Schwaller de Lubicz, R. A. 1999. *The Temples of Karnak.* Rochester: Inner Traditions.

Scott, Gerry D. 1989. "The History and Development of the Ancient Egyptian Scribe Statue." 3 vols. Ph.D. diss., Yale University.

Seele, Keith. C. 1959. *The Tomb of Tjanefer at Thebes.* Oriental Institute Publications 86. Chicago: University of Chicago Press.

Sethe, Kurt. 1907. "Die Berufung eines Hohenpriesters des Amon unter Ramses II." *ZÄS* 44: 30–35.

———. 1928. *Ägyptische Lesestücke zum Gebrauch im akademischen Unterricht: Texte des Mittleren Reiches.* 2nd edition. Leipzig: Hinrichs.

Sethe, Kurt and Wolfgang Helck. 1906–1958. *Urkunden der 18. Dynastie.* Leipzig: Hinrichs. Berlin: Akademie-Verlag.

Seyfried, Karl Joachim. 1987. "Entwicklung in der Grabarchitektur des Neuen Reiches als eine weitere Quelle für theologische Konzeptionen der Ramessidenzeit." Pages 219–53 in *Problems and Priorities in Egyptian Archaeology.* Edited by Jan Assmann, Günter Burkard, and Vivian Davies. Studies in Egyptology. New York: Kegan Paul International.

———. 1990. "Dritter Vorbericht über die Arbeiten des Ägyptologischen Instituts der Universität Heidelberg in thebanischen Gräbern der Ramessidenzeit." *MDAIK* 46: 341–53.

———. 1995. *Das Grab des Djehutiemhab (TT 194).* Theben 7. Mainz am Rhein: von Zabern.

Sheikholeslami, Cynthia May. 2002. "A Stela of Two Women from Abydos (Cairo JE

21797)." Pages 1109–18 in *Egyptian Museum Collections around the World: Studies for the Centennial of the Egyptian Museum, Cairo*. Edited by Mamdouh Eldamaty and Mai Trad. Cairo: Supreme Council of Antiquities.

Simpson, William Kelly, ed. 2003. *The Literature of Ancient Egypt: An Anthology of Stories, Instructions, Stelae, Autobiographies, and Poetry*. 3rd edition. With translations by Robert K. Ritner, William Kelly Simpson, Vincent A. Tobin, and Edward F. Wente. New Haven and London: Yale University Press.

Smith, Mark. 2006. "Osiris NN or Osiris of NN?" Pages 325–37 in *Totenbuch-Forschungen: Gesammelte Beiträge des 2. Internationalen Totenbuch-Symposiums Bonn, 25. bis 29. September 2005*. Edited by Burkhard Backes, Irmtraut Munro, and Simone Stöhr. Wiesbaden: Harrassowitz.

———. 1987. *The Mortuary Texts of Papyrus BM 10507*. Catalogue of Demotic Papyri in the British Museum 3. London: British Museum Publications.

Speleers, Louis. 1923. *Recueil des inscriptions égyptiennes des Musées royaux du Cinquantenaire à Bruxelles*. Brussels: n.p.

Stadler, Martin. 2004. "Ist Weisheit weiblich? Die Identität der ägyptischen Gottheit Thot auf dem Prüfstand." *Antike Welt* 35.3: 8–16.

Steindorff, Georg. 1935–1937. *Aniba*. 2 vols. Mission Archéologique de Nubie 1929–1934. Glückstadt: Augustin.

Strudwick, Nigel. 1994. "Change and Continuity at Thebes: The Private Tomb after Akhenaten." Pages 321–36 in *The Unbroken Reed: Studies in the Culture and Heritage of Ancient Egypt in Honour of A. F. Shore*. Edited by Christopher J. Eyre, Anthony Leahy, and Lisa Montagno Leahy. Occasional Publications 11. London: Egypt Exploration Society.

———. 2005. *Texts from the Pyramid Age*. SBL Writings from the Ancient World 16. Atlanta: Society of Biblical Literature.

Szpakowska, Kasia. 2003. *Behind Closed Eyes: Dreams and Nightmares in Ancient Egypt*. Swansea: Classical Press of Wales.

Tosi, Mario and Alessandro Roccati. 1972. *Stele e altre epigrafi di Deir el Medina n. 50001 – n. 50262*. Catalogo del Museo Egizio di Torino. Serie Seconda – Collezioni 1. Turin: Fratelli Pozzo.

Trapani, Marcella. 1995. "La carriera di Imeneminet, Soprintendente ai lavori di Ramesse II." *BSEG* 19: 49–68.

van den Boorn, Guido P. F. 1988. *The Duties of the Vizier: Civil Administration in the Early New Kingdom*. Studies in Egyptology. New York: Kegan Paul International.

van de Walle, Baudoin. 1975. "Biographie." Columns 815–21 in *Lexikon der Ägyptologie* I. Edited by Wolfgang Helck and Eberhard Otto. Wiesbaden: Harrassowitz.

van der Molen, Rami. 2000. *A Hieroglyphic Dictionary of Egyptian Coffin Texts*. PdÄ 15. Leiden: Brill.

van Dijk, Jacobus. 1988. "The Development of the Memphite Necropolis in the Post-Amarna Period." Pages 37–46 in *Memphis et ses nécropoles au Nouvel Empire: nouvelles données, nouvelles questions. Actes du colloque international CNRS, Paris, 9 au 11 octobre 1986*. Edited by Alain-Pierre Zivie. Paris: Editions du Centre National de la Recherche Scientifique.

———. 1993. *The New Kingdom Necropolis of Memphis: Historical and Iconographical Studies.* Groningen: n.p.

———. 1995. "Maya's Chief Sculptor Userhat-Hatiay: With a Note on the Length of the Reign of Horemheb." *GM* 148: 29–34.

———. 1997. "The Family and Career of Tia." Pages 49–62 in *The Tomb of Tia and Tia: A Royal Monument of the Ramesside Period in the Memphite Necropolis.* By Geoffrey Thorndike Martin. Excavation Memoir 58. London: Egypt Exploration Society.

———. 2000. "The Amarna Period and the Later New Kingdom (c. 1352–1069 BC)." Pages 272–313 in *The Oxford History of Ancient Egypt.* Edited by Ian Shaw. Oxford: Oxford University Press.

Van Siclen, Charles C. 1980. "The Temple of Meniset at Thebes." *Serapis* 6: 183–207.

Vercoutter, Jean. 1958. "Excavations at Sai 1955–7: A Preliminary Report." *Kush* 6: 144–69.

Vernus, Pascal. 1978. "Littérature et autobiographie: Les inscriptions de S^3-*Mwt* surnommé *Kyky.*" *RdE* 30: 115–46.

———. 1980. "Derechef les inscriptions de S^3-*Mwt* surnommé *Kyky.*" *RdE* 32: 145–46.

———. 2000. "La grotte de la Vallée des Reines dans la piété personnelle des ouvriers de la tombe (BM 278)." Pages 331–36 in *Deir el-Medina in the Third Millennium AD: A Tribute to Jac. J. Janssen.* Edited by Robert J. Demarée and Arno Egberts. Egyptologische Uitgaven 14. Leiden: Nederlands Instituut voor het Nabije Oosten.

———. 2002. "La déesse Hathor et la piété personnelle: La stèle de Qenherkhepeshef." Pages 239–43 in *Les artistes de Pharaon: Deir el-Médineh et la Vallée des Rois.* Exhibition Catalogue. Edited by Guillemette Andreu. Turnhout: Brepols.

———. 2003. "La piété personnelle à Deir el-Médineh: La construction de l'idée de pardon." Pages 309–47 in *Deir el-Médineh et la Vallée des Rois: La vie en Egypte au temps des pharaons du Nouvel Empire. Actes du colloque organisé par le Musée du Louvre les 3 et 4 Mai 2002.* Edited by Guillemette Andreu. Louvre Conférences et Colloques. Paris: Musée du Louvre, Editions Khéops.

Vigneau, André. 1935. *Encyclopédie photographique de l'art/The Photographic Encyclopædia of Art* I: *Les antiquités égyptiennes du Musée du Louvre.* Paris: Editions Tel.

von Beckerath, Jürgen. 1995. "Das Problem der Regierungsdauer Haremhabs." *SAK* 22: 37–41.

Warburton, David. 1997. *State and Economy in Ancient Egypt: Fiscal Vocabulary of the New Kingdom.* OBO 151. Fribourg and Göttingen: Universitätsverlag; Vandenhoeck & Ruprecht.

Wente, Edward F. 1966. "The Suppression of the High Priest Amenhotep." *JNES* 25: 73–87.

———. 1985. "A New Look at the Viceroy Setau's Autobiographical Inscription." Pages 347–59 in *Mélanges Gamal Eddin Mokhtar* II. Edited by Paule Posener-Kriéger. Bibliothèque d'Etude 97. Cairo: IFAO.

———. 2001. "Grammar: Late Egyptian." Pages 56–60 in *The Oxford Encyclopedia of Ancient Egypt* II. Edited by Donald B. Redford. Oxford: Oxford University Press.

White, Hayden. 1987. *The Content of the Form: Narrative Discourse and Historical Representation*. Baltimore: Johns Hopkins University Press.

Wildung, Dietrich. 1973. "Göttlichkeitsstufen des Pharao." *OLZ* 69: 549–65.

Wilkinson, John Gardner. 1878. *The Manners and Customs of the Ancient Egyptians*, III. Edited by Samuel Birch. London: Murray.

Willems, Harco. 1998. "The One and the Many in Stela Leiden V1." *CdE* 73: 231–43.

Wilson, John A. 1970. "The Theban Tomb (No. 409) of Si-Mut, Called Kiki." *JNES* 29: 187–92.

Winlock, H. E. 1924. "A Statue of Horemheb before His Accession." *JEA* 10: 1–5.

Yoyotte, Jean. 1951. "Un document relatif aux rapports de la Libye et de la Nubie." *BSFE* 6: 9–14.

———. 1957. "A propos de l'obélisque unique." *Kêmi* 14: 81–91.

Zayed, el-Hamid Abd. 1964. "A Free-Standing Stela of the XIXth Dynasty." *RdE* 16: 193–208.

Zivie, Alain-Pierre. 2002. "The Cow and the Royal Messenger." Paper Presented at the Annual International Egyptological Colloquium: Reconstructing Egyptian life: New Knowledge from Ancient Sources. British Museum: Department of Ancient Egypt and Sudan.

INDEX

Includes proper names, key terms and concepts, and selected themes. Some relevant passages that are indexed do not include the head word under which they occur. Page runs are given for the owners of texts translated (indicated by "no." in parentheses and "with notes" after the relevant page runs).